The Levellers in the English Revolution

1   to the world as Men, soe farre from being of that
peaceable spiritt which is suitable to the Gospell,
Wee would have bought peace of the world vppon such
Termes, wee would nott have peace in the world
vppon such Termes as should destroy all propert[y]
if the principle vppon which you move this alterac[i]on
or the ground vppon w[hi]ch you presse that wee should
make this alterac[i]on doe destroy all kinde of prop[erty]
or whatsoever a man hath by humane Constituc[i]on
Law of God doth nott give mee propertie, nor the a[lso]
of nature, butt propertie is of humane Constituc[i]on
have a propertie and this I shall enjoy, Constituc[i]on o[f]
propertie, If either the thinge itt selfe that you p[resse]
or the Consequence that you presse, though I shall
acquiesce in having noe propertie, yett I cannott giv[e]
heart or hand to itt because itt is a thinge evill in i[t]
and scandalous to the world, and I desire this A[ssembly]
may bee free from both.

I see that though itt were our End, I see there i[s]
Degeneration from itt, Wee have engaged in this Kin[gdom]
o ventur'd our lives, and itt was all for this to Recover[e]
birthrights and priviledges as Englishmen, and by t[he]
Arguments vrged there is none. There are many th[ousands]
of vs Souldiers that have venturd our lives, wee have ha[d]
propriety in the Kingdome as to our Estates, yett wee
had a Birthright butt itt seemes now Except a Man [hath]
a fixt Estate in this Kingdome, hee hath noe right[e in]
this Kingdome, I wonder wee were soe much dec[eaved]
If wee had nott a Right to the Kingdome, wee wer[e]
meere Mercinarie Souldiers. Ther are many in my Cond[ition]
that have as good a Condition, itt may bee little Esta[te]

DOCUMENTS OF REVOLUTION
General Editor: Heinz Lubasz

The Levellers in the English Revolution

EDITED BY G. E. AYLMER

Cornell Paperbacks
CORNELL UNIVERSITY PRESS
Ithaca, New York

FRONTISPIECE 'Wee have engaged in this
Kingdome and ventur'd our lives, and itt was
all for this: to recover our birthrights and
priviledges as Englishmen, and by the arguments urged there is none.' Edward Sexby's
sad and angry lament comes from the debates of
the Army Council at Putney, October–
November 1647. William Clarke, the Council's
secretary, recorded the debates, which were
transcribed some time before his death in 1666.

Picture research by Alla Weaver

First printing, Cornell Paperbacks, 1975

International Standard Book Number 0-8014-9153-3
Library of Congress Catalog Card Number 74-25313

Printed in Great Britain

Contents

Preface

I am grateful to the General Editor of the 'Documents of Revolution' series, Dr Heinz Lubasz, for having asked me to contribute this volume to it, and for all his help in the course of its preparation. I am grateful too to members of the staff of Thames and Hudson for their co-operation.

My thanks are due to the British Library, for allowing the reproduction of items from the Thomason Collection in the King's Library; also to the staffs of that and other libraries where I have worked in the course of its preparation. I am particularly indebted to the Provost and Fellows of Worcester College, Oxford, for allowing me to reproduce Clarke Manuscript LXV, folios 34 to 63, and other short extracts. I wish to thank the Librarian, Dr R. E. Sayce, and the Assistant Librarian, Miss Lesley Montgomery, for their unfailing help. I am also grateful to my typist, Miss Angela Cooper, for her skill and patience. As with the other books which I have written or edited, my wife's help and encouragement have been invaluable.

If I believed in dedications, I should inscribe this book to the memory and the example of those whose inspiration has helped me to be less untrue to radical good causes than I should otherwise have been.

G. E. Aylmer.
June 1974.

John Lilburne, the Leveller leader, portrayed (after his acquittal) at his trial for treason under the Commonwealth, in October 1649. He holds Sir Edward Coke's Institutes of the Laws of England *in his hand.*

Introduction

THE STORY of the Levellers and their ideas is interesting both in itself and as an aspect of English history during the Interregnum of 1640–60. The Levellers were defeated by Oliver Cromwell and his allies – twice, in 1647 and again in 1649 – and the 'revolution' which *they* wanted never took place. But the more conservative revolution which was carried through by Cromwell and others was more thoroughgoing and more effective than it would otherwise have been because of their contribution – both as allies and as opponents of Cromwell, of the other Army leaders, and of the so-called Independents in Parliament.

The leaders and others about whom enough is known are interesting in themselves, and many of them are colourful as individuals; their ideas are remarkable; and so is the organization they formed. Whether they wanted full manhood suffrage, or something more like male household suffrage (roughly what existed in this country between 1885 and 1918), it is no misnomer to call them the first democratic political movement in modern history. Indeed, it is fair to say that until the late eighteenth century in America, Britain and France, they were unique. Popular insurrections, whether peasant or urban; movements of extreme religious enthusiasm which sometimes led to violence on a large scale; and radical political theorizing – all these phenomena had been evident in England and in other parts of Europe for centuries. Instances of them can indeed be found contemporary with the Leveller movement itself. But no where else before the 1760s, or even perhaps before 1789, do we find the combination of radical journalism and pamphleteering, ideological zeal, political activism, and mass organization that prevailed in England from 1646 to 1649.

The circumstances of these years were, of course, exceptional. They alone made the Leveller movement possible as a major historical event. The essential elements were these: the personalities of the leading figures, of John Lilburne above all; the intellectual development of their ideas; and the juxtaposition of difficult economic conditions with the political and religious conflicts and dissatisfactions that followed the King's defeat in the First Civil War (1642–6).

Of the several necessary pre-conditions for the rise of the movement the most important was the parliamentarian military victory over Charles I, together with the constitutional and religious deadlock which accompanied and followed it. The main groups or factions on the winning side had been divided, almost continuously since the Civil War had first begun, over the relative priorities of winning the war and of reaching a compromise agreement with the King. Once victory had been won, disagreement merely shifted, focusing now on the terms which Charles must be made to accept as the price of being restored to his position as king.

Meanwhile there had also been chronic disagreements, going back even before the outbreak of the fighting, between those Puritans who wanted to replace the all-inclusive episcopalian state-church under royal headship with an all-inclusive presbyterian church under parliamentary control; those who wanted a loose, decentralized national church; and those who preferred a plural church system with equality for all Protestant denominations and with no establishment at all. The more rigid the structure and the more sweeping the claims of the established national church – whatever its denominational complexion – the more urgent became the issue of toleration for those outside it, of 'liberty for tender consciences' as Cromwell called it in 1644. By 1646 the Church of England as it had existed since the Elizabethan Settlement of 1559 had been effectively replaced by a Presbyterian Church. Even if to the 'high' Presbyterians (the Scots and their few English allies) it was 'a lame Erastian presbytery', to many radical Puritans and others it seemed to provide an all too grim and swift confirmation of Milton's poetic aphorism: 'New Presbyter is but old Priest writ large'. At the same time, the more radical Puritan sects themselves exhibited in an extreme form what their enemies were to call 'the dissidence of dissent'. Those of the Independents who were more heterodox in their beliefs, more strongly opposed to the establishment, and more committed to toleration now began to move away from the orthodox Congregationalists (who in fact differed from 'low', Erastian Presbyterians only on the issue of church government). The Baptists, who had never been closely united, now divided into two main groups, over the basic theological issue of divine predestination of human destiny versus salvation by God's free grace. Other small groups proliferated, even if they were less numerous, less extreme, and perhaps less colourful than was alleged by their enemies among the orthodox (Presbyterian) Puritans.

Besides the constitutional deadlock between King and Parliament and the deepening religious conflict, these were also years of continued, if not worsening, material hardship for many people: of economic dislocation due to the war and its aftermath, and of social disturbance and disharmony. These discontents were felt with particular sharpness, and the many remedies proposed for them found especially ready expression in London. By far the largest urban community in the country, the capital had grown with what seemed to many contemporaries portentous and deplorable speed during the previous few generations. It had, moreover, also been undergoing a precocious social development, one in which prevailing norms of hierarchy and discipline were more likely to be challenged than in the small towns and villages of provincial England.

Lastly, but by no means least, the parliamentary Army, especially after

A military manual of 1660 illustrates the elaborate procedure involved in contemporary arms drill. The main infantry weapons of the Civil War were musket and pike; those of the cavalry, sword and pistol.

its reconstitution in the 'New Model' of 1645, provided another unique element in the situation. Some of the foot-soldiers had been conscripted, but the officers and the horse-troopers were volunteers. Latterly, moreover, there had been a significant social change in the status of the senior officers, a tentative shift towards an 'opening of the careers to talents'. Whereas in 1642–3 the higher ranks on the parliamentarian side had been almost as upper-class (filled with men from noble and greater gentry families) as those on the King's side, by 1646–7 many more men of lesser, or even of non-gentry origin can be found among the majors and colonels (if not until 1649 among the Generals). At the same time the regimental chaplains seem to have tended to be more radical than the Puritan clergy in general. According to some conservative contemporary observers, the mental atmosphere of the Army resembled (in modern terms) something like a mixture of a revivalist religious congress and an extreme left-wing political debating society. A number of those in the non-commissioned ranks, perhaps especially in the cavalry regiments, may already have served as apprentices or have come direct from the middle levels of society. So the social gulf between officers and men may have been less than in ordinary armies before the French Revolution and Napoleon.

It is easy, perhaps all too tempting, to relate the rise and fall of the Leveller movement simply and directly to the situation of the Army. In

11

the spring and summer of 1647, the soldiers' grievances were capitalized upon and harnessed by the radical pamphleteers. Officers and soldiers alike wanted their arrears of pay made good; in many units it was months behind. Whether they were to be demobilized or not, they wanted guarantees against being sued in the law courts for actions committed in the course of their military duties, under the orders of the Army or of Parliament. Those who were to remain in service wanted their pay to be safeguarded for the future. Furthermore, if they were to be sent to Ireland (to re-conquer it for England), they wanted to go there freely and voluntarily and under leaders whom they trusted. These demands were repeatedly put forward until, in the autumn of 1647, the Generals re-asserted their authority, defeated the Agitators (or soldiers' delegates), and purged the few dissident or fellow-travelling field officers. Then, in 1648 the Second Civil War, and the Presbyterian come-back which accom-panied and followed it, brought the Levellers and the Independents together again. This threat was removed by Pride's Purge in December 1648. But very soon after the regicide of 30 January 1649, the Leveller challenge was renewed, only to be finally defeated in the ensuing months. This negative outcome is the more readily accounted for when one con-siders that the Leveller leaders were imprisoned, dispersed, or had died; that the Army had been purged, and that the soldiers' most urgent material grievances (as to indemnity, arrears, demobilization, and the leadership, pay and provisions for the projected Irish relief expedition) had been substantially met. The very issues which had so nearly enabled the Levellers to capture the Army in 1647 now provided the setting for their decisive defeat. Despite the evidence of continuing mass support in London (for example, signatures to petitions, and the demonstrations at Lilburne's two trials in October 1649 and August 1653), the movement disintegrated, and the Levellers were never a serious challenge to the republican regime after the summer of 1649.

Yet, if we consider the hierarchical nature of seventeenth-century society, the prevailing assumptions of the age, the deferential acceptance of upper-class rule, the cohesive nature of the local communities of rural and provincial England, the pervasiveness and force of preaching and writing against rebellion, popular tumult, anarchy and communism – then what is remarkable and needs to be explained is not the Levellers' failure, either to seize power or to see more of their demands implemented, but rather the amount of influence which they did exercise, and the part they man-aged to play on the stage of history during these few years.

The best authorities[1] tell us that there were two main sources of Leveller thinking. One was the radical, iconoclastic Calvinism of the Protestant Reformation; the other the more rationalist, optimistic temper of the Renaissance, and more specifically the neo-classical idea of Natural Law. There is no need to quarrel with this analysis to feel that it is only a starting point. For, if this were a sufficient explanation, then was it just coincidence and the accident of personality that the Leveller movement was set in the England of Charles I and Oliver Cromwell? The indigenous English contribution to Leveller ideas is both more particular and more elusive: it owed a great deal to the notion and partial practice of self-government, locally[2] if not nationally, and to the tradition, even if it were partly a hollow one, of the individual's rights at law. The attitude of the Levellers towards the Common Law, indeed towards the whole English legal system, was highly ambivalent. On the one hand, they were emphatic and persistent in claiming their full rights under Magna Carta and other statutes and legal traditions: not to have to answer to interrogation by which accused persons might incriminate themselves; and not to be arrested except on a magistrate's warrant, and not then to be tried save before a jury of their peers. Yet at the same time they subscribed to the historical myth of the Norman Yoke. They believed the native English to have been oppressed by their Norman conquerors, and saw all laws made since 1066 as having been largely the work of the enslaving monarchs and their military-cum-aristocratic supporters. Hence the crucial importance of how to interpret natural law and the law of God. For the law of God prescribed too that they should believe and worship according to their consciences, and should not be coerced by Milton's 'new Presbyter' any more than by his 'old Priest', such as Archbishop Laud. Natural law underlay the right of the commons, in the sense of the people, to take back the powers with which they had entrusted their elected rulers, in the House of Commons. All power originated in the people, who merely entrusted their elected representatives with as much of it as they chose, for the sake of safety, well-being, convenience, and so on. From this in turn was to be developed the characteristic Leveller idea of a sovereign legislative body, itself subject to recall by the electors and to frequent accountability, and bound by various fundamental laws which were unalterable by statute or other enactment.

The inception of the Leveller movement is correctly traced to the particular events and circumstances of the years 1644–6. In order to defeat the King, the Long Parliament had had to introduce numerous radical measures, which were no part of its original, pre-Civil War reform programme. These included the self-denying ordinance, which excluded peers and MPs from civil and military office; the New Model Army, which replaced one nominally national and a whole series of provincial armies; the entire new fiscal system, including an effective levy on wealth from property, penal taxation of royalists and neutrals, and the excise extending to a wide range of commodities; local as well as national rule by an elaborate network of committees, many of whose members and their staffs would have had little or no part in the governing process before 1642. These measures were *ad hoc* responses to problems that arose as the conflict proceeded, a process which I have elsewhere called 'functional radicalization', to emphasize that it was primarily a response to practical needs and not the result of an ideologically motivated policy. At the same time some of Parliament's own erstwhile supporters became increasingly suspicious of the self-interest of MPs and committee-members. The deepening rift between the Presbyterian clergy (and their parliamentary allies) and the other Puritan or ex-Puritan sects was paralleled by a widening gap between the conservative parliamentarians in both Houses (almost always a majority in the Lords and in the Commons too for most of 1646–7 and part of 1648), and their radical ex-allies in London, in the Army, and among the sects. Here the position of the Army leadership and of the radical minority in the House of Commons was crucial precisely because it was equivocal in relation to this split. A unique position within this radical group was occupied by Oliver Cromwell: Lieutenant-General of Horse in contravention of the self-denying ordinance, radical parliamentary leader, and 'darling of the sectaries' because of his championing of toleration for all brands of Protestant dissenters. The Levellers' fluctuating relations with Cromwell provide a vital thread in any understanding of the movement, and one explanation of its varying fortunes.

By the mid-1640s John Lilburne was already a well-known popular hero. He had been sentenced in Star Chamber, for helping to distribute seditious pamphlets, and flogged through London at the cart's tail before being pilloried in Westminster, aged only twenty-two or twenty-three, back in 1638. And he had spent the next two-and-a-bit years in prison, part of the time under very severe conditions of restraint. Ironically two of the three Puritan pamphleteers with whom he was involved – the lawyer William Prynne and John Bastwick, doctor of medicine – later became his implac-

A propaganda attack on Archbishop Laud published in the Netherlands in 1645 shows part of Lilburne's ordeal after his trial and sentence in Star Chamber.

Laud, party and judge in the Star Chamber case, is shown dining off the ears of Prynne, Burton and Bastwick.

able enemies. The third – the Reverend Henry Burton – although subsequently a Congregationalist, and hence an ally of Lilburne against the Presbyterians – was in many ways hardly more radical than the others, and no ally of Lilburne in his other causes. By 1639, from a conviction that the bishops were an outgrowth of Popery, and that therefore they and the whole Anglican Church were the creatures of anti-Christ, Lilburne had already arrived at a belief in complete separation: the true believers must totally quit the established church, and separate themselves from it, and must worship according to their consciences in their own congregations. Although there were sixteenth-century precedents, in ecclesiastical terms this step was revolutionary. Theologically, however, Lilburne's beliefs were in many respects orthodox and even conventional. There is little evidence that he deviated from Calvinist teaching on the doctrines of election and reprobation until his final conversion to Quakerism in the last years of his life. Indeed, apart from the principle of not being coerced by a state-church, and an innate, perhaps emotional anti-clericalism, it is hard to see doctrinally why Lilburne was not a mainstream, 'low profile' non-separating Congregationalist Puritan himself. Having suffered under the lash and in the pillory for bringing copies of one of Bastwick's anti-episcopalian pamphlets in from Holland and for having helped to distribute them in London, Lilburne himself began to write clandestine pamphlets after his 'martyrdom' and, in spite of all difficulties and dangers, to get them published. In particular, two which appeared in May and June 1639 were addressed direct to the apprentices of London (of whom Lilburne himself had earlier been one), at the very time when Charles I's relations with the Scots were approaching a climax in the first of the two so-called Bishops' Wars. This was a testing time for the whole system of the King's 'Personal Rule', of government without parliament.

The external opposition from the Scots, against Charles's religious policies for Scotland, also put to the test – fatally, as it turned out, for the King and his regime – the extent of support for royal policies in Britain as a whole, and (closely linked to this) the Crown's solvency and credit-worthiness. Thus the Puritan pamphleteers pilloried in 1637, together with the young John Lilburne, were the harbingers of the storm which was to break in its full fury three years later.

After his release from prison, first called for by Oliver Cromwell MP and effected by the Long Parliament, Lilburne took part in the great demonstrations of May 1641 demanding Strafford's execution, and in those against the bishops and the peers during the following winter. On the outbreak of civil war in 1642, he became a Captain under the pro-separatist Puritan peer, Lord Brooke. As he was the younger son of a gentleman, and one whose mother's family had held a minor office in the royal household, it is not surprising that the twenty-seven-year-old Lilburne, even though he had no military experience whatever, could move straight to as high a commissioned rank. This serves as a useful reminder that, when the Civil War began, Parliament's army was officered on much the same assumptions of social hierarchy as was that of the King. After being twice in action, Lilburne was captured while resist-ing Prince Rupert's attack on the western outskirts of London in Novem-ber 1642. Initially the royalists made as if to treat their captives as felons or traitors, not as prisoners-of-war. A timely threat of reprisals by Parliament against royalist prisoners not merely saved Lilburne from almost certain condemnation and execution, but humanized this aspect of the Civil War – at least in England – for the remainder of its course. The following spring Lilburne was exchanged and soon became an officer in the army of the Eastern Association. Just as it was Cromwell who had moved for his immediate release in November 1640, so it was apparently Cromwell who recruited him to this position in 1643. Lilburne soon quarrelled with his immediate commanding officer, a certain Colonel Edward King, whom he believed – probably correctly – to be intolerably high-handed if not positively dishonest, and – probably with less justice – a virtual traitor. In 1644 he served directly under the Association's general commanding, the earl of Manchester; and he fought as a Lieutenant-Colonel of Dragoons (in the seventeenth century these were mounted infantry) at the battle of Marston Moor on 2 July 1644. Unable in conscience to subscribe to the Solemn League and Covenant – the price of Parliament's alliance with the Scots – and having by now also quarrelled with Manchester (partly by taking Cromwell's part against the earl), Lilburne left the army and returned to civilian life in the spring of 1645.

He was already in touch with other discontented radical supporters of Parliament in London, and he had already begun to engage in public controversy with Prynne – on the issue of whether the new Presbyterian state-church was to be all-inclusive or to allow toleration to the sects outside the establishment. If an ideological label is to be attached to

Lilburne's re-arrest and imprisonment by the House of Lords in June 1646 provides an apt frontispiece for his ally Overton's Remonstrance of Many Thousand Citizens, and other Free-born People of England, . . . , *published in the following month.*

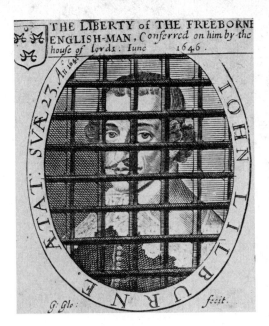

THE LIBERTY of THE FREEBORNE ENGLISH-MAN, *Conferred on him by the house of lords. Iune* 1646.

Lilburne and his associates at this time, it should be that of Independents – with Cromwell still their natural ally and parliamentary champion.

In the mid-1640s, Lilburne came into collision with authority on three counts. Initially he was involved in the printing and dissemination of clandestine anti-Presbyterian tracts, contrary both to the Long Parliament's censorship laws and the monopoly enjoyed by the Stationers' Company of London; next the House of Lords took up his attack on Manchester; finally the Commons were affronted by his joining in a bitter attack on the honesty and loyalty of their own Speaker, William Lenthall, whose brother Sir John was Warden of the King's Bench prison and one of the most hated men of his time. After various questionings before different committees, he was first actually imprisoned by order of the Commons on the third count, in August 1645, but was released on a legal technicality in October. Next it was the House of Lords which had him arrested, in June 1646, on a charge arising out of the old row with Manchester and Colonel King. This time he was sentenced to a heavy fine plus indefinite imprisonment, and from August 1646 until the autumn of 1647 he was in the Tower of London. For much of this time Lilburne had an appeal pending to the House of Commons, denying the jurisdiction of the House of Lords over him as a commoner. Lilburne and his allies enjoyed a somewhat ambivalent relationship with the chairman of the Commons' committee in charge of hearing such appeals – Henry Marten. Marten was a radical republican, but no Puritan; ultimately he was no Leveller either, though he was more sympathetic than other MPs.

17

The year 1645 marks the beginning of Lilburne's breach with the Long Parliament, his first close association with his future political partners Richard Overton and William Walwyn, and the development of his own thought in a more radical direction. He is not a writer whose works lend themselves to reproduction. Too many of his pamphlets are overloaded with citations and references, ill-organized, rambling from personal narrative to general principles and back again. But the passages from *Englands Birth-Right Justified* (no. 1, p. 56) give a good idea of the way in which his thought was now moving. His general principles are better illustrated by a statement appended to another pamphlet of a year or so later (no. 4, p. 71).

Obviously there are more ways than one in which a political and social ethic can be derived from Christian beliefs, but in this postscript to *Londons Liberty In Chains* Lilburne's argument is fairly concise and direct. What someone states his beliefs to be must have a certain validity for the historian. The statement itself does not, of course, tell us how or why Lilburne came to hold these beliefs in the first place, though in his case the process by which he arrived at them is perhaps clearer than it is with many of his contemporaries. For, as his biographers and others have pointed out, an astonishingly high proportion of his works are in some measure autobiographical, which also helps to explain why his writings are of uneven quality as pieces of political theory.

Meanwhile Lilburne was not alone. Other spokesmen of popular radicalism, partly lay, partly ecclesiastical in character, were also becoming increasingly disillusioned with the Long Parliament, the Assembly of Divines, and all their works. And they were coming more and more into conflict with Parliament itself, or its subordinate authorities.

Foremost among these was Richard Overton. Virtually nothing is known for certain of his early years. Possibly the son of a Midland clergyman, and himself a member of a refugee Baptist congregation in the Netherlands as a youth (in 1615–16), he may have been an assistant printer helping his brother or cousin Henry, who became free (that is, a Master) of the Stationers' Company in 1629. At any rate by 1641–2 he was engaged in clandestine printing and publishing in London; he was probably sole or part author of various tracts attacking episcopacy and the bishops and of subsequent tracts attacking presbyterianism and the ortho-dox, conservative Puritan divines in 1645. He had already written in favour of the doctrine of the mortality of the individual soul until the general resurrection (a question incidentally which had been open to philosophical debate in the Middle Ages: individual immortality did not become a dogma of the Catholic Church itself until the very eve of the Reformation). Despite this probable Baptist background and commit-ment as a spokesman of heterodoxy against either an episcopalian or a presbyterian state-church, the whole tone of Overton's writing is un-mistakably more secular than that of Lilburne. In editing extracts from
18   writers as copious, as diverse, and at times as inconsistent as the Levellers,

especially Lilburne, one must of course beware of stating too categorically that one particular passage is 'typical' of an author's viewpoint or ideas. But with this warning, the opening section of Overton's *An Arrow against all Tyrants* of October 1646 (no. 3, p. 68) and the postscript to Lilburne's *Londons Liberty In Chains* of November may fairly be taken to illustrate this contrast. Not that we should exaggerate Overton's rationalism, or his rationality. At a critical stage later in his career (in 1648) he consulted a fashionable London astrologer as to whether or not he should act with the Agitators in the Army.[3] Like Lilburne, Overton was imprisoned for an attack on the Lords: he was in Newgate, August 1646–autumn 1647.

William Walwyn, the third member of the trio, was a more respectable, if perhaps a less heroic figure, who nevertheless seemed to his enemies more sinister than the other two because of his subtlety and cunning. The younger son of a Worcestershire gentleman, and on his mother's side the grandson of a bishop, he – like Lilburne and other future Levellers – had been apprenticed in London. He was even admitted as a member of the Merchant Adventurers Company, the body whose monopoly of the export trade in cloth was one of Lilburne's most burning grievances. Walwyn was drawn into radical pamphleteering gradually in the course of 1642–4 through his concern with religious freedom. A man of cultivated tastes, moderate affluence, and with a good library of his own, Walwyn seems by the early 1640s to have developed two habits which, besides being features of his way of life, contributed materially to the future evolution of Leveller ideas. At the same time they infuriated the more orthodox Puritans. He made a practice of going round systematically from sermon to sermon, lecture to lecture, comparing the utterances of different pastors and teachers on the same general topics, and weighing up critically their disagreements, their merits and their failings – especially as exponents of true Christian charity (not least their charitableness towards each other's deviations!). Secondly, both at home and in other private gatherings in London, he seems to have pursued an almost Socratic method of group discussion. At these meetings, Walwyn and his friends and disciples would pursue questions to their extreme logical conclusions, even if such conclusions turned out to be highly subversive of the established order in Church and State, indeed of basic contemporary ethical notions and social mores. Although normally a retiring man, a 'private person' in the best sense, Walwyn evidently exercised what appeared to his enemies a disproportionate influence over others, comparable perhaps to that of a few rather old-fashioned Oxford or Cambridge dons in recent times, or to such present-day university teachers as excel in seminar discussions; his activities, like theirs, sometimes had a disturbing impact on the minds of pupils and disciples. It was the combination of his respectability, reasonableness and urbanity, together with his ultra-radical ideas, plus perhaps an added talent for undercover political organization, that made Walwyn the most hated of the Levellers among some of their opponents.

William Walwyn portrayed at the end of his life as a be-wigged professional man of Charles II's time. His post-Restoration career as an unlicensed medical author and practitioner explains this frontispiece. Opposite. The proliferation of radical sects produced a violent counter-attack. The author of The Dippers Dipt *was a Calvinist episcopalian; but even the more orthodox of the Baptists were in turn to attack Walwyn and other so-called 'antinomians'.*

Although he eschewed any denominational label, by 1641 or 1642 Walwyn's ecclesiastical position was one of extreme Independency, or separatist congregationalism. In theology, however, he was early converted to the doctrine misnamed by its enemies antinomianism. By this, he meant 'that part of doctrine (called then, Antinomianism) of free justification by Christ alone'. This question is one on which more analysis of sermons and other theological writings is needed before we can speak with any confidence. But 'free justification' seems to have meant that, if the believer's heart was truly opened through his or her spontaneous effort, then God's irresistible grace freely operating would open the possibility of salvation to anyone, even potentially to all. Along this route, which was travelled by Walwyn, as also by his eminent contemporaries Milton, the younger Vane, and the radical Independent divine John Goodwin, there therefore developed a fundamental breach with the central Calvinist tenet of predestination. Ironically, on this one, vital point of theology some break-away Puritans were nearer to the Arminians and other non-Calvinist Anglicans than they were to orthodox Presbyterians, Congregationalists, and Particular Baptists. It is arguable that the belief in potentially open-ended, general salvation was more consonant with toleration and with democracy than was the narrow, exclusive élitism of the strict predestinarian. In his earliest avowed defence of Lilburne, *Englands Lamentable Slaverie* of October 1645 (no. 2, p. 63), Walwyn makes no secret of this divergence. Addressing Lilburne in the form of 'A private Letter of publique use', he begins, 'Although there is some difference between you and mee in matters of Religion, yet, that hath no whit abated in me, that great love and respect justly due unto you, for your constant zealous affection to the Common Wealth, and for your undaunted resolution in defence of the common freedoms of the People'.

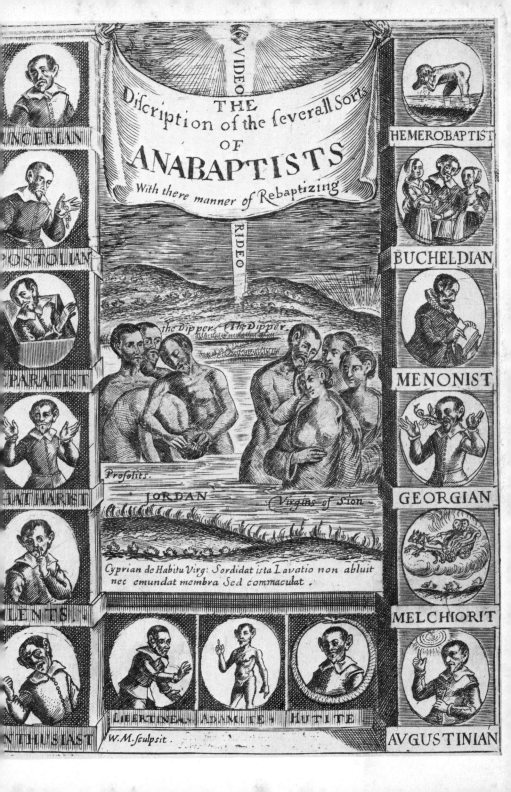

VIDEO

THE
Discription of the severall Sorts
OF
ANABAPTISTS
With there manner of Rebaptizing

RIDEO

VNCERIAN

APOSTOLIAN

SEPARATIST

CATHARIST

SILENTES

ENTHUSIAST

the Dipper.   The Dipper

Profelits.

JORDAN   Virgins of Sion

Cyprian de Habitu Virg: Sordidat ista Lavatio non abluit
nec emundat membra Sed commaculat.

LIBERTINE   ADAMITE   HUTITE

W.M. sculpsit.

HEMEROBAPTIST

BUCHELDIAN

MENONIST

GEORGIAN

MELCHIORIT

AVGUSTINIAN

To Overton belongs the credit for having first put forward a general reform programme, wider and more far-reaching than that implied in Lilburne's *Englands Birth-Right*. In July 1646 *A Remonstrance of Many Thousand Citizens, and other Free-born People of England to their own House of Commons* carried a stage further than had previous radical pamphlets the principle of parliamentary accountability to the electors. Moreover, its tenor was explicitly republican, which earlier writings of the three had not been; it was also more emphatically anti-Norman, and so more guarded towards Magna Carta, as towards all other laws passed since 1066 when the Norman Yoke had been imposed on the free people of England. But until the end of 1646 it is still unclear how large and organized a following the three leaders enjoyed, and whether they were thought of by others, or thought of themselves, as belonging to a coherent, defined movement, for they were apparently still sometimes known simply as 'Lieut-Col Lilburne and his friends'.

1647 was both the *annus mirabilis* of Leveller writings and the year of crisis for the Levellers as an organized movement. By its end, the very name 'Levellers' had been given to them by their enemies.

In March the first of a long series of collective petitions was presented to the House of Commons. Known subsequently as the 'large' *Petition* (no. 5, p. 75), it may have been mainly drafted by Walwyn. Its cool and rational tone, its text unclogged with references, citations or biographical asides, together with its concern for a wide range of social and other reforms, certainly point to his having had a large share in its authorship. After two months of toing and froing, the Presbyterian, or conservative majority condemned it and ordered it to be publicly burnt by the common hangman. The Levellers, it must have seemed, could by then (that is, late May 1647) expect no reasonable, voluntary response to their proposals from the present parliament as it was then constituted. What was the answer: a purged parliament, a new parliament, or a radically different constitution? But by the time the Levellers' challenge to Parliament had raised these issues, the Long Parliament's parallel collision with the Army had opened up new and dramatic possibilities for the radical, popular cause.

The first publication ostensibly on behalf of the non-commissioned ranks, as distinct from their officers, is dated 26 March.[4] Its tone is eminently respectful, but the authors portray themselves as fearful of being let down by their officers, who are allegedly being offered estates by Parliament, 'like the trun[d]ling of a goulden bal before you, to make you run after it, with an intent never to let you have it . . .' If the officers should allow the Army to be disbanded before its interests were safeguarded (as to arrears of pay and indemnification for acts committed, during the war or otherwise, under military or parliamentary orders), then the officers too would be at the mercy of Parliament. The soldiers, or those writing on their behalf, went on to protest that their liberties as Englishmen were 10,000 times more important to them than their pay arrears, and defended 'those honest people who have shown themselves with us, and for us in

A woodcut of 1620: successive regimes had difficulty in enforcing censorship.

these our sad calamities . . .', and criticized such persons being held in prison without trial or legal redress. This can only refer to Lilburne, Overton, and perhaps also the radical printer William Larner (though he had been released in autumn 1646) and others being held with them.

The soldiers turned to acting and debating through representatives. The first Agitators, or 'adjutators' (two delegates from each regiment), were elected during the last week of April. The cavalry troopers then, as at other stages, apparently tended to show themselves more militant, more politically conscious, than the foot soldiers. The earliest open appeal to the Army, along what might be called pro-Leveller lines (though at this stage addressed to the officers as well as to the soldiers) was published on 18 April.[5] From May onwards we have evidence – both from Leveller writings and from contemporary documents (in print only since the 1890s) concerning the Agitators – of the links between the two groups. In view of the works already cited, and of what some contemporaries had been saying for two years about Lilburne's hold over sections of the Army, it is reasonable to see some Lilburnian or Leveller influence in the Army's resistance to Parliament's plans – for their being either demobilized or sent off to Ireland – in March–April 1647, and in the action which was taken by the other ranks on their own account in April and May. According to one of Lilburne's later pamphlets, Edward Sexby, then a trooper in the Lord General's own regiment of horse, served as an active go-between. Sexby may have been yet another cadet member of a minor gentry family who had served an apprenticeship in London. Originally from Suffolk, he was in Cromwell's cavalry by 1643, and had been transferred to Fairfax's when the Army of the Eastern Association was absorbed into the New Model in the spring of 1645. At least as much a man of action as Lilburne himself, Sexby was to a greater extent than any of the three leading pamphleteers the stuff of which actual revolutionaries are made. His career, it can safely be said, is one which only the most reckless historical novelist would dare to invent! By 1646–7, he was already regarded as the chief means for the dissemination of Lilburne's ideas in the Army; he may have acted as a kind of go-between for the Army radicals and the civilian Levellers in London. After his political prominence in 1647, he seems to have played little part in politics for a time. In the spring of 1649 he appears as a commissioned officer engaged in secret work for the new republican authorities; in the next year he rose rapidly to the rank of Lieutenant-Colonel and Governor of Portland in Dorset. Posted to join the English Army in Scotland with a scratch force of ex-garrison soldiers and men drafted in from other units, he had to suppress a mutiny (or at least quite serious disorders) on the way north. After his arrival he was court-martialled in Edinburgh, early in 1651; and, although exonerated from the disciplinary charge of having wrongly executed a deserter for plundering, he was found guilty of having stopped several men's pay unwarrantably (and possibly of having pocketed the money himself). In consequence he was cashiered. In 1652 he was sent by the government of the Commonwealth – perhaps by Cromwell and Sir Henry Vane on their own private initiative – to negotiate with the French rebels, the *Frondeurs*, in the far south-west. Whatever his other successes in this role, Sexby persuaded the popular, radical wing of the movement in Bordeaux, the *Ormée*, to adopt the programme of the English Levellers, one of the key pamphlets being duly translated into French. Back in England by 1653, he soon became an implacable enemy of the Cromwellian Protectorate, and was fully committed to underground conspiracy by 1654–5; after a series of intrigues and adventures, and the issue of a brilliant anonymous pamphlet advocating tyrannicide (namely Cromwell's assassination)[6] he was caught by Secretary Thurloe's agents, and died a few months later in the Tower in 1658.

From May to November 1647, the fortunes of the Leveller movement were largely bound up with those of the Agitators and their few supporters among the more senior officers. Besides the issues already described (arrears, indemnity, the proposed Irish relief expedition and its commanders, etc.), the parliamentary majority led by Denzil Holles were in conflict with the Army over relations with the King and over the religious settlement. Pushed on by some of the Presbyterian clergy and their lay allies in London, Parliament began to organize its own military force, as a kind of 'anti-Army'; and by June renewed civil war, this time between two factions of ex-parliamentarians, seemed a real possibility. In the face of this situation, it looked at first (May–June) as if the wishes of the Agitators and their allies might even determine the policy of the Army as a whole. Cornet Joyce's seizure of the King and his moving him from Holdenby to Newmarket; the securing of the artillery train at Oxford; the establishment of the General Council of the Army, on which Agitators sat along with generals and other field officers; above all Cromwell's decision to take his stand with the Army rather than to side with Parliament – all must have seemed to point in the same direction. But, despite these appearances, and despite the rapidly developing showdown between the Presbyterian-controlled Parliament, its London and Scottish allies, and its own newly formed army, on the one side, and the New Model on the other, realities were different. Cromwell and his son-in-law, Commissary-General Henry Ireton, and probably other senior officers too, had their own ideas about reaching a settlement with the King, if necessary at the expense of Parliament – and perhaps of their radical allies as well.

If we take the writings of the individual pamphleteers together with the 'large' *Petition*, the Levellers had by this time put forward quite a comprehensive programme of reforms. Their demands included the sole sovereignty of the House of Commons (if not the abolition of the monarchy and House of Lords); a purge of the present Parliament and a fixed term for its existence; elections for future parliaments on a new basis (the details had not yet been specified); fuller protection for all men at law, against the state and against over-mighty groups or individuals; drastic reform of the legal system; equal legal rights and liabilities for all, regardless of birth, wealth or influence; the abolition of all monopolies, including corporate ones like the Merchant Adventurers and the Stationers' Company; the abolition of the excise tax and of compulsory tithes, and the reform of taxation in general so that it fell more equitably on the rich as well as the poor; protection for all dissenting Puritan sects against the intolerance of the Presbyterians (some already went further, and pointed towards the complete separation of Church and State). But the corner-stones on which all else depended were the effective safeguarding of the individual's rights at law, and the genuine answerability to the people (however they were to be defined) of a House of Commons which itself enjoyed sole legislative power. While borrowing several points from Agitator and Leveller writings, the programme which Ireton and his collaborator Colonel John Lambert embodied in *The Heads of the Proposals*, pointed in an utterly different direction, towards a constitutional monarchy, with a strong executive and a legislature which, even if substantially reformed, would be far from democratic and only marginally more answerable to the electors than parliaments had been hitherto. Moreover, although the first draft of the *Declaration*, in which the Heads were included, was seen by the General Council, the final published version was not. And in addition, it was alleged to have been seen, and in principle – worthless as this was to be

Rainsborough is portrayed here in pro-Leveller propaganda after his death. He proved less popular in the Navy than the Army, and lost control of the Fleet in the pro-royalist mutiny of spring 1648: indiscipline and direct action were not confined to the popular radicals.

for its authors – approved by the King before it appeared in print. Nor were the Army's bloodless occupation of London and the overthrow of the abortive Presbyterian counter-revolution in Parliament and the City, at the beginning of August, followed by other changes that might have accorded with Leveller–Agitator wishes. Lilburne remained in the Tower, and Overton in Newgate; the presses were not freed; monopolies in trading, preaching and printing were not abrogated; taxes remained as high as ever. Meanwhile it was a year of near-famine prices for the poor, so the soldiers' inability – because of heavy arrears – to make regular remittances home in cash to their families must have come especially hard. Fairfax virtually handed over control of military appointments and other important matters to a small standing committee, dominated by Cromwell and Ireton. This body, together with Parliament, still fundamentally anti-radical and anti-Army despite the forced withdrawal of eleven conservative leaders, soon took action to remove the individual most likely to provide a focus for the soldiers' discontents – Thomas Rainsborough – the one field officer of any real standing who might have replaced Lilburne as the link between the Army and the civilian Levellers in London.

Colonel Thomas Rainsborough's background was a blend of the courtly and the maritime. His father had been a merchant-navy man who became a captain and finally an acting vice-admiral in the service of Charles I, and had died as an MP in 1642. After serving initially in the parliamentary navy, Rainsborough had a distinguished Civil-War career as a colonel of foot, first under Manchester and then under Fairfax. He was elected to the Long Parliament as a 'recruiter', that is in one of the series of by-elections held to replace those members who had died and the royalist MPs who had been expelled. He is first recorded as having crossed swords with Cromwell in the third week of September 1647.

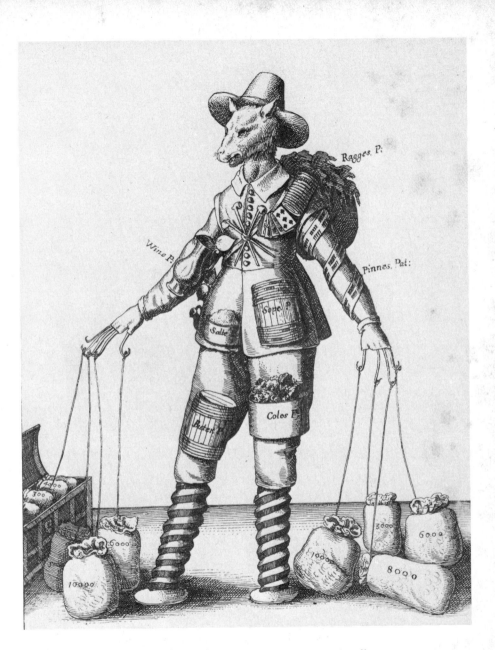

The 'Picture of a Pattenty': a monopolist or patentee was conventionally regarded as an exploiter of the ordinary consumer and an obstacle to other merchants and tradesmen. Lilburne extended the term 'monopoly' to include restraint on freedom of speech and publication.

Already Leveller–Agitator suspicions of the Generals were intensifying, as can be seen from further pieces by Lilburne and Overton, and one purportedly addressed to Fairfax by the Agitators.[7] Two months earlier Overton had produced his own version of a wider, more comprehensive reform programme, in 'Certain Articles . . .', appended to his *Appeale from the Degenerate Representative Body, the Commons of England assembled at Westminster: To the Body Represented The free people in general of . . . England, and . . . Wales* (no. 6, p. 82). But in the circumstances of late summer–early autumn 1647 a narrower concentration on the issues of political power and responsibility was not surprising. Cromwell interviewed Lilburne in the Tower on 6 September. Apparently it was a friendly meeting, but the failure to bring about his release predictably exacerbated Lilburne's suspicions of his old comrade-in-arms and his champion since 1640.

Rainsborough, on the other hand, is not known to have visited Lilburne until 31 October, and it is not clear to what extent the Levellers – or the Agitators – were aware that he was their staunchest ally until the Putney Debates actually began on 28 October. If the Levellers did not realize that he was one of them until the end of October 1647, posterity could not know the extent of Rainsborough's commitment to democracy, or his decisive role at Putney, until the text of the Army debates, set down by William Clarke, was published by C. H. Firth in the 1890s. A cynic might argue that Rainsborough espoused the popular cause out of pique or thwarted ambition – because he was appointed vice-admiral at the end of the previous month (27 September) and therefore knew that he would be forced to give up command of his regiment, and to leave the Army.[8] More interesting and to the point is whether he had got his ideas from reading previous radical or proto-Leveller writings; for otherwise he must have arrived at democratic conclusions by his own separate process of political reasoning. His doctrine of consent, for example, as enunciated on the second day of debate in Putney church (no. 8, p. 97), if anything goes beyond Overton's theory of the relationship between representers and the represented and the accountability of the former to the latter. For it not only implies that any parliament must be inferior to, and limited in power by, the people who choose its members, but that every individual's consent to what is done by the government depends upon his personal enjoyment of some actual (and not merely nominal) share in the political process: that is, at least in his possession of the franchise. Despite their strongly 'popular', anti-aristocratic, anti-plutocratic bias, neither Overton nor Lilburne had previously gone beyond annual parliaments, the separation of powers, and a redistribution of seats among constituencies; whereas by Rainsborough's reasoning every inhabitant should logically have had the vote – the position of lunatics, convicted criminals and children being perhaps unclear. The extent to which several of the Levellers were prepared to qualify this, notably to exclude apprentices (who might well be up to twenty-three or twenty-four years old), paupers, political opponents and servants, provides the basis for Professor C. B. Macpherson's analysis of their ideas in terms of what he has called 'the political theory of possessive individualism'. Whether or not one agrees with him that by 'servants' they meant to exclude all wage-earners, there is no doubt about the Levellers being ready to accept something less than complete manhood suffrage. But why only manhood suffrage? On Rainsborough's premises, why should not women have had the vote too? Considering the prominence of women in the Leveller cause (notably Elizabeth Lilburne and Mary Overton, but numerous others as well), it is curious that no mention of women's rights ever appears in their programme; only one Leveller petition claims to speak for the women supporters of the movement.

Meanwhile the growing disillusionment of the radicals with the Army leaders, in particular about their negotiations with the King, and the election of new Agitators (in some cases different from and more militant than those of April to September) provide the immediate background to the Putney Debates.[9] On 15 October one of the most important but unfortunately not one of the most readable of the Leveller–Agitator pamphlets appeared: *The Case of the Armie Truly Stated*. It was ostensibly by the 'Agents' (alias Agitators) of five cavalry regiments – one of whom, Robert Everard, admittedly later took a modest part in the debates. It is generally thought to have been a composite work, which may account for its rather unsatisfactory style and organization. None the less, as one modern editor has well expressed it, the *Case* is important in having provided 'the necessary ideological bridge' between the soldiers' grievances and the Levellers' constitutional programme – as this was about to be formulated.[10] Part or even principal authorship is sometimes ascribed to another leading Leveller in 1647–8: John Wildman.

The ex-Leveller and future republican Wildman, portrayed by the famous, Bohemian-born engraver, Wenceslaus Hollar, in 1653. Unlike many of the other Levellers, Wildman did not acquire his politics from Puritan religious convictions.

Detail from a contemporary attack on ex-apprentices and tradesmen as preachers. A wide range of types was portrayed, from traders and skilled craftsmen to unskilled labourers.

The only prominent Leveller whose career outlasted the Restoration era and who also lived to hold office after the Revolution of 1688, Wildman's biography – like Sexby's – verges on melodrama. But in spite of the interest of his career and his writings, very little indeed is known for sure about his background and early years. He is said to have studied at Cambridge, but this statement, made by the royalist historian Edward Hyde, earl of Clarendon, has not been confirmed from university or college records. He may also have been a law student; certainly he showed unusual forensic skill on more than one occasion, and perhaps more than casual, amateur legal knowledge. He was sometimes known as 'Major' Wildman, apparently on the strength of brief, post-Civil War service in Fairfax's lifeguard, but he took part in the Army Council's debates by mutual agreement, as one of two non-Agitator spokesmen for the Levellers. The other was a man probably of Oxfordshire gentry origin and London apprentice training, Maximilian Petty, on whose contributions at Putney Professor Macpherson places particular stress. Wildman's precise age and – apart from his alleged lifeguard service – his means of livelihood remain unknown, in spite of such questions being closely examined in an excellent modern biography.[11] Suggestions that, because he had married a Berkshire girl and was a republican, he therefore provided a link between the other Levellers and the republican MP for Berkshire, Henry Marten, or that he was an intellectual convert and disciple of Lilburne and/or Walwyn, are at present no more than plausible speculations. It may be that he helped to write *The Case of the Armie*; but Wildman's subsequent works certainly have a very different character.

Although it was noted by George Thomason,[12] the great collector of tracts and pamphlets, as having been published as late as 3 November, the first of the famous Leveller manifestoes entitled *An Agreement of the People* (no. 7, p. 88) must have been available, as the basis for discussion, either

The General Council of the Army, with Fairfax presiding, in 1647. Possibly the officers are shown hatted and the Agitators bare-headed; the figure in the black skull-cap is probably William Clarke.

Putney church lies just to the south-east of the modern bridge. It has been much re-built since the time of this picture. The church was a convenient meeting-place for the Army – and less provocative than Westminster or the City would have been.

in printed or handwritten copies, by 28 October at the latest: its first substantive clause (on the redistribution of seats and enlargement of the electorate) provided the main basis for the second day's debate at Putney on 29 October (no. 8, p. 97).

The debates on the first day were equally important at the time, but they are harder to comprehend today. The other great issue in the General Council of the Army, besides the Levellers' programme for constitutional reform, was that of 'engagements'. The Agitators and their Leveller or pro-Leveller allies set out to pillory Cromwell and Ireton for having gone back on the Army's various declarations issued in the previous May and June, through their subsequent negotiations with the King, and their failure to force a more drastic settlement on Parliament. The argument, particularly of Wildman and Sexby, supported by Rainsborough, was that everything depended on the Army leaders remaining constant to these 'engagements', and to the principles which they embodied. The insistence on keeping strictly to previous agreements and declarations was not logically consistent with the Levellers' other demand – on the franchise issue – for a settlement based on natural right. This, as Ireton was quick to point out, might well be incompatible with previous engagements and would mean 'an end to all civil right'. Nor, in the cut and thrust of debate,

32

as opposed to later retrospective pamphlets, was it at all easy to prove conclusively that the Generals had reneged on the Army's earlier undertakings. We must also remember the composition of the audience. A lot of those present are recorded as having said something, but others apparently remained mute; it was they whom both sides in the debates wanted and needed to convince: the colonels, majors and captains present from most of the regiments in the New Model. By contrast with earlier discussions in the General Council (for example, at Reading in July),[13] many of the other officers seem to have been to a great extent spectators and listeners to a kind of dialectical duel between Ireton and Cromwell on one side and the radical spokesmen on the other, especially during part of the second day, although several of the others present had something to say then as well as on 28 October and again on 1 November. Thus the part of the debates which is included here, while it contains the most remarkable statements of political principles, is not representative of William Clarke's text as a whole.

Because Ireton and Cromwell chose to make their stand in opposition to clause I, the rest of the *Agreement* was never really debated, or was discussed only in committees of whose deliberations we have no full record. It would, for instance, have been particularly interesting to have seen what the various contesting parties made of the sub-clauses 1–5 of clause IV – that is, of the matters specifically reserved as being outside the scope of parliamentary enactment (no. 7, p. 88). This list of reserved powers, based on the earlier doctrines of trust and recall in the relationship between representers and represented, and implying as it does a fundamental law above, and prior to, statute law, now becomes a central plank of the Leveller political platform. As opposed to the specific demands made under these or other headings, their contemporary opponents had surprisingly little to say about the actual principle of reserved powers in the constitution. Indeed the compromise, or so-called 'Officers' Agreement' (presented by the Army Council, without Agitators any longer on it) in January 1649, accepts their existence, and adds a further distinction – reminiscent of Richard Hooker's between 'things necessary' and 'things indifferent' – between 'Articles . . . Fundamentall to our common Right, Liberty, and Safety' and other desirable changes, 'not fundamentall, but . . . most convenient . . .' As we shall see, if the Levellers gave way over the franchise, it is arguable that the Grandees and the Independents conceded at least as much in other respects – that is, if we assume that the Officers' Agreement was meant honestly and as more than a political delaying tactic.

However, the more immediate aftermath to Putney was damaging to the Levellers. Refusing their demand for a general rendezvous of the whole Army – to be presided over jointly by the Army Council with the Lord General, and presumably to be used for getting signatures to the Agreement – the commanders determined on a series of separate rendezvous for different groups of regiments (that is, brigades or divisions) of the Army. Such was the background to the 'Ware mutiny'. Two regiments, one of which should not have been there at all and whose men came in defiance of all but one of their officers, joined the rendezvous on Corkbush Field outside Ware (a little way north-east of Hertford), on 15 November, with Leveller slogans and papers, directly contrary to military discipline. If it deserves to be called a mutiny at all, rather than an indisciplined demonstration, it was one that went off at half-cock. Lilburne – now at last out of the Tower on parole – was at Ware, lurking in the background. Despite the presence of Rainsborough (at least for part of the time – the accounts are not quite clear about this), the soldiers allowed themselves to be overawed by the prestige of Fairfax and the sheer personality and courage of Cromwell. The 'mutiny' was suppressed at the cost of one soldier executed (out of three who were sentenced to die), and three officers arrested, one of whom being an MP was at once sent off to Parliament to be dealt with there.[14] But the cost to the Leveller cause was in fact much heavier than this. For they had played their trump card – direct action by the rank and file of the Army – and it had failed. As events turned out, they were to try it only once more, and then under even less favourable circumstances.

During the winter of 1647–8 the Leveller movement was as much influenced by outside events as by its own internal growth. The renewed breach between King and Parliament, Charles's secret (and treacherous) alliance with the Scots, the build-up of tension which culminated in the Second Civil War (of April to September 1648), and the resurgence of Presbyterian strength in Parliament and in London – all this tended to bring Independents and more extreme radicals together again into alliance for sheer self-preservation.

The bare outline of developments from 1646 to 1648 that has been given here, far from exhausts all the activities in which individual Leveller writers and organizers were engaged, or else which were alleged against them by their enemies. In 1646 a good part of Walwyn's polemical energies must have been consumed in his prolonged pamphlet controversy with the Reverend Thomas Edwards, one of the most prolix and vituperative of the Presbyterian heresy-hunters. Edwards' writings also brought him into collision with Lilburne and, more interestingly, with the radical Independent divine, John Goodwin of St Stephen's, Coleman Street. Goodwin, like Walwyn, was later to be accused of theological deviations, both antinomian and arminian. That they had – at least to the modern liberal mind – much the best of their running battle with Edwards, is not to say either that this was the general view at the time, or even indeed that the whole exchange was of much practical consequence. The same, of course, might be said of Milton's prose writings, both on divorce and on freedom of speech, though his more 'mainstream' early pamphlets on church government are known to have had some contemporary influence.

His
Excellencie
Sir Thomas Fairfax
Generall of the forces
raised, by the
Parliament

Fairfax is portrayed here as a victorious military leader and hero, rather than a political simpleton. While criticizing the high command collectively, the Levellers seldom attacked him by name.

35

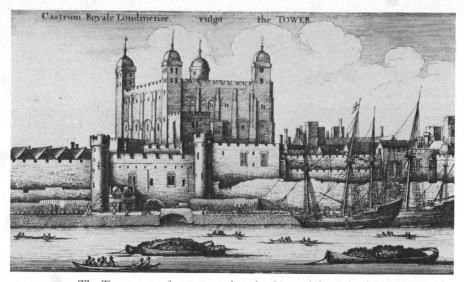

The Tower was a fortress, guarding the City and the trade of the Thames; it was also a state prison. Lilburne had four separate spells there, besides being in other prisons.

In September–October 1647, besides trying to negotiate his own release and to strengthen Leveller ties with the Army, Lilburne was also engaged in somewhat curious discussions with various royalists, imprisoned like himself in the Tower. He may have toyed with the idea of a direct Leveller–Agitator alliance with the King, to be achieved at the expense of the Army leaders as well as the Parliament. Perhaps fortunately for his reputation it came to nothing, being overtaken by events such as Putney and Ware, and by Charles's flight from Hampton Court to the Isle of Wight (11–14 November). The details were only fully brought to light by Lilburne's most recent and best biographer in 1961.[15]

Hard on the heels of this came the totally contradictory charge, which literally made contemporary headlines, that a group of Levellers had been planning to murder the King! On 25 November five men were imprisoned partly in connection with this, on the basis of an anonymous letter to Charles dated the 9th, which was said to have precipitated his escape two days later. One of those arrested was William Larner (the publisher, described on this occasion as a book-binder). It is also here that we first meet as active Levellers two other men who were important organizers of the movement, as its co-treasurers in 1648–9: Thomas Prince, a wholesale trader in cheese and butter, and Samuel Chidley, a stocking-maker and seller, who together with his redoubtable mother was already a known organizer of separatist congregations. In answer to this, the Levellers claimed that Cromwell and Ireton had wanted to frighten the King into fleeing from Hampton to the Isle of Wight, in order to get him further away from Parliament and more completely into their own power. The truth of all this is hard to seek. Whatever the private views of some Agitators and Levellers about the desirability of getting rid of Charles I, it is scarcely credible that men such as Prince and Larner were actually planning to assassinate him. Equally, however, the Levellers' accusation against Cromwell and Ireton makes them too clever by half: there was no certainty that the King would go to the Isle of Wight, or what his reception would be on arrival there. His flight might well have worked to Cromwell's disadvantage. A further lurid touch is afforded by the Leveller belief that the anonymous informer concerned in the 'plot' was Free-born John's own brother, Lieutenant-Colonel Henry Lilburne, who was indeed to be killed in action fighting for the royalists in August 1648 (and was then treated as a traitor for having changed sides). As a final twist to the story, John Lilburne persuaded himself that the influential MP and senior garrison commander in the north-east, Sir Arthur Hesilrige (a future republican), had somehow trapped Henry into this defection, as part of his vendetta against the Lilburne family, who were an obstacle to his own dishonest estate-building in county Durham. Resentment against Hesilrige for his actual, or supposed, misdeeds was to play a major part in Lilburne's final downfall.

The next series of charges against the Levellers came in February 1648. An informer called George Masterson had attended some of their meetings, in particular one held in east London to discuss future tactics. Lilburne had presided, dressed in the red coat of a lieutenant-colonel of dragoons, and Wildman had also taken a prominent part. Ironically the publication of Masterson's account, together with two further Leveller petitions (edited by Gualter Frost, the secretary to the main parliamentary executive, the Derby House committee) helped both to preserve these ephemeral documents for posterity, and to give the Levellers additional contemporary publicity.[16] This pamphlet also tells us more about Leveller organization than any other surviving record. It reveals an elaborate network of agents in different districts, with regular subscriptions from supporters coming in via local collectors to the two treasurers Chidley and Prince.

Up to this time Lilburne had been enjoying liberty on bail. But while the approach of the Second Civil War brought Levellers and Army leaders together again, the end of 1647 had seen the bitterest and most trenchant onslaught yet made in print on Cromwell and Ireton. Written by Wildman, under the pseudonym or anagram 'John Lawmind', *Putney Projects* (dated by Thomason to 30 December 1647) is a closely argued attack on the two generals. It compares their professions with their actions, concentrating on the events of May to September 1647. Considering its date of appearance, the pamphlet's silence on the events in Putney church and afterwards at Ware is, to say the least, remarkable. Did Wildman perhaps sense that these internal Army divisions and conflicts would be less telling polemically than a recital of Cromwell's and Ireton's dealings with Parliament and with the King, set beside the Army's various declarations made earlier in the summer? Much of it is taken up with a detailed criticism of *The Heads of the Proposals* in their final, published form. The same technique appears in Wildman's less well-known piece, *The Lawes Subversion*, published under a different pseudonym in March 1648. In this he used the arrest and imprisonment without trial of the conservative parliamentarian Sir John Maynard as the basis for a further indictment of the two generals. And in this way it forms an important minor sequel to his *Putney Projects*.

Wildman's writing is less inspired than that of Lilburne or Overton at their best, less effective to the modern reader than Walwyn's urbane approach; but it is relevant, consistent, and – polemically – deadly. Thus, he keeps strictly to one theme; there is little overlap with his supposed earlier work, *The Case of the Armie*. Here, as in other ways, he is untypical of Leveller authors. There are no autobiographical asides to interrupt the flow of the argument, a temptation which Lilburne, and to a lesser extent Overton and Walwyn, could seldom eschew. Wildman is concerned to discredit Cromwell and Ireton, not to advertise himself, or even – at least overtly – to propagate his own, contrary beliefs. To know about the Levellers, as individual people, or as a group, we turn to their other spokesmen. Not that Wildman was unable to defend himself; he did so effectively in an extended postscript to *Putney Projects*, but his two purposes are kept distinct, and both gain in effectiveness from this separation.

After so devastating an indictment of Cromwell's and Ireton's trustworthiness and credibility, it is remarkable how much of a Leveller detente with them was still to prove possible.

During part of 1648 the history of the Levellers is superficially less sensational than in the preceding and in the following years. It is tempting to say that the movement had entered into a period of consolidation, filling out its programme, improving and extending its organization, which is a necessary phase in the evolution of any political party. But this is to take an anachronistic nineteenth- or twentieth-century view of the situation. The England of the late 1640s was not like that. The upper classes, whether Cavalier or Roundhead, Anglican or Puritan, were simply not going to allow a qualitatively different kind of political movement to enter the political arena on its own terms and to compete with them on that basis.

The House of Commons voted for 'No Further Addresses', in effect to break off negotiations with the King, on 3 January. On the 20th, after being cross-examined but also allowed to defend themselves at the bar of the House, Lilburne and Wildman were remanded in custody on the basis of Masterson's and another informer's depositions. Lilburne was in prison again from then until a combination of more Leveller petitions and an eloquent plea by the Presbyterian MP, Maynard (now himself back in Parliament), saw the two Houses order his release and cancel the 1647 sentence against him at the beginning of August. This may even have been done with the deliberate hope of putting him at odds with the Generals and thus of weakening Cromwell; if so, the manoeuvre misfired, at least in the short-run.

Another change of circumstances was now operating to the Levellers' disadvantage. In the aftermath of the Corkbush Field fiasco, and the recovery of full control by the Generals and the main body of field officers, several regiments had been persuaded to re-call their Agitators. And – apparently by mutual consent – during the winter of 1647–8 the General Council of the Army once more became a body consisting exclusively of commissioned officers. The Levellers had therefore lost their platform inside the Army for the legitimate ventilation of grievances and for advancing their other views. Perhaps partly because of this, we find a renewed emphasis on the petitioning of Parliament through most of 1648. But, counter-balancing their loss of any constitutional footing in the Army, from June 1648 (until September 1649) the Levellers possessed in *The Moderate*, if not their very own weekly newspaper, at least one that was normally well disposed and provided space for their news and opinions. The next attempt at a general summing up of their demands came in another so-called 'large' (that is, comprehensive) *Petition* of 11 September (no. 9, p. 131). In this they were concerned to remonstrate with Parliament for its many failings, and certainly not to attack the leaders of the Army either collectively or by name. Indeed, in its context at the time, this petition could be seen as an extraordinarily polite ultim-atum to the Long Parliament, from a radical, but pro-Army, standpoint.

By this time the Second Civil War had been fought and won. Only a few scattered garrisons still held out for the King. Yet concurrently with this, the conservative, so-called Presbyterian majority in the two Houses had re-embarked on their policy of negotiating a settlement with Charles, on very much the same terms which they had offered him back in 1646. In one important respect, it now emerged that the Levellers were, if anything, less ruthless than their erstwhile allies and more recent oppo-nents, the officers who controlled the Army Council. In Cromwell's absence and with Fairfax's apparently uncomprehending complaisance, Ireton now enjoyed a singular pre-eminence within this body. And it soon began to press not only for a final breach with the King, but for steps to bring him to justice as well. As the main part of the Army again neared London, its tone stiffened. Meanwhile the Levellers lost one of their out-standing potential leaders. Rainsborough had left the Navy again when the sailors (less radical than some at least of the Army rank and file) had mutinied in the name of King and Parliament, and had only been quietened by the return of their previous Presbyterian commanders. He had been re-posted to the Army, and had just taken charge of siege operations in south Yorkshire. A group of royalist officers and soldiers broke out of their beleaguerment in Pontefract Castle, and – possibly meaning to kidnap him alive – killed him in his lodgings at Doncaster. His funeral in London provided the occasion for a large-scale demonstration and for the display of the sea-green Leveller colours by huge numbers of people. There was, and is, no evidence that his assassination was other than either an abortive attempt to use him as a hostage, or a reprisal for the executions of the royalist commanders after the fall of Colchester to Fairfax in late August. But in the poisoned atmosphere of suspicion even Rainsborough's death became part of the Levellers' indictment of the Grandees and their supporters. This, however, was a retrospective interpretation. For, in the face of the apparently imminent conclusion of a treaty between Charles I and the 'Presbyterian' majorities in both Houses, Cromwell and Ireton evidently decided that they ought to re-open relations with the Leveller leaders.

Accordingly the first of a series of meetings between Leveller representatives and the Army leaders took place early in November. Spokesmen for other groups were added later. It is indicative of their intense dislike of Walwyn that the London Independents, who were scheduled to join in the next stage of the discussions, refused to do so if he were one of the Leveller team. As a conciliatory gesture, Lilburne agreed to Walwyn's withdrawal, so to start with the Leveller spokesmen were Lilburne himself, Wildman, and a fellow-travelling London militia colonel called William Wetton. Why Overton was so much in the background at this stage is not clear, unless he disapproved in principle of these negotiations, although apparently he later took part in them. According to one modern historian,[17] at the end of November Colonel Thomas Harrison, the future regicide and millenarian general, acting on Ireton's behalf, made a substantial – and honestly intended – concession to the Leveller viewpoint. It was then agreed that a joint committee of four parliamentary (political) Independents, four London (religious) Independents, four of the Army leaders and four Levellers should set about drafting an *Agreement of the People* – presumably as the basis for a new constitutional settlement. This time the Leveller team included Walwyn and Petty as well as Lilburne and Wildman; together with Henry Marten, the only non-Army MP who would participate, they actually drew up a new *Agreement*. But it seems that the officers were soon working on their own text, which in some respects turned out to diverge considerably from Leveller ideas.

This is the background to the so-called Whitehall Debates of December 1648–January 1649. These too were noted down in shorthand by William Clarke and, like the Putney Debates, written up some years later but not published until the end of the nineteenth century.[18] The last meeting in the series at which any of the Levellers seem to have been present was on 14 December, and on the very next day they published their own (second) *Agreement of the People*. In this they accepted, and even extended, the restrictions on the franchise which had first been expounded at Putney.

They produced a detailed scheme for the redistribution of seats in a reformed parliament. They enlarged the powers reserved as fundamental and beyond the reach of statute to include the strict separation of the legislative and executive branches of government, as well as to prohibit 'levelling', in the sense of fixed equality of wealth, not to speak of the replacement of private property by communism. And they distinguished numerous 'particulars', or grievances – all drawn from earlier pamphlets and petitions – from the articles of the *Agreement* itself.[19] A week later another well-wishing, or fellow-travelling officer, Lieutenant-Colonel John Jubbes, produced his own individual *Agreement*, perhaps in a vain attempt to act as a bridge between Ireton (to whom his work is addressed on the title page) and the Levellers.[20] It is notable for the breadth of the religious toleration proposed, which was to embrace Roman Catholics as well as episcopalians; for a touch of humanity towards the Irish; and for listing the members whom he wanted to see in a kind of 'popular-front' government (ranging from Fairfax, Cromwell – who was to be sent off to Ireland as commander-in-chief – and the earl of Northumberland, to Lilburne and Wildman). It is too easy to dismiss a man like Jubbes as sincere but unpractical. His scheme was no more impracticable than others mooted by less radical spokesmen, especially coming as it did during the tense weeks between Pride's Purge and the execution of the King. Certainly it was no more so than the officers' *Agreement*, mainly the work of Ireton, which was presented to Parliament in the form of a petition on 20 January 1649. This lifted a great deal from the second Leveller *Agreement* of December, while appreciably narrowing its provisions for religious freedom.[21]

In the debates at Whitehall, of which the fullest record survives, the civil magistrate's power in matters of religion was the principal point at issue. Interestingly, it was the radical Independent John Goodwin, and not any of the Levellers, who gave Ireton (himself, as far as we know, an orthodox Congregationalist) his worst hammering on this. One or two of Wildman's interventions are notable for their coolly secular tone. Was he perhaps a deist? (no. 10, p. 139).

Before the end of December, perhaps from the date at which he withdrew from the debates, Lilburne had once again become disillusioned with the other parties to the negotiations. He reported back to his associates in London, 'and so absolutely discharged myself for medling or making any more with so perfidious a generation of men as the great ones of the Army were, but especially the cunningest of Machiavilians Commissary Henry Ireton . . .' Very soon after this he left London for his home county in the far north-east of England. Admittedly, as well as feeling disgruntled over the rival Agreements, he may also have been embarrassed by the offer of a place as commissioner on the High Court of Justice for the King's trial. But unless, like Lenin's withdrawal to Finland in the summer of 1917, this was a case of *reculer pour mieux sauter*, it was a strange move for a potential revolutionary leader to make at such a critical time.

The sincerity of the Army officers in presenting their compromise *Agreement* to the Rump House of Commons is a matter for debate. Certainly, in the aftermath of the regicide, when monarchy and House of Lords were abolished, and a unicameral Commonwealth established, no further move was made by the Army to press acceptance of the *Agreement* on the House. On the other hand, the second Leveller and the officers' *Agreements* did provide a starting point for parliamentary discussions of the redistribution of seats and other reforms, later in the year.

By February 1649 the Levellers found themselves confronted by a situation in which the Army leaders and their parliamentary allies were in firm control of events. The King had been executed. And, however unpopular this action may have been, no one had tried to proclaim Charles II as his successor, or made any other move in the royal interest. While the changes of government proceeded, the country remained quiescent. Taxes went on being collected; the law courts continued to function; law and order were maintained. What was worse, to Lilburne – now back in the south – and the others, the new rulers seemed to be setting up as tight-knit and oligarchical a regime as any which had been seen in England before, and one which would be harder to influence – let alone to dislodge – because of its military basis.

It was this combination of partly political, partly institutional features that the Levellers meant by the expressive phrase 'Englands New Chains' (no. 11, p. 142). Two pamphlets so entitled were presented in the form of Petitions to the Commons by Lilburne and others; in all probability he was their principal author. Legal proceedings by a 'high court of justice', with nominated commissioners as both judges and jurors (instead of the traditional system of trial by one's peers, or failing that, by any twelve free-born men of the neighbourhood), was an abhorrence to him, even when it was used against Charles I or other royalist leaders. A Council of State, which was elected by the purged House of Commons, and itself consisted largely (nine-tenths) of MPs, linked the executive and the legislature together in a way which the Levellers considered illegal as well as wrong in principle. The role of the Army Council (consisting of officers only), and the use of courts martial to maintain military discipline when no war was going on, formed additional fetters in the 'new chains'.

Between the two parts of *Englands New Chains Discovered*, the second of which seemed, and must have been intended, to be a direct incitement to the soldiers and others to revolt against the newly established republic, appeared *The Hunting of the Foxes from New-Market and Triploe Heaths to Whitehall, By five small Beagles (late of the Armie). Or, the Grandie-Deceivers Unmasked*. Ostensibly written by five recently cashiered (pro-Leveller) troopers, it was probably by Lilburne or Overton, or the two of them jointly. In concentrating on the perfidy of Cromwell and Ireton and the hypocrisy of the former (no. 12, p. 149), it forms a kind of second instalment of *Putney Projects*. But stylistically it is very different.

42   In the meantime Wildman had apparently dissociated himself from the

Leveller movement at some stage between December 1648 and February 1649. Although he was not lost to all radical causes (as for example in London in 1650, and in the Fen country in 1651), and was subsequently to re-emerge as an active republican opponent of Cromwell's Protectorate, he had decided to cut his losses. He now began to earn a living as a solicitor specializing in property transactions, and as a speculator in confiscated lands. Walwyn too remained out of the limelight, and temporarily uninvolved with his old allies. Like his earlier battle with Thomas Edwards, he was again engaged in a long running duel with clerical enemies in 1649; this time his attackers were various Baptist and Congregationalist ministers and some members of their congregations. This pamphlet warfare produced several fascinating pieces,[22] which tell us quite a lot about Walwyn – and his enemies – but are tangential to the main Leveller story.

It was the presentation and publication of *Englands New Chains Discovered*, part two, and the evidence of renewed disaffection in the Army, including demands for the election of new Agitators, that brought matters to a climax. Anticipating the habits of the police in the twentieth century (and not only of 'political' police in totalitarian states), the military authorities struck in the early hours of the morning of 28 March 1649, arresting Lilburne, Overton, Prince and Walwyn, on the Council of State's express orders. The four men, especially the first two, naturally made the most of the situation, defying the Council when they were brought before it, refusing to answer possibly incriminating questions, and very soon managing to publish graphic accounts of what had happened from their quarters in the Tower.[23] None the less, this pre-emptive blow, together with the death or defection of other one-time leaders (Sexby had by this time begun his ascent through the commissioned ranks of the Army), probably put paid to any prospects which the Levellers might otherwise have had of overthrowing the Commonwealth, or even of extracting concessions from the Rump and the Army commanders. Without adequate leadership, without effective organization either in the Army or in the capital and its surroundings, Leveller defeat was perhaps inevitable.

Events came rapidly to a head. On 14 April appeared the collective self-justification of the four imprisoned leaders. *A Manifestation* . . . (no. 13, p. 150), although ostensibly a joint work, is quite unlike other known pieces by Lilburne or Overton, and it seems certain that Walwyn was the main, if not in effect the sole author. In style and content (that is, both as a piece of prose literature and as a political statement) it is the most nearly perfect, the most persuasive and moving of all Leveller pamphlets. It is short, consistent, and entirely devoted to one central theme. But if the Levellers got the best of it on paper, at least with posterity, events at the time worked out very differently.

In April a very small mutiny of soldiers in London resulted in the execution of an ex-Agitator trooper, Robert Lockyer. His funeral was

The mutineers had bedded themselves down in the village of Burford when Fairfax and Cromwell caught up with them there. After the attack, all the prisoners were shut up in the church until their fates were decided. Graffiti by one or two of them are still visible.

turned into another massive pro-Leveller demonstration; whether this was spontaneous and, if it was not, who organized it, we have no means of telling. On the 1 May (a nice anticipatory coincidence!) the third and final Leveller *Agreement of the [Free] People* was issued from the Tower (no. 14, p. 159). Petitions continued for the release of the four leaders and of others, like Captain Bray, who was again in prison for his activity on behalf of the Levellers and against the Generals. As in 1647, the only real threat to the authority of the high command, and so to the stability of the state itself, came from within the Army.

The mutinies of May 1649 were the most serious and sustained attempt at popular revolution by physical force in seventeenth-century England. Yet they were in truth very feeble and easily suppressed. The ex-soldier

44 William Thompson, who had been at constant odds with the Army

authorities since he had been cashiered for misconduct back in 1647, brought out between one and two hundred men in north Oxfordshire, and began a spontaneous revolt, based on the strongly Puritan (but orthodox) town of Banbury. Meanwhile, partly precipitated by fears of being sent off to Ireland, the best part of two regiments mutinied at Salisbury, and after some hesitation marched north. They failed to make contact either with other hoped-for mutineers from Buckinghamshire, or with Thompson and his party north of Oxford; eventually they turned west along the Thames valley, and then across it and up the little river Windrush to Burford. Fairfax and Cromwell pursued them with a picked force from London, and by an almost incredible feat of endurance caught up with them on 14 May, having covered fifty miles that day. Having sent a once pro-Agitator officer on ahead as an emissary to negotiate, perhaps deliberately to put the mutineers off their guard, they stormed into Burford in the middle of the night. The mutineers were overwhelmed in a matter of minutes, and with remarkably few fatal casualties on either side. Although all four hundred of those captured were in principle liable to the death penalty for armed mutiny (another seven or eight hundred having escaped and dispersed in the darkness), only four were actually sentenced to be executed. Of these, three were shot (including Thompson's brother, a cornet). Colonel Ayres or Eyres, although apparently captured in arms with the men, was merely remanded in custody to Oxford, where his presence was to be one cause of another, less serious disturbance in another regiment a few months later. Despite rumours of risings, military or civilian, elsewhere, and defiantly pro-Leveller publications from Bristol, which may have been the intended destination of the men caught at Burford, nothing else happened. Finally, abandoned by all his colleagues, who surrendered or dispersed, William Thompson fought it out to the death in Northamptonshire – as C. H. Firth wrote disapprovingly – 'with a courage worthy of a better cause'.[24] Considering the potential seriousness of these outbreaks, and the severity of normal seventeenth-century military discipline, the authorities showed genuine restraint. Why Colonel Ayres was not tried on a capital charge is a mystery, unless the rulers of the Commonwealth instinctively wanted to avoid making more martyrs. Also he was by then, it seems, a civilian and no longer a member of the Army.

Lilburne himself, however, was not left unmartyred for lack of trying. On 10 August he published *An Impeachment of High Treason against . . . Cromwell and . . . Ireton*, and on the 29th *An Outcry of the Youngmen and Apprentices of London*, the former self-explanatory from its title, the latter another open appeal for direct action against the regime. It was this which led to the preliminary steps being taken, in September, for his trial on charges of treason in late October. Lilburne's successful conduct of his own defence, his duel with the presiding judges (let alone with the Attorney-General leading for the prosecution), his effective appeal to the London jurors, and his triumphant acquittal and subsequent release – once more all make a dramatic story, whether told by Lilburne himself, or by other opponents of the republic.[25] And it was indeed, by any standards, a remarkable as well as a heroic achievement. It is notable that he was tried in the traditional way (under a special commission issued to the judges), and not before a High Court of Justice appointed by Parliament. Was this out of humanity or sheer oversight? We cannot read the motives of Cromwell and Ireton (both by then in Ireland), or of the Commonwealth's civilian rulers. As with the penalties inflicted after the suppression of the Army mutinies, in severity they do not compare at all badly with many twentieth-century governments – of all ideological shades.

The other three Leveller leaders were released on condition only of taking the Engagement, the republic's new loyalty oath, which had replaced the Solemn League and Covenant. This they did, with Overton making some trenchant qualifications at the expense of several leading political figures, but this was disregarded. Lilburne too enjoyed unconditional freedom from November 1649. But although he also took the Engagement, he was not allowed to take his seat as a lawfully elected member of the Common Council of London. Pro-Leveller publications continued, despite the censorship being stricter again from late summer 1649; occasional mass petitions were still presented to Parliament in the Leveller interest.

Yet nothing could, or can today, disguise the fact that by the autumn of 1649 the Levellers had been decisively defeated. Indeed as an organized political movement they scarcely any longer existed. Material conditions for ordinary people were as bad as ever in 1649, though things began to improve markedly in 1650. The flower of the Army was now engaged upon the bloody, bitter reconquest of Ireland – a terrible contrast to the relative clemency and humaneness shown in England. Relations with the Scots steadily deteriorated, and in 1650 reached the point of preventive war being launched against them by the Commonwealth, in response to the Covenanters' unholy alliance with Charles II. So there was much else to occupy people's attention during the early years of republican rule. But, to return to a question already asked earlier, does this really explain why the Levellers failed?

Besides the defeat of the mutineers and the dispatch of many units to Ireland and elsewhere (in all cases away from the area of London and the home counties), 1649 also saw the large-scale use of ex-Crown lands to settle military pay arrears. In some cases the officers exploited the needs of their men. They or other middle-men bought up the debentures (or tickets of entitlement to so much land for so much back pay owing) at a discount from the soldiers, and then themselves acquired the property concerned, often re-selling it at a large profit. But in other cases, whole regiments acted collectively – officers and men together appointing a few selected 'attorneys' to act on their behalf. Besides settling one of the acutest of earlier material grievances (in the conflict between Parliament and Army back in 1647), these transactions may have helped psychologically

This pamphlet, dating from the time when the four Leveller leaders were in the Tower, portrays William Everard the Digger (and not Robert, the ex-Agitator) before Fairfax. It would encourage identification of the Levellers with the Diggers.

THE

Declaration and Standard

Of the *Levellers* of *England* ;
Delivered in a Speech to his Excellency the Lord Gen.*Fairfax*,
on *Friday* last at White-Hall, by Mr.*Everard*, a late Member of the
Army, and his Prophesie in reference thereunto ; shewing what will
befall the Nobility and Gentry of this Nation, by their submitting to
community ; With their invitation and promise unto the people, and
their proceedings in *Windsor* Park, *Oatlands* Park, and severall other
places ; also, the Examination and confession of the said Mr.*Everard*
before his Excellency, the manner of his deportment with his Hat on,
and his severall speeches and expressions, when he was commanded
to put it off. Togsther with a List of the severall Regiments of Horse
and Foot that have cast Lots to go for *Ireland*.

Imprinted at *London*, for *G. Laurenson*, *Aprill* 23. 1649.

to re-impart a sense of corporate solidarity among all ranks. Equally, however, the role of some officers as speculators, profiteering at the expense of their men, may have contributed to a general atmosphere of political cynicism. This is certainly evident in the non-commissioned ranks by the eve of the Restoration, in 1659–60.

In another way the Levellers were more vulnerable to counter-attack, by government propagandists and other conservative opponents, in 1649 than they had been in 1646–8: movements and writings more radical than their own were to make their appearance. Gerrard Winstanley, the leader of the so-called Diggers, had begun to publish his earliest mystical tracts during 1648; and one of his most important works, combining pantheism and idealistic communism, appeared at the beginning of 1649.[26] But the actual Digger experiment in communal occupation and cultivation of the   47 common land on St George's Hill in Surrey, together with pamphlets explaining and justifying this 'digging' only began in April. The Diggers called themselves True Levellers, and this made their appearance all the more convenient a stick with which to beat the Levellers. Not surprisingly Leveller disavowals of 'levelling' and of the Diggers soon followed. They had already included a ban on levelling and communism being imposed by Parliament, as a 'fundamental' or reserved power, in their second *Agreement of the People* the previous December. This may have been in response to a pamphlet called *Light Shining in Buckinghamshire: or, a Discovery of the main ground, originall cause of all Slavery in the World, but chiefly in England*, which appeared earlier that month[27] and went a long way in a levelling direction (if not yet as far as Winstanley and the Diggers were to go). Unless the Leveller pamphleteers were intellectually inconsistent – rather than politically circumspect (as, for example, over taking the Engagement) – not even Walwyn can be clearly identified as a crypto-communist, despite the charges which were brought against him.

This makes all the more mysterious the authorship and provenance of another most remarkable pamphlet which appeared in August 1649. *Tyranipocrit, Discovered with his wiles, wherewith he vanquisheth. Written and printed to animate better Artists to pursue that Monster*,[28] is neither in style nor in content the work of Winstanley. It deploys a wealth of symbolism and metaphor in identifying the worst enemy of true religion and human well-being as the 'white devil' of hypocrisy, who – compounded with the black devil of godless tyranny – makes the monster of the title, Tyranipocrit. In theology it is antinomian, or at least very strongly against predestination. On the secular side, it includes a moving denunciation of imperialist exploitation, whether of the 'Indians' or of the Irish, and calls for the strict equalization of wealth and incomes (though not, it should be noted, for community of property). In all this, it is not totally isolated. Overton had struck a pro-welfare note in some of the Articles appended to his *Appeale* in the summer of 1647 (no. 6, p. 82), and this was continued in the anonymous but pro-Leveller *Mournfull Cryes of many thousand Poor Tradesmen* (early 1648). The same was definitely to be true of the obstetric surgeon Peter Chamberlen in *The Poore Mans Advocate, or, Englands Samaritan* a little later.[29] Conceivably the imprint of *Tyranipocrit* is genuine, and the author was an Englishman then living in the Netherlands;[30] or a foreigner, much taken up with what was happening in this country.[31] In the last resort it is simply another illustration of the extraordinary flowering of radical ideas, that besides Winstanley and the Levellers, 1649 should also have seen the appearance of such a pamphlet as *Tyranipocrit*.

On the basis of these apparent divergences, the Soviet historian M. A. Barg, followed by the foremost authority in this country, Christopher Hill, have seen a fundamental cleavage in the Levellers' ranks, going back to the inception of the movement and running right through its history. In Hill's brilliant and moving book, *The World Turned Upside Down*, the

48

notion of a contrast, of a distinction if not a division, between 'Levellers' and 'True Levellers' becomes part of the central thesis concerning the abortive popular revolution, which nearly happened but did not, in Interregnum England.[32] For Dr Hill, as for Professor Barg, only the socially more radical of the Levellers (probably Overton and Walwyn) were in this sense true Levellers; only they belong – with the Buckinghamshire spokesmen, the Diggers, and the author of *Tyranipocrit* – among the genuine revolutionaries, who would (if they could) have turned the world upside down. One can readily agree that a range of varying ideas on social problems may have been held by men who were political allies. There is less evidence of what one might call 'social democracy' in Lilburne's writings, despite his hatred of oppression and sympathy for the underdog, than there is in Overton's; but at least equally important is the fact that Overton and Wildman (whom Barg and Hill bracket with Lilburne as an 'untrue' Leveller) strike an altogether more secular tone, while between Lilburne and Walwyn we have seen that there was a deep divergence of theological principle. Ironically, the case for such an overall split seems to involve accepting and extending the argument used in *Walwins Wiles* and other hostile works, which tried to drive a wedge between a notionally respectable but misled Lilburne and Prince, and a truly devious and sinister Walwyn, with Overton as a kind of shadowy rogue figure on the sidelines. It is also true that pro-Leveller and pro-Digger writings are not always distinct, as with another pamphlet ostensibly emanating from Buckinghamshire in May 1649.[33] But the Barg–Hill thesis requires much too sustained and systematic a division; and it suggests greater consistency and self-awareness than is evident in many of the sources. It also implies that differences of outlook and emphasis on economic and social questions underlay, or can be equated with, a general ideological division between true Levellers and pseudo ones, between revolutionaries and reformists. I cannot disprove this, any more than Professor Barg and Dr Hill can prove it. Those who are interested must take the matter further for themselves, not only by means of the documents printed here but by reading more widely in contemporary sources.

As has been suggested here, the Levellers are best understood in the general context of their time. We must remember the exceptional outpouring of pamphlet literature during these years, of which their publications formed only a small fraction – the sudden, massive use of the printed as well as the spoken word to advocate a multitude of varied reforms and innovations. To set them in this context, with other authors, preachers, and so on, does not make the Levellers less remarkable as the leaders of a popular political movement in their own time, or less interesting for posterity, only – it is hoped – more credible and explicable. But no individual or group in the past is well served by uncritical admiration on the part of historians who happen to share their sympathies, and even – albeit three centuries later – their aspirations.

Two main criticisms can be brought against the Levellers. The first count is that their economic ideas were unconstructive. Their opposition to monopolies and special privileges, coupled with their strong defence of private property, pointed to an ideal world of owner-occupiers on the land, plus self-employed craftsmen and independent traders. They had little to offer the landless peasants, or those whose holdings were simply too small for them to subsist upon, and little too for the urban wage-earners. Nor had they any real grasp of what the needs of a developing capitalism might be, as Henry Robinson and some other reforming pamphleteers did have. In matters concerning finance, trade, industry, agriculture, they can therefore be called unprogressive, even reactionary, despite their insistence on particular reforms like the overthrow of monopolies. But this was certainly not the case in other respects. Even if we take their modified franchise proposals of 1648–9, and discard the idea that they ever wanted unqualified manhood suffrage, it is still clear that in contemporary terms their plans for parliamentary reform were revolutionary. Even something like male household suffrage, together with their other demands, might well have ended the landed gentry's predominance both nationally and in the countryside, together with that of the mercantile oligarchies in London and other towns. The direct election of local magistrates and officials, the creation of local and the abolition of central law courts, strict and brief rotation in office, the rigid separation of powers, and generally the maximum of decentralization in government and restriction of its powers (together, of course, with the absence of monarchy and House of Lords) – these features suggest something not too unlike the aspirations, if not the realities, of Jacksonian America, the United States of the 1820s to 1840s, but without the Senate, the Supreme Court and the complications of the South and Slavery.

The second count against them relates to their sense of tactics and political realities. To put it bluntly, there was no prospect of their programme being realized by consent; the upper classes would never have abdicated without a struggle. Yet the Levellers were unprepared for armed conflict and violent revolution; moreover, if they had been readier to face this, it would have been self-defeating for their ideals and for much of their political programme. They had a healthy suspicion of the excessive concentration of power in too few hands, whether other people's or their own. But they showed less awareness of the inevitable need for extraordinary measures to effect the changes which they wanted, and of the further difficulties in dismantling such emergency powers once created. In considering whether a constitution such as that outlined in the second or third *Agreement of the People* could conceivably have been implemented in the England of 1647–9, we move into the world of 'might-have-been', perhaps of fantasy. All one can reasonably say is that, given the balance of forces in the country at that time, a victory for the Agitators and the Levellers not in alliance with the Independents and the Army leaders (let alone against them) is hard to imagine. It could only have come

Was it a basic weakness of the Levellers' programme that they had too little to offer the mass of rural workers – whether self-employed or landless labourers – like those portrayed here at harvest time?

about through some extraordinary combination of circumstances, probably including large-scale violence, bloodshed, and temporary dictatorship. Can one not then imagine Winstanley, or some other critic to the left of the Levellers (the author of *Tyranipocrit*?), excoriating them, along much the same lines as they excoriated the rulers of the Commonwealth in *Englands New Chains Discovered*?

The Levellers, or some of them, may perhaps have lost sight of the fact that, in an imperfect world, politics is inevitably about power, even if it should also be about justice. But simply to dismiss them as unpractical idealists, whose programme had no basis in reality, is wide of the mark. Some of their proposed reforms were in fact adopted under the various republican governments of the 1650s: the use of English in legal proceedings (and of normal contemporary handwriting on legal documents); less imprisonment of insolvent or recalcitrant debtors; some measure of religious toleration outside a Puritan state-church (Cromwell was nearer to them on this than he was to many of his own allies and supporters); the redistribution of parliamentary seats among constituencies, to take some account of changes in wealth and population. This of course was only a fraction of the full Leveller programme of 1646–9. But it is a reminder that by no means all their demands were considered unpractical even by their enemies.

This raises a final question, of whether at any stage events could have gone differently. Outside the realms of imagination and complete historical unreality, might the Levellers have achieved more than they did if circumstances had been more favourable to them? First and foremost, despite the generalship and high standing of Fairfax, the intellectual and debating capacity of Ireton, and the military and political abilities of various other commanders, none of the Levellers' other opponents had the same combination of qualities – or the same standing in Army, Parliament and Puritan sects – as Cromwell did. If he, rather than Rainsborough, had been removed by sudden death, then in the short-run the differences would have been incalculably great. Even so, if the Agitators had given the Generals more trouble, they might well simply have been more bloodily suppressed; but as allies of a weaker Army against stronger conservative forces in Parliament, they might have exercised greater influence – up to a point – on Army policy. Looking at particular stages in the history of the Leveller movement, Ware and Burford are usually singled out as the turning points. But there were others. If Cromwell had not decided to throw in his lot with the Army in May 1647, the Agitators would have enjoyed greater power at least temporarily; it still seems very unlikely that they could have gained complete control of the Army against the opposition of nine-tenths of the officers. If the antecedents to the scene on Corkbush Field had included more careful planning before 15 November, by Lilburne, Rainsborough, Ayres and others, might the outcome have been different? Moving forward in time, could Lilburne have rallied immediate opposition to the purged Parliament and its

This Dutch cartoon of 1652, a product of the war between the two republics, shows Oliver Cromwell as Lord General being wooed and petitioned from many sides, the Levellers included: not so fanciful considering that even Winstanley dedicated his principal work to Cromwell in 1652.

military masters if he had stayed on the scene and gone all-out in December 1648–January 1649? By late March 1649 should the Leveller leaders not have seen that they were logically committed to a policy of organized, if not armed, resistance, and have gone underground, rather than waiting to be arrested in their beds? Finally, were the mutinies of May 1649, if not a case of 'premature insurrectionism', at least gravely inopportune? It is often too easy to be wise after the event; but if history teaches any lessons at all, one surely is the damage done to any public cause by direct action which fails. Somewhat more intangibly, in the realm of ideas and propaganda, did the Levellers allow themselves to be out-flanked, even by-passed, by more thorough-going revolutionaries of different kinds: Diggers, Ranters, Fifth Monarchy Men (and others who may be met in   53

The victorious Puritan-parliamentarian of the late 1640s is here contrasted both with the old Cavalier and with the new popular 'fanatic': a curiously Aristotelian defence of the conservative revolution as a middle way. The text advocates limited religious toleration.

the pages of Christopher Hill)? In so far as they did, these groups had even less prospect of achieving any practical success than the Levellers had.

We must not try to be too knowing, to explain everything. At the same time excessive scepticism about explaining the past, by invoking the inadequacies of the evidence or the inscrutability of human motives, all too often ends up in a kind of unthinking or irrational chronicling of events. But this too involves its own implicit assumptions about what happened and why.

Like the Victorian novelist, the historian likes to be able to tidy up the scene in his last chapter. Here we can safely say that none of the principal characters lived happily ever afterwards. Following his last and fatal collision with the Rump, and in particular with Sir Arthur Hesilrige in 1651–2, Lilburne spent the whole of his remaining years either in enforced exile (1652–3) or in prison (1653–7). He achieved the final triumph of another acquittal after a second trial (this time for returning from banishment after the dissolution of the Rump by Cromwell); but this time (1653) he was not released, either by the Barebones Parliament which was then sitting, or subsequently by the government of Cromwell's Protectorate. He was, however, treated with a modicum of kindness and respect, as was his widow in the years that remained before the Restoration. Lilburne was converted to Quakerism some time during his final imprisonment; he was only about forty-two when he died. Meanwhile, from around 1654 Overton and Sexby (now a Leveller again) embarked on the hopeless task of trying to engineer a Cavalier–Leveller alliance to overthrow the republic. Overton survived the Restoration; and, if his origins are identified correctly, was in his sixties when we last find an order for his arrest (in 1663). His eventual fate is unknown. Wildman, as we have seen, survived his years of republican conspiracy against Cromwell (having possibly been a double-agent for part of this time!) and survived the whole Restoration era too, to become a senior public official (temporarily) under William and Mary, a London alderman and a knight. Along with his one-time partner at Putney, Maximilian Petty, he took part in the revived republican political discussions of 1659. These took place at a theoretical, 'coffee-house' level only. One or two lesser figures, like Captain Bray, also re-appeared in the brief, abortive radical revival of 1659, only to disappear the following year. A few others re-appear as conspirators, plotters, or secret agents during the reign of Charles II. Of the leading men, Walwyn (like the Digger leader, Winstanley) disappeared totally into private life. He took up medical practice, and at the ripe old age of eighty was advertising and dispensing 'cordials', that is, patent medicines. These at least sound tastier and less noxious than many remedies then in regular use by qualified practitioners.[34] But of numerous ex-Levellers, as of other ex-radicals from the Interregnum, nothing more is known; not even whether they regretted their oppositions to Cromwell and the Rump if they survived into the England of Charles and James II. And very little was to be discovered about them, until the seventeenth-century pamphlet literature began to be re-explored in the nineteenth century, and until the Army debates were published in the 1890s. Yet this temporary near-oblivion was ill-deserved. Nothing fails in history like failure, but when it can be recovered and reconstructed, the story of some failures is of greater interest to posterity – and more rewarding in its own right – than many superficial historical success stories.

1 Englands Birth-Right Justified

JOHN LILBURNE

John Lilburne (1615–57) had begun his career as a radical pamphleteer, in opposition to the bishops, as early as 1638. This extract is from the first of his publications (of October 1645) to cover a wide range of secular as well as religious grievances. When it was written he had already been imprisoned by order of the very Parliament in whose service he had been fighting from the outbreak of the Civil War until earlier in the same year. He was to be released, on a legal technicality, later in the same month, but was re-arrested on the orders of the House of Lords in the following June (1646).

In these passages, Lilburne's main concern is with the nature of law and its role in preserving the individual's rights in society. Out of his criticisms of the Long Parliament's misdeeds, he develops the notion of a 'monopoly', extending the idea from trade or industry to the clergy, the lawyers and the printers. The Londoners' petition of the previous spring, which he includes in his text, also covers other social and economic grievances, as well as a biting attack on the Speaker's brother, who was in charge of one of London's most notorious prisons. Lilburne then turns to Parliamentary reform, demanding strict enforcement of the Self-Denying Ordinance (by which MPs were meant to be barred from holding civil or military office), annual parliaments, the elimination of lawyers from the Commons, and other safeguards against improper influence. Finally he returns to monopolies and to the rights and grievances of the Londoners, especially over taxation. He ends with a plea that all public offices should change hands annually by people volunteering in turns and receiving minimal salaries.

ENGLANDS BIRTH-RIGHT Justified Against all Arbitrary Usurpation, whether REGALL or PARLIAMENTARY, or under what Vizor soever.

With divers Queries, Observations and Grievances of the People, declaring this Parliaments present Proceedings to be directly contrary to those fundamentall Principles, whereby their Actions at first were justifyable against the King, in their present Illegall dealings with those that have been their best Freinds, Advancers and Preservers: And in other things of high concernment to the Freedom of all the Free-born People of England; By a Well-wisher to the just cause for which Lieutenant Col. JOHN LILBURNE is unjustly imprisoned in New-gate. (October 1645).

[p. 2] It is confessed by all rationall men, that the Parliament hath a power to annull a Law, and to make a new Law, and to declare a Law, [p. 3] but

known Laws in force & unrepealed by them, are a Rule (so long as they
so remain) for all the Commons of England whereby to walk; and upon
rationall grounds is conceived to be binding to the very Parliament themselves as well as others. . . . where there is no Law declared, there can be
no transgression; . . . But take away this declared Law: and where will
you find the rule of Obedience? . . . Yea, take away the declared, unrepealed Law, and then where is Meum and Tuum, and Libertie, and
Propertie? But you will say, the [p. 4] Law declared, binds the People, but
is no rule for a Parliament sitting, who are not to walk by a knowne Law.
It is answered: It cannot be imagined that ever the People would be so
sottish, as to give such a Power to those whom they choose for their
Servants; for this were to give them a Power to provide for their woe,
but not for their weal, which is contrary to their own foregoing Maxime;
therefore doubtlesse that man is upon the most solid and firm ground,
that hath both the Letter and equity of a known, declared, and unrepealed
Law on his side, though his practise doe crosse some pretended Priviledges
of Parliament.

[p. 5] From the equity and letter of which Lawes, it is desired that our
learned Lawyers would Answer these insuing QUERIES.

[p. 6] 1. Whether the Letter and equity of this Law doe not bind the very
Parliament themselves, during the time of their sitting, in the like cases
here expressed, to the same Rules here laid downe? Which if it should
be denied, Then

2. Whether the Parliament it self, when it is sitting, be not bound to the
observation of the Letter and equity of this Law, when they have to doe
with Free-men, that in all their actions and expressions have declared
faithfulnesse to the Common-wealth? And if this be denied; Then

3. Whether ever God made any man law-lesse? Or whether ever the
Common-wealth, when they choose the Parliament, gave them a lawlesse
unlimmited Power, and at their pleasure to walke contrary to their own
Laws and Ordinances before they have repealed them?

4. Whether it be according to Law, Justice, or Equity, for the Parliament
to Imprison or punish a man for doing what they command him, and by
Oath injoyne him?

5. Whether it be legall, just, or equall, that when Free-men doe endeavour
according to their duty, Oath, and Protestation, to give Information to
the Parliament of Treason acted and done by Sir John Lenthall, against the
State and Kingdome, . . . that he shall be present to out-face, discourage,
and abuse the Informers and Witnesses in the face of the Committee,
without any check or controll from them? . . .

[p. 8] 8. Whether it be not just and equall, that seeing Monopolisers were
thrown out of the House about Foure yeeres agoe, as infringers upon the
Common right of all the free-men of England, in setting up Pattents of
Soape, Salt, Lether, etc. why should not those be partakers of the same
justice now, that have been chief sticklers in setting up greater Patentees
then ever the former were?

57

Complain
against Monopoli
1) Preaching
2) sole trade of
woollen com.
3) printing
4) bread/beer

As first the Patent of ingrossing the Preaching of the Word only [p. 9] to such men as weare Black and rough garments to deceive, Zech. 13.4. and have had a Cannonical Ordination from the Bishops, and so from the Pope, and consequently from the Divell, although the Spirit of God doth command every man that hath received a gift, to minister the same one to another, as good Stewards of the manifold grace of God, 1.Pet.4. 10,11. . . . The second Monopoly is the Patent of Merchant Adventurers, who have ingrossed into their hands the sole trade of all woollen Commodities that are to be sent into the Netherlands, the mischievousnesse you may at large read in a late discourse consisting of motives for the inlargement and freedome of trade, especially that of Cloath, & other woollen manufactures ingrossed at present contrary to the Law of Nature, the law of Nations, and the lawes of this Kingdome, by a company of private men, who stile themselves Merchant Adventurers . . .

[p. 10] The third Monopoly, is that insufferable, unjust and tyrannical Monopoly of Printing, whereby a great company of the very same Malignant fellows that Canterbury and his Malignant party engaged in their Arbitrary Designes, against both the Peoples and Parliaments just Priviledges . . . are invested with an Arbitrary unlimmitted Power, even by a generall Ordinance of Parliament, to print, divulge and disperse whatsoever Books, Pamphlets and Libells they please, though they be full of Lyes, and tend to the poysoning of the Kingdom with unjust and Tyrannicall Principles.

And not only so, but most violently . . . to suppresse every thing which hath any true Declaration of the just Rights and Liberties of the free-borne People of this Nation, and to brand and traduce all such Writers and Writings with the odious termes of Sedition, Conspiracie and Treason, but to countenance and authorize such as shall calumniate them . . .

[p. 11] The next Monopoly, it is to be feared will be upon Bread and Beere, for as justly may there be a Monopoly upon them, as upon the former. Oh Englishmen! Where is your freedoms? and what is become of your Liberties and Priviledges that you have been fighting for all this while, to the large expence of your Bloods and Estates, which was hoped would have procured your liberties and freedomes? . . .

[p. 22] To the Right Honourable, The LORD MAJOR, and the Right Worshipfull, the Aldermen, and Common-Councell of the City of LONDON: In Common Councell Assembled.

The humble Petition of divers Citizens of
this Honourable City.
(April 1645)

SHEWING,

That the afflictions and sorrows of our hearts are unexpressible, in regard of the manifold miseries that are upon us, and thousands of our deer Brethren, and fellow Citizens complaints being generall, and very grievous. As amongst many other;

58

I. That the Poore is in great necessity, wanting wherewith to set themselves on worke, their Children uneducated, and thereby prepared to wickednesse and beggary.

II. That Trading is exceedingly decayed, whereby thousands that have lived in a free and plentifull way, are many fallen, and are more falling into great extremity.

III. That Assessments are made very unequall, whereby the Taxes laid upon the City, are made burthensome, and paid with much repining.

IV. That the Forces of the Citie are very much abated, and that the Citie is not in a Posture of Warre answerable to its greatnesse, or its danger. . . .

[p. 25] 6. Sir John Lenthall having acted and done many things of extraordinary prejudice against the State, one Captaine Cob, . . . out of duty and affection to the well-fare of the Publique, informed by a Letter the Speaker of the House of Commons of it, . . . But the Speaker, contrary to his duty, never caused him to be called in, . . . And therefore assuredly, if so foule and hainous a businesse as this is, be smothered up againe, I am very confidently perswaded, some one or other will publish all the particulars of it (ere long) in print, to the view of all the Commons of England, that so they may see and judge how they are jugled with, by some of those they have reposed their greatest trust in, . . .

[p. 28] The Lawyers rule Committees, the Speaker rules the Lawyers, Sir John Lenthall rules the Speaker; Thomas Dutson rules Sir John Lenthall, and the Devill rules Dutson. . . .[1]

[p. 30] 12. Whether it be not most agreeable to Law, Justice, equitie and conscience, and the nature of a Parliament mans place, that during the time of his being a member, hee should lay aside all places of profit in the Common-wealth, and tend only upon that function for which he was chosen; or if he be poor, or have lost his Estate, whether he ought not at present, to be content with his masters wages, that is to say, with so much a day, as the Common-Wealth by the Law of the Land is to pay him for his dayes labour, . . . 4s. per diem to every Knight, and to every Citizen and Burgesse 2s. a day, or more, as heretofore hath been accustomed, etc. or with some reasonable Competency, being the Commonwealth is grown so poor, that it is not able to pay her common Souldiers their 8d. a day, though they constantly adventer their lives to preserve her, which the Parliament men seldome doe, not to thirst after great and rich Places, farre lesse to possesse or enjoy them. . . .

Object. But would you have those Parliament men, that had their Places before the Parliament sate, turned out of theirs?

Yes, . . .

[p. 31] But you will say, This will fetch that gallant man Cromwell from the Army, which will be a mighty losse to the Kingdome, seeing he is so

---

[1] The Speaker (William Lenthall) was the brother of Sir John (Warden of the King's Bench Prison); Dutson was the chief jailer, the actual prison 'boss'.

able and active a Souldier, and so extraordinarily beloved of the Officers and Souldiers in the Army, yes, and such a stay to that unparralleld General Sir THOMAS FAIREFAX.

I answer, it is very true, that the Kingdome will have a mighty losse of him indeed, if he should be taken out of the Army, and be made unserviceable to them anywhere else; but if he come into the House of Commons (that proper seat whereunto hee was chosen) and doe them ten times more service there, then he doth, or can doe in the Army, what losse hath the Common-Wealth then? Consider seriously the grand service he did the last Winter, when hee was in the House, and see whether any action that ever he did in his life can be parralleld to it, and I beleeve it will be found good to have him at home: for he is sound at the heart, and not rotten cored, [p. 32] hates particular and selfe-Interests, and dares freely speake his minde. . . .

O for self-denying Cromwell home againe, . . .

Againe, Whether is not agreeable to Law, Justice, Equity and Conscience, . . . That for maintenance of the Laws, and the redresse of divers mischiefs and grievances, which daily [p. 33] happen, a Parliament shall be holden every yeere, . . . that seeing this present Parliament, (by reason of the extraordinary necessities of the Kingdom) have sate foure yeeres, and many of the members betray'd their trust, and those that remain, ingrosse Law-making, and also Law-executing into their own hands contrary both to reason, and to the true intent and meaning of the Law, . . .

[p. 35] Take heed how you fill up Elections with these kind of men (meaning Lawyers) . . . my Reasons against such Elections follow:

1. The Knowledge of the Common Law, doth no way conduce to the making of a States man: . . .

4. The Reformation of Courts of Justice, is a worke of absolute necessitye, without which . . . you shall have no Peace: . . .

5. It is necessary to make a Law for limitation of exorbetant fees, extortion, and prevarication (or collusion) amongst Lawyers, as it is used in other Countries.

6. It is necessary to limit the certaine number of practisers in each Court, that they swarme not (like Locusts) over the land, devouring and impoverishing it. . . .

[p. 35 points taken from *Some Advertisements, for the new Election of Burgesses for the House of Commons*, p. 6].

[p. 38] Yet let us not be idle or secure, but observe and indeavour these insuing means for our part.

I. By Petitioning, and by all other lawfull wayes and addresses, strive to procure from the Parliament, and all other just Authority, that they . . . will administer JUSTICE impartially . . .

one Moneths doing of which, would procure the Parliament more Cordiall freinds then the fighting of all their Armies, or the forcing of all their Covenants, or the Pressing of all their Souldiers, or persecuting all their Sectaries will doe in ten moneths space.

Monopoly of selling Bibles, extent yt to obtaine by force or compulsion.

II. To endeavour to set the City of London right in the enjoyment of her Priviledges: . . .

III. To rise as one man under faithfull, honest, experienced, constant, well-affected Commanders, such as those that rise, shall chuse to adventure their lives with, and beleager all the Kings Garrisons before the storme grow so great in the North, that no man dare travell under paine [p. 39] of his life, . . .

IV. To call to a just and strict account all Fingerers, and Receivers of money, whatsoever, even Parliament men as well as others; . . .

[p. 41] But to returne to our former matter, especially the grievances of the Nation; (through the mistake of the Printer, in omitting of some Manuscripts) and the absence of the Author, when the Monopolies in the former part of this Book were expressed; as chiefly that soul-starving, or murthering Monopoly, in hindering the free passage of [p. 42] the Gospel, by extorting the prices of Bibles, which the false self-loving Stationers, as deadly enemies to all goodnesse, have been enterprizing a long time to obtaine, and against all common freedom, to engrosse into their owne hands the sole and only selling of them, by which meanes, they intend to sell at what rates soever they please, though already they sell at double the rate that honest wel-affected Common-wealths men may print and sell them, and also be conscionable gainers by them:

So of all Monopolies or Patents, next the monopolizing of ingrossing the Preaching of Gods Word into the Tything and gripeing clawes of the Clergy: this is the most wicked and intollerable, because it deprives many, both poore servants, and others of meane condition to buy any Bibles at all, by reason of the extraordinary dearth or dearnesse of them, . . .

[p. 44] Innumerable instances there are throughout these three mourning and bleeding Kingdomes, to prove all these businesses, but I will onely chuse a Citie instance, and let every man who is in his profession after that manner grieved and wronged, turne the simile home to himself, according to his smart; Though the poore Hatmakers, who earne their living with heavy and hot labour, both early and late, doe pay Excise both for all the materialls, and fire which they use, for the bread they eate, for the liquor they drinke, and clothes they weare, yet when they have made their Hatts, and [p. 45] done all they can with great trouble and toyle, day and night, they are forced to pay Excise over againe out of their very labour, not-withstanding it was both so deare and heavy in buying all the necessaries before. . . .

When this Kingdom was in any way or possibility of subsistance, the auntient custome was, that Taxations should be raised by way of Subsidie, which is the most just, equitable, and reasonable way of all, for it sets every tub on its owne bottome, it layes the burthen upon the strong shoulders of the rich, who onely are able to beare it, but spareth and freeth the weake shoulders of the poore, because they are scarcely able to subsist, pay rent, and maintain their families.

But our new invented pay, layes the burden heavily upon the poore,

61

and men of middle quality or condition, without all discretion, and scarcely maketh the rich touch it with one of their fingers: yea, many of them are more and more advanced in their prosperous estate, by their great salleries they have for executing their places, . . . besides all the bribes they get, and the false Accounts they make; So that in this life, the rich have their pleasure, but poore Lazarus paines. . . .

[p. 48] The Postscript. . . . That in regarde the Kingdome is in so pittiful and great distresse, and that the most and best things that ever this Parliament did, were first motioned by private men, and then authorised and established by them: it would be excellent and needfull, if they would ordaine, that every freeman of England, who is able, would bestow his service one yeere at least, freely for the good of the Civill State, in any Place or Office of Trust, whereof his skill and breeding doe fit him to be most capable, according as they shall be chosen, and those who are not able to serve freely for a yeere, [p. 49] and to have competent maintenance allowed unto them, to the value of 50. or 60 l. a yeere, according to their charge; if such be chosen for their skill and diligence, though they want outward means: for which allowance, those that are conscienscious, will doe as good service, at least, as some others, who have 1000. or 2000. a yeere.

The like rule is no lesse, but rather farre more excellent and needfull, to be observed and established in matters concerning the Church-state, wherein her servants are to perform their duties freely, . . . otherwise, to have the like allowance . . .

2 *Englands Lamentable Slaverie*
WILLIAM WALWYN

William Walwyn (1600–80) first emerged as a pamphlet-writer in support of religious toleration. Here he is seen coming to Lilburne's aid, while not disguising the theological differences between them. Walwyn shows here that his own principles of individual rights rest on political, legal, religious and moral grounds. He praises Lilburne for invoking Magna Carta against the Long Parliament's abuses: arbitrary arrest, cross-examination of accused persons, and imprisonment without trial. Yet even Magna Carta and other statutes ostensibly concerned with the liberty of the subject are shown to be only qualified and limited defences of individual rights. Here too, while taking Lilburne's part, he reveals a difference of emphasis, if not of principle, between them – Lilburne making too much of Magna Carta for Walwyn's liking.

By the time that Lilburne was in prison again in the following summer the association between the future Leveller leaders had taken clearer shape. Even so, they were never to take exactly the same line on every issue. The mass petitions to Parliament and the successive 'Agreements of the People' are the nearest that they came to collective statements of policy or principle.

ENGLANDS LAMENTABLE SLAVERIE
Proceeding from the Arbitrarie will, severitie, and
Injustices of Kings, Negligence, corruption, and
unfaithfulnesse of Parliaments, Coveteousnesse, ambition
and variablenesse of Priests, and simplicitie, carelesnesse,
and cowardlinesse of People.
Which slaverie, with the Remedie may be easily observed.

By the scope of a modest & smooth Letter, written by a true Lover of his Countrey and a faithfull friend to that worthy Instrument of Englands Freedome, Lieuten. Collonnell Lilburn, now unjustlie imprisoned in Newgate

Being committed first by Order and Vote of Parliament without cause shewed, and then secondly for refusing to answer upon Interrogatories to their Committee of Examinations, Contrarie to

1 The Great Charter of England.
2 The very words of the Petition of right.
3 The Act made this present Parliament; for the abolishing the Star-Chamber.
4 The Solomne Protestation of this Kingdome.   63

5 And to the great Vow and Covenant for uniting the two Kingdomes together.

The Copie of which Letter (with the Superscription thereof) hereafter followeth.

A private Letter of publique use, to the constant maintainer of the Just Liberties of the People of England, Lieuten. Coll. John Lilburn Prisoner in Newgate by command of Parliament.

Sir,

Although there is some difference between you and mee in matters of Religion, yet, that hath no white abated in me, that great love and respect justly due unto you, for your constant zealous affection to the Common Wealth, and for your undaunted resolution in defence of the common freedome of the People.

The craft and delusion of those that would master, and controle the People, hath not availed (by fomenting our differences in Religion, which is their common practice) to make me judge preposterously, either of your or any other mens sufferings.

We have a generall caution, that no man suffer as an evill doer; but if any suffer for well doing, who are they that would be thought Christians, and can exempt themselves from suffering with them? No certainly, it is neither pettie differences in opinions, nor personall frailities in sufferers, nor both, that can acquite or excuse us in the sight of God. So we are not simplie to be spectators or beholders of them a far off (as too many doe.) but if one suffer, all ought to suffer with that one, even by having a sympathie and fellow feeling of his miserie, and helping to beare his burden; so that he may be eased in the day of tentation; yea and the sentences both of absolution and condemnation shall be pronounced at the great day, according to the visiting or not visiting of Prisoners, and hearing of their mourning sighs, and groanes.

This is my judgement, from whence hath issued this my practice, that when I heare of the sufferings of any man, I doe not enquire, what his judgement is in Religion, nor doe I give eare to any tales or reports of any mans personall imperfection. (being privie to mine owne) but I presently labour to be rightly informed of the cause of his sufferings (alledged against him) whether that be evill or good, and of the proceedings thereupon, whether legall or illegall, just or unjust.

And this hath been my course and practice in things of that nature for almost a score of yeares, whoever have been the Judges, whether Parliament, King, Counsell-board, Star-Chamber, High Commission, Kings-Bench, or any Judicatory, yea what ever the accuser, or the accused, the judgement or punishment hath been; I have taken this my just and necessary liberty; for having read, observed, debated and considered both ancient and latter times, the variations and changes of Governments and Governors, and looking upon the present with an impartiall judgement,

I still find a necessity of the same my accustomed watchfullnesse, it never being out of date; [the more my hearts grief] for worthy and good men (nay the most publique spirited men) to suffer for well doing, unto whom only is promised the blessing, and the heavenly Kingdome; Mat. 5.10.

Your suffering at present, is become every good mans wonders for they all universally conclude your faithfulnesse and zeale to the publique weale to be such, as no occasion or tentation could possibly corrupt, and the testimonies you have given thereof to be so great, as greater could not be.

They observe likewise, the large testimonie given of your deserts, by your honourable and worthy Friend in the Armie, Lieuten. Generall Cromwell.

And therefore, that you should now be kept in safe custodie, was very sad newes to all that love you; knowing how impossible it was, to make you flee or start aside; but when they heard that you were sent to that reproachfull prison of Newgate, they were confounded with griefe.

It should seeme, that you being questioned by the Committee of Examinations, stood upon your old guard, alledging it to be against your liberty, as you were a free borne Englishman, to answer to questions against your selfe, urging MAGNA CHARTA to justifie your so doing; And complaining that contrary to the said Charter, you had been divers times imprisoned by them.

Now it is not much to be wondred at, that this your carriage should be very offensive unto them; for you were not the first by divers, (whom I could name) that have been examined upon questions, tending to their own accusation and imprisonment too, for refusing to answer, but you are the first indeed, that ever raised this new doctrine of MAGNA CHARTA, to prove the same unlawfull.

Likewise, You are the first, that compareth this dealing to the crueltie of the Starre Chamber, and that produced the Vote of this Parliament against those cruelties (so unjustly inflicted on your selfe by that tyrannous Court) And how could you Imagine this could be indured by a Committee of Parliament? No, most Parliament men are to learne what is the just power of a Parliament, what the Parliament may doe, and what the Parliament (it selfe) may not doe. It's no marvell then that others are ignorant, very good men there be, who affirme, that a Parliament being once chosen, have power over all our lives estates and liberties, to dispose of them at their pleasure whether for our good or hurt. All's one (say they) we have trusted them, and they are bound to no rules, nor bounded by any limits, but whatsoever they shall ordaine, binds all the people, it's past all dispute, they are accountable unto none, they are above MAGNA CHARTA and all Lawes whatsoever, and there is no pleading of any thing against them.

Others there are (as good wise and judicious men) who affirme, that a Parliamentary authority is a power intrusted by the people (that chose them) for their good, safetie, and freedome; and therefore that a Parliament cannot justlie doe any thing, to make the people lesse safe or lesse free, then they found them: MAGNA CHARTA (you must observe) is but a part of the peoples rights and liberties, being no more but what with much striving and fighting, was by the blood of our Ancestors, wrestled out of the pawes of those Kings, who by force had conquered the Nation, changed the lawes and by strong hand held them in bondage.

For though MAGNA CHARTA be so little as lesse could not be granted with any pretence of freedome, yet as if our Kings had repented them of that little, they alwaies strove to make it lesse, wherein very many times they had the unnaturall assistance of Parliaments to helpe them: For Sir, if we should read over all the hudge volume of our Statutes, we might easily observe how miserablie Parliaments assembled, have spent most of their times and wee shall not find one Statute made to the enlargement of that streight bounds, deceitfully and improperlie called MAGNA CHARTA, (indeed so called to blind the people) but if you shall observe and marke with your pen, every particular Statute made to the abridgement of MAGNA CHARTA, you would make a very blotted booke, if you left any part unblotted,

Sometimes you shall find them very seriously imployed, about letting loose the Kings prerogatives, then denominating what should be Treason against him (though to their owne vexation and continuall danger of their lives) sometimes enlarging the power of the Church, and then againe abridging the same, sometimes devising punishments for Heresie, and as zealous in the old grossest superstitions, as in the more refined and new, but ever to the vexation of the people.

See how busie they have been about the regulating of petty inferiour trades and exercises, about the ordering of hunting, who should keep Deere and who should not, who should keep a Greayhound, and who a Pigeon-house, what punishment for Deere stealing, what for every Pigeon killed, contrary to law, who should weare cloth of such a price, who Velvet, Gold, and Silver, what wages poore Labourers should have, and the like precious and rare businesse, being most of them put on of purpose to divert them from the very thoughts of freedome, suitable to the representative, body of so great a people.

And when by any accident or intollerable oppression they were roosed out of those waking dreames, then whats the greatest thing they ayme at? Hough[1] with one consent, cry out for MAGNA CHARTA (like great is Diana of the Ephesians) calling that messe of pottage their birthright, the great inheritance of the people, the great Charter of England.

And truly, when so choice a people, (as one would thinke Parliaments could not faile to be) shall insist upon such inferiour things, neglecting greater matters, and be so unskilfull in the nature of common and just freedom, as to call bondage libertie, and the grants of Conquerours their Birth rights, no marvaile such a people make so little use of the greatest

66   [1] ?How

advantages; and when they might have made a newer and better Charter, have falne to patching the old.

Nor are you to blame others for extolling it, that are tainted therewith your selfe, (saving only that its the best we have) Magna Charta hath been more precious in your esteeme then it deserveth; for it may be made good to the people, and yet in many particulars, they may remaine under intolerable oppressions, as I could easily instance:

3 An Arrow against all Tyrants
RICHARD OVERTON

Richard Overton (?1600–?60s) had already clashed with the Presbyterian puritans, who wanted to preserve a state-church with coercive powers and to deny liberty of worship to the puritan sects. Like Lilburne he was imprisoned by order of the House of Lords in 1646. Most of the Arrow is a detailed attack on the usurpation of the Lords in trying to exercise an illegal jurisdiction over Commoners, and on the Presbyterian clergy for their encroachments on the rights of free expression and free association, which should be available at least to all non-episcopalian Protestants. In the opening passage which is printed here, Overton develops a non-religious doctrine of natural rights as the basis of political rights. These rights are implanted in Man by Nature. While God is the creator of Nature, and so their indirect author, no particular theology – Christian or other – and certainly no doctrine of Revelation, is required in order to accept these premises. It would be unwise, on the evidence available, to portray Overton as a sceptic or materialist in the modern sense, and toleration was certainly of great importance to him. Yet his political principles do seem to owe less to his religious convictions than is the case with Lilburne and perhaps – initially at least – with Walwyn.

AN ARROW AGAINST ALL TYRANTS
And Tyrany, shot from the Prison of Newgate into the
Prerogative Bowels of the Arbitrary
House of Lords, and all other Usurpers and Tyrants
whatsoever.

Sir,

To every Individuall in nature, is given an individuall property by nature, not to be invaded or usurped by any: for every one as he is himselfe, so he hath a selfe propriety, else could he not be himselfe, and on this no second may presume to deprive any of, without manifest violation and affront to the very principles of nature, and of the Rules of equity and justice between man and man; mine and thine cannot be, except this be: No man hath power over my rights and liberties, and I over no mans; I may be but an Individuall, enjoy my selfe and my selfe propriety, and may write my selfe no more then[1] my selfe, or presume any further; if I doe, I am an

[1] Here, as frequently elsewhere, for 'then' read 'than'.

encroacher & an invader upon an other mans Right, to which I have no Right. For by naturall birth, all men are equally and alike borne to like propriety, liberty and freedome, and as we are delivered of God by the hand of nature into this world, every one with a naturall, innate freedome and propriety (as it were writ in the table of every mans heart, never to be obliterated) even so are we to live, every one equally and alike to enjoy his Birthright and priviledge; even all whereof God by nature hath made him free.

And this by nature every one desires aimes at, and requires, for no man naturally would be befooled of his liberty by his neighbours craft, or inslaved by his neighbours might, for it is natures instinct to preserve itselfe, from all things hurtfull and obnoctious, and this in nature is granted of all to be most reasonable, equall and just, not to be rooted out of the kind, even of equall duration with the creature: And from this fountain or root, all just humain powers take their original; not immediatly from God (as Kings usually plead their prerogative) but mediatly by the hand of nature, as from the represented to the representors; for originally, God hath implanted them in the creature, and from the creature those powers immediatly proceed; and no further: and no more may be communicated then stands for the better being, weale, or safety thereof: and this is mans prerogative and no further, so much and no more may be given or received thereof: even so much as is conducent to a better being, more safety and freedome, and no more; he that gives more, sins against his owne flesh; and he that takes more, is a Theife and Robber to his kind: Every man by nature being a King, Priest and Prophet in his owne naturall circuite and compasse, whereof no second may partake, but by deputation, commission, and free consent from him, whose naturall right and freedome it is.

And thus Sir, and no otherwise are you instated into your soveraign capacity, for the free people of this Nation, for their better being, discipline, government, propriety and safety, have each of them communicated so much unto you (their Chosen Ones) of their naturall rights and powers, that you might thereby become their absolute Commissioners, and lawfull Deputies, but no more; and that by contraction of those their severall Individuall Communications confer'd upon, and united in you, you alone might become their own naturall proper, soveraign power, therewith singly and only impowred for their severall weales, safeties and freedomes, and no otherwise: for as by nature, no man may abuse, beat, torment, or afflict himselfe; so by nature, no man may give that power to another, seeing he may not doe it himselfe, for no more can be communicated from the generall then is included in the particulars, whereof the generall is compounded.

So that such so deputed, are to the Generall no otherwise, then as a Schoole-master to a particular, to this or that mans familie, for as such an ones Mastership, ordering and regulating power is but by deputation, and that *ad bene placitum*, and may be removed at the parents or Head masters pleasure, upon neglect or abuse thereof, and be confer'd upon another (no parents ever giving such an absolute unlimited power to such over their children, as to doe to them as they list, and not to be retracted, controuled, or restrained in their exorbitances) Even so and no otherwise is it, with you our Deputies in respect of the Generall, it is in vaine for you to thinke you have power over us, to save us or destroy us at your pleasure, to doe with us as you list, be it for our weale, or be it for our wo, and not to be enjoyned in mercy to the one, or questioned in justice for the other, for the edge of your own arguments against the King in this kind, may be turned upon your selves, for if for the safety of the people, he might in equity be opposed by you in his tyranies oppressions & cruelties, even so may you by the same rule of right reason, be opposed by the people in generall, in the like cases of distruction and ruine by you upon them, for the safety of the people is the Soveraigne Law, to which all must become subject, and for the which all powers humaine are ordained by them, for tyrany, oppression and cruelty whatsoever, and in whomsoever, is in it selfe unnaturall; illegall, yea absolutly anti magisteriall, for it is even destructive to all humaine civill society, and therefore resistable.

Now Sir the Commons of this Nation, having impowred their Body Representative, wherof you are one, with their own absolute Soveraignty, thereby Authoritively and legally to remove from amongst them all oppressions and tyranies, oppressors and tyrants, how great soever in name, place or dignity, and to protect, safegard, and defend them from all such unnaturall monsters, vipers and pests, bred of corruption or which are intrusted amongst them & as much as in them lie, to prevent all such for the future. And to that end, you have been assisted with our lives and fortunes, most liberally and freely, with most victorious and happy successe, whereby your Armes are strengthned with our might, that now you may make us all happy within the confines of this Nation, if you please; and therfore Sir, in reason, equity and justice, we deserve no lesse at your hands, and (Sir) let it not seem strange unto you, that we are thus bold with you for our own.

For by nature we are the sons of Adam, and from him have legitimatly derived a naturall propriety, right and freedome, which only we require, and how in equity you can deny us, we cannot see; It is but the just rights and prerogative of mankind (whereunto the people of England, are heires apparent as well as other Nations) which we desire: and sure you will not deny it us, that we may be men, and live like men; if you doe it will be as little safe for your selfes and posterity, as for us and our posterity, for Sir, look what bondage, thraldome, or tyrany soever you settle upon us, you certainly, or your posterity will tast of the dregs: if by your present policy and (abused) might, you chance to award it from your selves in particular, yet your posterity doe what you can, will be liable to the hazard thereof.

4 Postscript to Londons Liberty
JOHN LILBURNE

Appended to one of his many pamphlets written from prison, this is one of two 'Postscripts' in which Lilburne tries to formulate a general statement of his political beliefs.[1] Starting, as will be seen, from a strictly religious position (invoking texts in both New and Old Testaments), he arrives at a doctrine of political rights which is democratic and also highly individualist. Moreover, it is hard to see how – either logically or morally – these rights can be denied to anyone, at least anyone adult and in their right mind, be they male or female, rich or poor, lord or servant. At any rate, no such qualifications are made, and no restrictions are placed on the scope of these political rights. Historians who see Lilburne as less radical than, for example, Overton or Walwyn, might argue either that there is an element of sheer rhetorical flourish here, that every word is not meant to be taken literally, or else that Lilburne was simply not consistent in his different writings and in his line on different issues. At the end he comes back characteristically to his own collisions with the authorities and his current involvement with the popular opposition to the ruling oligarchy in the City of London.

A POSTSCRIPT WRITTEN BY LIEUTENANT
COLONELL JOHN LILBURN, Prisoner in the Tower
of LONDON, Octob. 1646.

The omnipotent, glorious, and wise God, creating man for his own praise; made him more glorious then all the rest of his Creatures that he placed upon earth: creating him in his own Image, (which principally consisted in his reason and understanding) and made him Lord over the earth, and all the things therein contained, Gen. 26, 27, 28, 29, and chap. 5.1. and 9.6. I Cor. 11.7. Col. 3.10; But made him not Lord, or gave him dominion over the individuals of Mankind, no further then by free consent, or agreement, by giving up their power, each to other, for their better being; so that originally, he gave no Lordship, nor Soveraignty, to any of Adams Posterity, by Will, and Prerogative, to rule over his Brethren-Men, but ingraved by nature in the soule of Man, this goulden and everlasting principle, to doe to another, as he would have another to do to him; but man by his transgression, falling from his perfection of reason (that Image in which God created him, Col. 3.10.) became tyran-

---

[1] For the other, from *The Free-man's Freedom Vindicated*, of 23 June 1646, pp. 11–12, see Woodhouse, *Puritanism and Liberty*, pp. 317–18.

nicall, and beastly in his principles and actions; the effect of which, we see in Caines flaying of Abel; for which he was accursed of God, and all things hee went about, Gen.4.8, 10, 11, 12. but God taking mercy of Mankind in some measure, and not executing the fulnesse of his wrath, in the 9. of Gen. to revenge that beastlinesse, bloody, revengfull, and devouring temper of Spirit, that, by the fall, had now entred into the Spirits of all Mankind; institutes a perpetuall, morall, unchangeable, and everlasting Law; that is to say, That whosoever he was, that would be so beastly, bearish, and Woolvish, as to fall upon his neighbour, brother, or friend, and to do unto him that, which he would not he should do to him, by taking away his life and blood from him; God ordaines, and expresly saith he shall lose his life, without mercy or compassion for so doing, vers. 5.6. Yea, and afterwards, when he chuseth unto himself Israel, out of all the Nations of the world to be his peculiar people, Levit. 19.15, 16, 17, 18 ordaines this for a standing Law amongst them; Yee shall do no unrighte-ousnesse in judgment; thou shalt not respect the person of the poore, nor honour the person of the mighty; but in righteousnesse shalt thou judge thy Neighbour. Thou shalt not go up and down as a Tale-bearer amongst thy people; neither shalt thou stand against the bloud of thy neighbour: I am the Lord. Thous shalt not hate thy Brother in thy heart: thou shalt [not] in any wise rebuke thy neighbour, and not suffer sinne upon him. Thou shalt not avenge nor bear any grudge against the Children of thy People; but thou shalt love thy Neighbour as thy selfe: I am the Lord.

And when the fulnesse of time was come, that Christ the Restorer and Repairer of mans losse and fall, should come and preach Righteousnesse & Justice to the world; He saith, it is the Law, & the Prophets, that what-soever we would that men should do to us, that wee should do to them, Matth.7.12. Luke 6.31. Yea, and further saith, That as it is the great Commandement that we should love (our Soveraign Creator, and Preserver) the Lord our God with all our hearts, and all our soules, and with all our minds; so the second Commandement, which is like unto it, is, That we should love our neighbours as our selves; and on these two, saith hee, hang all the Law and the Prophets: so that by this, it is cleerly evident, that Religion, Christianity, or the knowledge of Christ, doth not destroy morality, civility, justice, and right reason; but rather restores it to its first perfection, beauty, splendor and glory: and therefore the Apostle exhorts Saints and Believers, Ephes. 4.17, 18, 19, 20, 21, 22, 23, 24. Not to walk as other Gentiles do, in the vanity of their mind, having their understanding darkened, being alienated from the life of God, through the ignorance that is in them, because of the blindnesse of their heart. Who being past feeling; have given themselves over to lasciviousnesse, to work all uncleannesse with greedinesse. But (saith the Apostle to all that love Christ,) Ye have not so learned Christ: If so be ye have heard him, and have been taught by him, as the truth is in Jesus. That ye put off, concern-ing the former conversation, the old man; which is corrupt, according to the deceitfull lusts: And be renewed in the Spirit of your mind. And that ye put on that new man, which after God is created in righteousnesse, and true holinesse; and excellent to this purpose, is that of the Apostle, Col. 3.7, 8. where speaking of, and to those that have put off the old man, with his deeds; and have put on the new man, which (saith he) is renewed in knowledge, after the Image of him that created him.

And therefore the same Apostle layeth down his exhortation at large, and declareth, it is not only the duty of the Saints, to doe good each unto other, but as much as in them lyes, to doe good unto all the Sons of Adam; saying, Gal.6.10. as we have therefore opportunity, let us do good unto all men; especially, unto them, who are of the Household of Faith. But the greatest good that I know of, that any man can do unto the Sons of Men besides the discovery of the knowledge of Christ, and the benefits and priviledges that are to be injoyed by him; is, rationally to discover the privilege, that is, the Right, Due, and Propriety of all the Sons of Adam, as men: that so they may not live in beastlinesse, by devouring one another: and not onely so, but also to stand for, and maintain those Rights and Priviledges in any Kingdome, or Nation, wheresoever they are in any measure established: that so the trusted, made great and potent, by a power conferred upon them; may not there-with (as is too commonly seene) Lord it, domineer over, and destroy by their Prerogative-will and pleasure, the Betrusters: yea, and also to maintain the liberties and priviledges established in a Land, by Law, against the incroaching usurpations of some great and mighty Nimrods of the world, made so by wayes and meanes, more immediatly and properly flowing from the Divell, then God: and by their false-assumed incroaching power, tyrant-like tread under their feet, all just, and innocent persons: and protect, defend, and countenance none but those, that will comply, applaud, and assist them, in their brutish, woolvish and tyrant-like proceedings: which practises are contrary to the very end of Government, and Magistracy; as is largly declared by the Apostle, Rom. 13.3, 4. where he plainly saith, Rulers are not (no nor ought not to be) a terrour to good Workes, but to the evill: wilt thou then not be afraid of the power? Do that which is good, and thou shalt have praise of the same. For he is the Minister of God to thee for good: But if thou do that which is evill, be afraid, for he beareth not the sword in vain; for he is the Minister of God, a Revenger to execute wrath upon him that doth evill, but not upon him that doth good. The knowledge of which, in some measure, in my own soule, hath been the true ground, that conscienciously made me out of duty to my selfe, and neighbours, and obedience to God; stand against, and oppose my self against the Bishops, and with resolution so often since, in the middest of many deaths; hazard my life for my liberties, and the lawes, liberties, and rights of all the people of this Land, & which is the only principle that now carryes me on in opposition against the Lords: unto whom, as so many men, I have and must confesse, I am ten times more oblieged, for my own particular, than to the house of Commons it self, having found at their hands several times cordiall and speedy Justice, which I never enjoyed from the House of 73

Commons in my life; although I have waited upon them therefore, these six years, and followed them as close as any man (I think) in England: and I dare safely say it, without vain or lying boasting; for these nine or ten years together, I have been as serviceable to the Common-wealth of England in my place and condition as any one man whatsoever that sits in the house; though I have been as ungratefully dealt with by them, as ever man in England was: yet I say, when the Lords forced me to contest with them, which I professe, I was as unwilling to do, as I was to run my head against the wall, the which I told unto one of themselves; yet I say, before I would have parted with my reason and understanding, and so have defaced, obliterated, and annihilated, as much as in me lay, the Image that God created me in, (and which Christ by communicating of himself to me; hath restored, confirmed, and inlarged) and degenerated into the habit of a beast, (which all slaves that live in the World without a rationall and just Law are in) by parting with, and betraying my native, naturall, just liberties, which the fundamentall lawes of this Land give me; I will part with my very heart-blood first; yea, and if I had a thousand lives, they should all go, before I will part with my just liberties, either to them, or any power on earth, what ever it be, that dare assume unto themselves so much tyranny, and satanicall pride as to go about it, or endeavour it. And it is this very principle that now engageth to write this Postscript, to beget a Contest with the Prerogative-men of London, Englands mighty Nimrods, who haue inslaved not only this City, but beene strong Instruments from time to time, to doe the same to the whole Land.

5 The 'large' Petition

The so-called 'large' Petition *was presented to Parliament some months before the name 'Leveller' came into use for its authors, and perhaps also precedes the existence of a coherent party organization. None the less, it is usually taken as the first systematic, collaborative exposition of Leveller views. The authors make clear the strength of their parliamentarian sympathies, yet explain how – more in sorrow than in anger – they have become more and more critical of the Long Parliament. Their present grievances are skilfully contrasted with the reforms achieved by the Parliament back in 1640–2. Unless there were other draftsmen of whom we know nothing, Walwyn's pen seems likely to have been at work here. The similarity with parts of his* Englands Lamentable Slaverie *(no. 2) will be obvious. Amongst the targets of the 'large' Petition are monopolies, arbitrary arrest and imprisonment, the unreformed legal system, the compulsory maintenance of a coercive state-church, indefinite imprisonment for debt, and the condition of the prisons. Interestingly, the general problem of poverty and the need for action to alleviate it are also brought to Parliament's attention.*

The Petition is couched in the form of an appeal to the House of Commons to assert their authority against the Lords as much as against the monarch. Essentially, indeed, they are being called upon to be true to their own better selves. The numerous requests made here rehearse the contents of earlier pamphlets, and would also have meant the release of Lilburne and Overton.

The immediate historical context of the Petition is as important as its content. Its presentation coincided with the widening and deepening of the breach between Parliament and Army. During the time from its submission to its final rejection, the Army refused to accept Parliament's orders, the first Agitators (or soldiers' delegates) were elected, and the officers moved – or were forced – towards a common front with the soldiers. Meanwhile the Levellers increasingly emerged as protagonists of the Agitators in the Army's resistance to Parliament.

We can only guess how much the course of events would have been altered if Parliament had accorded a more sympathetic reception to the 'large' Petition. But the long delay, followed by its brutal rejection and condemnation, can only have helped to cement the new alliance between the London radicals and the militants in the Army.

TO THE RIGHT HONOURABLE AND SUPREME AUTHORITY OF THIS NATION, THE COMMONS IN PARLIAMENT ASSEMBLED.

The humble Petition of many thousands, earnestly desiring the glory of God, the freedome of the Common-wealth, and the peace of all men.

Sheweth,

That no Government is more just in the Constitution, then that of Parliaments, having its foundation in the free choice of the People, and as the end of all government is the safety and freedome of the governed, even so the people of this Nation in all times have manifested most hearty affections unto Parliaments, as the most proper remedies of their grievances, yet such hath been the wicked pollicy of those who from time to time have indeavoured to bring this Nation into bondage, that they have in all times, either by the disuse or abuse of Parliaments, deprived the people of their hopes; for testimony whereof, the late times foregoing this Parliament will sadly witnesse, when 'twas not only made a crime to mention a Parliament, but either the pretended Negative voice (the most destructive to freedome) or a speedy dissolution blasted the fruit and benefit thereof, whilest the whole Land was overspread with all kind of oppression and tyranny, extending both to soule and body, and that in so rooted and settled a way, that the complaint of the people in generall witnessed, that they would have given any thing in the world for one six moneths freedome of Parliament, which hath been since evidenced in their instant and constant readinesse of assistance to this present Parliament, exceeding the Records of all former ages, and wherein God hath blessed them with their first desires, making this Parliament most free and absolute of any Parliament that ever was, and inabling it with power sufficient to deliver the whole Nation from all kind of oppression and grievance though of never so long continuance and to make it the most absolute and free nation in the world.

And it is most thankfully acknowledged, that you have in order to the freedome of the people, suppressed the High-Commission, Star-Chamber, and Councell Table, called home the banished, delivered such as were imprisoned for matters of conscience, and brought some Delinquents to deserved punishment; that you have suppressed the Bishops and popish Lords, abolished Episcopacy, and that kind of prelatick and persecuting government, that you have taken away Ship-money, and all new illegall Patents whereby the hearts of all the well-affected were inlarged, and filled with a confident hope, that they should have seen long ere this a compleat removall of all grievances, and the whole people delivered from all oppression over soule or body. But such is our misery, that after the expence of so much precious time, blood and treasure, and the ruine of so many thousands of honest Families, in recovering our liberty. Wee still find the Nation oppressed with grievances of the same destructive nature as formerly though under other notions, and which are so much the more grievous unto us, because they are inflicted in the very time of this present Parliament [under God] the hope of the oppressed; For as then all the men and women in England, were made liable to the Summons, Attachments, Sentences and imprisonments of the Lords of the Councell board, so wee find by wofull experience, and the suffering of many particular persons, that the present Lords doe assume and exercise the same power, then which nothing can be more repugnant and destructive to the Commons just liberty. As then the unjust power of the Starchamber was exercised in compelling men and women to answer to interrogatories tending to accuse themselves and others, so is the same now frequently practised upon divers persons, even your cordiall friends, that have been, and still are punished for refusing to answer questions against themselves, and neerest relations. As then the great oppression of the High-Commission, was most evident in molesting of godly peaceable people for non-conformity, or different opinion, or practice in religion, in judging all who were contrary-minded to themselves, to bee Hereticks, Sectaries, Schismatiques seditious, factious, enemies to the State, and the like; and under great penalties, forbidding all persons not licensed by them to preach or publish the Gospell; even so now at this day, the very same, if not greater molestations are set on foot and violently prosecuted by the instigation of a Clergy, no more infallible then the former, to the extreme discouragement & affliction of many thousands of your faithfull adherents, who are not satisfied that controversies in religion can be trusted to the compulsive regulation of any, & after the Bishops were suppressed, did hope never to have seen such a power assumed by any in this Nation any more. And although all new illegall Patents are by you abolished, yet the oppressive Monopoly of Merchant adventurers, and others do still remain to the great abridgement of the liberty of the people, and to the extream prejudice of all such industrious people, as doe depend on Clothing or woollen manufacture, it being the staple commodity of this Kingdom and Nation, and to the great discouragement and disadvantage of all sorts of Tradesmen, Seafaring-men, and hinderance of Shipping, and Navigation, also the old tedious and chargeable way of deciding Controversies or suits in law is continued to this day, to the extreme vexation, and utter undoing of multitudes of Families (a grievance as great and palpable as any in the world) that old and most unequall punishment of malefactors, is still continued whereby mens lives and liberties are as liable to the lawes corporall paines as much inflicted for small, as for great offences, and that most, most unjustly upon the testimony of one Witnesse, contrary both to the law of God and common equity (a grievance very great) but little regarded; And also Tithes and other inforced maintenance are still continued, though there be no ground for either under the Gospel, and though the same have occasioned multitudes of suits, quarrells and debates both in former and latter times. In like manner multitudes of 77 people, poore distressed prisoners for debt, lye still unregarded, in a most miserable and wofull condition throughout the Land, to the great reproach of this Nation; Likewise Prison-keepers or Jaylors are as presumptuous as ever they were both in receiving and detaining of prisoners, illegally committed, as cruell and inhumane to all, especially to such as are well-affected, as oppressive and extorting in their Fees, and are attended with under Officers of such vile and unchristian demeanour as is most abominable; Also thousands of men and women are permitted to live in beggery and wickednesse all their life long, and so breed their children to the same idle and vicious course of life, and no effectuall meanes used to reclaime either, or to reduce them to any vertue or industry.

And last as those who found themselves agrieved formerly at the burdens and oppressions of those times, that did not conforme to the Church government then established, refused to pay Ship-money, or yeild obedience to unjust Patents, were reviled and reproached with Nick-names of Puritans, Hereticks; Schismaticks, Sectaries, or were termed factious or seditious, men of turbulent spirits, despisers of government, and disturbers of the publike peace; even so it is at this day, in all respects with those, that shew any sensibility of the fore-recited grievances, or move in any manner or measure, for remedy thereof, all the reproaches, evills, and mischiefs that can be devised, are thought too few, or too little to be layd upon them, as Round-heads, Sectaries, Independants, Hereticks, Schismaticks, factious, seditious, Rebellious, disturbers of the publike peace: destroyers of all civill relations, and subordinations, yea and beyond what was formerly, non-conformity is now judged a sufficient cause to disable any person (though of known fidelity) from bearing any offices of trust in the Common-wealth, whiles Neuters, malignant and disaffected, are admitted and countenanced; and though it be not now made a crime to mention a Parliament, yet it is little lesse to mention the supreme power of this Honourable House, so that in all these respects this Nation remaines, in a very sad and disconsolate condition and the more, because it is thus with us, after so long a Session of so powerfull, and so free a Parliament, and hath been so made and maintained by the abundant love, and liberall effusion of the blood of the people, and therefore knowing no danger nor thraldome, like unto our being left in this so sad a condition by the Parliament, and observing that you are now drawing the great and weighty affaires of this Nation to some conclusion, and fearing that ere long you may be obstructed, by something equally evill to a Negative voice, and that you may be induced to lay by your strength, which under God hath hitherto made you powerfull to all good workes, whilest we have yet time to hope, and you power to helpe, and lest by our silence we might be guilty of that ruine and slavery, which without your speedy help, is like to fall upon us, your selves and the whole Nation, we have presumed to spread our cause thus plainly, and largely before you and do most earnestly intreat that you will stir up your affections to a zealous love and tender regard of the people, who have chosen and trusted you, that you will seriously consider that the end of your trust was freedome and deliverance from all kind of grievances and oppressions.

1 And that therefore in the first place you will be exceeding carefull to preserve your just Authority from all prejudices of a Negative voice in any person or persons whatsoever, which may disable you, from making that happy returne unto the people which they justly expect, and that you will not be induced to lay by your strength till you have satisfied your understandings in the undoubted security of your selves, and of those who have voluntarily, and faithfully adhered to you in all your extremities, and untill you have secured and setled the Common-wealth in setled peace, and true freedome, which is the end of the primitive institution of all government.

2 Secondly, that you will take off all sentences, fines, and imprisonments imposed on Commoners by any whomsoever, without due course of Law, or judgement of their equalls, and to give due reparations to all those who have been so injuriously dealt withall, and for preventing the like for the time to come, that you will enact all such arbitrary proceedings, to be Capitall crimes.

3 Thirdly, that you permit no authority whatsoever to compell any person or persons, to answer to any questions against themselves or neerest relations, except in cases of private interest between party and party in a legall way, and to release such as suffer by imprisonment, or otherwise, for refusing to answer to such interrogatories.

4 Fourthly, that all Statutes, Oathes, and Covenants may be repealed so farre as they tend, or may be construed to the molestation and insnaring of religious peaceable and well affected people, for non-conformity or difference of opinion, or practice in religion.

5 Fifthly, that no man for preaching or publishing his opinion in Religion, in a peaceable way, may be punished or persecuted as hereticall, by Judges that are not infallible, but may be mistaken as well as other men in their judgements, lest upon pretence of suppressing errors, Sects or Schismes, the most necessary truths, and sincere professions thereof may be suppressed, as upon the like pretence it hath been in all ages.

6 Sixthly that you will for the incouragement of industrious people, dissolve that oppressive company of Merchant-Adventurers, and the like, and prevent all such others by great penalties for ever.

7 Seventhly, that you will settle a just, speedy, plain, and unburdensom way for deciding of Controversies, and suits in Law, and reduce all lawes, to the neerest agreement with Christianity, and publish them in the English tongue, and that all processe and proceedings therein, may be true, and also in English, and in the most usuall Character of writing, without any abreviation, that each one who can read, may the better understand their owne affaires, and that the duties of all Judges, Officers, and practisers in the Law, and of all Magistrates and Officers in the Common-wealth, may be prescribed, their fees limited under strict penalties, and published in Print, to the knowledge and view of all men, 79

by which just and equitable meanes, this Nation shall be for ever freed of an oppression, more burdensome and troublesome then all the oppressions hitherto by this Parliament removed.

8 Eighthly, that the life of no person may be taken away under the testimony of two witnesses at least, of honest conversation, and that in an equitable way you will proportion punishment to offences, so that no mans life be taken away, his body punished, nor his estate forfeited, but upon such weighty and considerable causes, as justly deserve such punishment, and that all prisoners may have a speedy tryall, that they be neither starved nor their Families ruined by long and lingring imprisonment, and that imprisonment may be used only for safe custody untill time of tryall, and not as a punishment for offences.

9 Ninthly, that tythes, and all other inforced maintenances, may be for ever abolished, and nothing in place thereof imposed, but that all Ministers may be payd only by those who voluntarily choose them, and contract with them for their labours.

10 Tenthly, that you will take some speedy and effectuall course, to relieve all such prisoners for debt as are altogether unable to pay, that they may not perish in prison through the hard-heartednesse of their Creditors, and that all such who have any estates, may be inforced to make payment accordingly, and not shelter themselves in prison to defraud their Creditors.

11 Eleventhly, that none may be Prison-keepers, but such as are of approved honesty, and that they be prohibited under great penalties, to receive or detaine any person or persons without lawfull warrant, that their usage of Prisoners may be with gentlenesse and civility, their fees moderate and certaine, and that they may give security for the good behaviour of their under officers.

12 Twelfthly, that you will provide some powerfull meanes to keepe men, women, and children from begging and wickednesse, that this Nation may be no longer a shame to Christianity therein.

13 Thirteenthly, that you will restraine and discountenance the malice, and impudency of impious persons in their reviling, and reproaching the well-affected with the ignominious titles of Roundheads, factious, seditious, and the like, whereby your reall friends have been a longtime, and still are exceedingly wronged, discouraged, and made obnoxious to rude and prophane people, and that you will not exclude any of approved fidelity, from bearing offices of trust in the Common-wealth for Nonconformity, but rather Neuters, and such as manifest disaffection or opposition to common freedome, the admission and continuation of such, being the chiefe cause of all our grievances. These Remedies, or what other shall seeme more effectuall in your grave wisdomes, we humbly pray may be speedily applied, and that in doing thereof you will be confident of the assistance of your Petitioners, and of all considerate well-minded people, to the utmost of their best abilities against all opposition whatsoever, looking upon our selves, as more concerned now at last to

make a good end, then at the first to have made a good beginning, for what shall it profit us, or what remedy can we expect, if now after so great troubles and miseries this Nation should be left by this Parliament, in so great a thraldome both of body, mind, and estate; Wee beseech you therefore, that withall your might, whilest you have time, freedome and power, so effectually to fulfill the true ends of Parliaments in delivering this Nation, from these, and all other grievances, that none may presume or dare to introduce the like for ever; And we trust the God of your good successe, will manifest the sincerity of our intentions herein, and that our humble desires are such, as tend not only to our owne particular, but to the generall good of the Common-wealth, and proper for this honourable house to grant, without which this Nation cannot be safe or happy; And that he will blesse you with true Christian fortitude, suitable to the trust and greatnesse of the worke you have undertaken, and make the memory of this Parliament blessed to all succeeding generations.

Shall ever be the prayer of your humble Petitioners. SIR,

6 'Certain Articles'
RICHARD OVERTON

*The title of Overton's Appeale from the Degenerate Representative Body
... to ... The free People ... of England (July 1647) speaks for itself. It
expresses the utter disillusionment of the popular radicals with the Long Parliament, and invokes the people's right to withdraw their trust from legislators who
have flagrantly and repeatedly betrayed it. These Articles, appended as a
Postscript, form one of the fullest versions of the Leveller reform programme. And
they show that Overton was not exclusively concerned with immediate matters of
political tactics. Some historians would indeed argue that if heavier and more
consistent emphasis had been laid on the social and economic proposals presented
here, and if the Levellers had not been side-tracked into excessive concentration
on the issues of the parliamentary suffrage, and then of church–state relations,
they might have enjoyed wider popular support.*

*Having appealed from parliament to people in the main part of the pamphlet,
Overton here addresses himself to Fairfax and the Army under his command. The
Articles display a characteristic Leveller insistence on decentralization, the
accountability of governors to governed, together with suspicion of excessive or
arbitrary power wherever these might be located. Among the many other positive
reforms listed, some are familiar from earlier writings, but others appear for the
first time. The sections concerning Schools, Hospitals (including Poor Relief)
and Enclosed Commons show the basis of a possible social and economic programme
which the Levellers never really developed.*

Certain Articles for the good of the Common
wealth, presented to the consideration of his
Excellencie, Sir Thomas Fairfax, and to the
Officers and Souldiers under his Command.
By R. O.

Concerning Parliaments,

1 That for the future, the election and expulsion of Parliament Members may be so setled in the Electors, that none may be hindered, debard, or
expulsed from serving his Country under any colour or pretence whatsoever, as for refusing the Covenant or other wise without order first,
assent or concurrence of their Countrey.

2 That for the better security of the interest and power of the people,

all titles, by Prerogative, Priviledge, Pattent, Succession, Peerage, Birth or otherwise to sit and act in the Assembly of Parliament, contrary to, and without the free choice and Election of the People, be utterly abrogated, nuld and made voide, and that all such so sitting, may be removed from sitting therein.

3 That the authority of Parliament may bee preserved and secured for the future from the obstructions and prejudice of a negative voyce in any person or persons whatsoever.

4 That every County may have liberty to choose some certaine number amongst themselves, to inquire and present to the Parliament, what be the just Lawes, Customes, and Priviledges of each County, and that those County Commissioners, be bound to receive all and every impeachment, and impeachments, by any person or persons whatsoever, of the respective Counties, against any of their owne respective Knights or Burgesses in Parliament, for falsifying and betraying his or their Countries trust, or any wise indeavouring the introduction of an arbitrary power in this Land. And that the said Commissioners have power and be firmely bound to impeach and attach in the name of their respective Counties, their said Member or Members, and to bring him or them to a legall and publique tryall. That in case such be found guilty, justice may be executed, and others in their roome, by the free choyce of the People bee sent. And in case any such Commissioner, or Commissioners shall refuse to prosecute any such complaint or impeachment, that then hee or they be ajudged guilty of Treason.

Articles concerning Courts of Judicature, offices and Officers of the Law.

1 That all Courts which are not established by the just old Law of the Land: and all illegall offices, and Officers, belonging to the same, and all other vexatious and unnecessary Courts, be abolished by act of Parliament. And that provision bee made that for tyme to come, no Courts or Officers whatsoever may be obtruded upon the free Commoners of England, either by Royall grant, Pattent, Act of Parliament, or otherwise contrary to the old Law of the Land.

2 That according to the old Law and custome of the Land, long before, and sometime after the Conquest, There may bee Courts of Judicature for the speedy tryall and determination of all causes, whether Criminall or Civill, erected and established in every Hundred, for the ease and benefit of the Subject, to be holden according to the old custome once or twice every moneth, for the ending of all causes Criminall and Civill whatsoever, which shall happen in the respective Hundreds. That the Freemen of England may have a sudden, quick and easie dispatch of their suits, and be eased also of their vexations and chargable travellings from all parts of the Kingdome, for processe and tryall of their suits unto Westminster Hall.

3 That all such Officers, as by the ancient and common Lawes of this 83

Nation, are illegible,[1] and to be chosen by the free Commons, as Mayors, Sheriffes, Justices of peace, &c. may be left to the free Election of the people, in their respective places, and not otherwise to bee chosen. And that all such publique affaires (now in being) Not so elected and allowed, may be forthwith removed, and others by the free choice of the people be constituted in their roomes.

Articles concerning Goales, Goalers, and Imprisonment.

1 That the extortions, and oppressive fees of Goalers may bee redressed and eased, and that strict and severe provision be made against all Goalers, and their deputies, to restraine them for the future from the like extortions and cruelties, now frequent in all Goales of the Land. And that there may be a strict and severe Inquisition after the blood of such prisoners as have beene murthered and starved by the cruelties of Goalers, that so the persons guilty thereof may have justice executed upon them.

2 That no Prisoners be put in Irons, or to other paine, before conviction and condemnation.

3 That there may be cleanly and wholesome provision made in all the Goales of England, for the lodging of Prisoners, at the charge and cost of the State, and that no fees for Chamber-rent, for entering or deliverance, or any thing in lieu thereof, be exacted or demanded under a severe penalty.

4 That neither the high Court of Parliament, nor any other inferior Court or Magistrate whatsoever, may commit any free man of England to prison upon any pretended contempts, as is frequent in these dayes, but onely for transgression and breach of the knowne Lawes of the Land. And for the future (to award[2] the free Commons of England from the revenge of arbitrary spirits,) that strong provision be made by Act of Parliament to that end.

5 That there may be a severe penalty provided against all Goalers and their Deputies, which shall receive any prisoner persons whatsoever, without a lawfull charge or commitment drawne up in writing, according to the true forme of the Law, with a lawfull cause therein expressed, and with a lawfull conclusion, him safely to keepe untill hee shall be delivered by due processe or Law, according to Magna Charta, and the Petition of Right, and not at the will and pleasure of the Committee.

6 That strong provision be made against all such Goalers as shall detaine any person or persons in prison after a lawfull discharge, as is frequent in all the Goales of the Land, whereby many poore free Commoners of England have been starved and dyed of hunger.

7 That all criminall persons that are condemned and reprived, may be acquit and set free.

---

[1] eligible

[2] ?safeguard

Articles concerning the Lawes, and corruptions thereof,
with other publique Grievances.

1 That all Lawes of the Land (lockt up from common capacities in the Latine or French tongues,) may bee translated into the English tongue. And that all records, Orders, Processes, Writs, and other proceedings whatsoever, may be all entered and issued forth in the English tongue, and that in the most plaine and common Character used in the Land, commonly called Roman, or Secretary, and that without all or any Latine or French Phrases or Tearmes, and also without all or any abreviations or abridgements of words, that so the meanest English Commoner that can but read written hand in his owne tongue, may fully understand his owne proceedings in the Law.

2 That no free Commoner of England be inforced to put either by the high Court of Parliament, or by any subordinate Court, Officer or Minister of Iustice, whatsoever in the Land to make Oath, or to answer to any Interrogatories concerning himselfe in any criminall case, concerning his life, liberty, goods or free-hold. And that neither the High Court of Parliament, not any subordinate Court, Officer or Minister whatsoever, before Indictment, presentment, verdict of 12 men, or other due processe of Law, may take away any free Commoners life, liberty, goods, or freehold, contrary to the Stat[ut]e of Magna Charta, cap. 29–25. Edw. 3. cap. 4.28. Edw. 3. cap. 3.41. Edw. 3.C.3. I Eliz. cap. 1 &c.

3 That all Statutes made for the compulsion of persons to heare the Common Prayer Booke, and for the exercise of other Popish Rit[e]s, and Ceremonies, may be abrogated and taken away, and that all and singular persons indicted, imprisoned, or otherwise molested upon the aforesaid Statutes may be inlarged and relieved.

4 That neither Membership in Parliament, Office nor function, whatsoever in the Magistracy of the Land, may be any protection or demurre in any wise against the due processe or course of the ancient and common Lawes of this Realme, but that in all cases of treason, murther, Burglary, and fellonie, in all Actions, Suites, and civill proceedings whatsoever, the greatest Man or men in the Realme, may be made equally lyable at all times and seasons, and in all places in the Land to the tryall, sentence and execution of the Law, with the meanest Commoner.

5 That all wicked persons that shall beare false witnesse against any free man of England concerning his life, liberty, goods or free-hold upon legall discovery, and probation thereof, be adjudged, and condemned of their lives, liberties, and free-holds, according to that which they would have done unto their Neighbours.

6 That the cruell practise of imprisoning Debtors may be provided against, and that due Rights and properties may be recovered upon more mercifull tearmes then by way of imprisonment.

7 That according to the Law of God, and the old Law of the Land, matters of theft may not be punished with death, and that such Malefactors may make satisfaction either by just restitution to the party wronged, or

by an answerable servitude, and that such offenders upon the second conviction (lawfully had) be brand markt visibly in the most eminent part of their face, and confind to a singular habit. And upon the third lawfull conviction, to be put to perpetuall servitude, for the benefit of the State, saving to the party wronged, a competent deduction thereon, for restitution according to the theft, that upon all occasions of warre, such Bondmen may be taken for the Military service, and the impressing of free-men on that behalfe in some measure spared.

8 That every English Native, who hath goods, Wares and Merchandize, may have freedome to transport the same to any place beyond the seas, and there to convert them to his owne profit, it being his true and proper inheritance to doe, according to the Statutes of 14. Edw. 3.2.12. Hen. 7.6. and therefore to the end the old trade ingrosing Company of Merchants may be dissolved, and the like for the future prevented.

Concerning the Clergy.

1 That the grievous oppressions by Tythes and forced-maintenance for the Ministry be removed, and that the more easie and Evangelicall practice of contribution be granted, and confirmed for the benefit of the Subject, and his freedome therein, for prevention of the Lordlinesse, in and the Commotions, oppressions and tyrannies, that might happen by the Clergy.

Concerning Schooles.

That all ancient Donations for the maintenance and continuance of Free-Schooles which are impropriate or converted to any private use, and all such Free-Schooles which are destroyed or purloyned of any freedome for propriety may be restored and erected againe, and that in all parts or Counties of the Realme of England, and Dominion of Wales destitute of Free-Schooles (for the due nurture and education of children) may have a competent number of Such Schooles, founded, erected, and indowed at the publique charges of those respective Counties and places so destitute, that few or none of the free men of England may for the future be ignorant of reading and writing.

Concerning Hospitalls.

That all ancient charitable Donations towards the constant reliefe of the poor, impropriate, and converted to other use, and all Hospitalls that are either impropriate, corrupted or vitiated from their primitive constitution and end, or be deprived of any of their franchise, profits or emoluments, may be restored, relieved, and rectified, and safely preserved to the reliefs and ·maintenance of poore Orphants, Widowes, aged and impotent persons, &c. And that there be a convenient number of Hospitalls, founded, erected, and constituted in all the Counties of England and Wales, at the publique charge of the respective Counties, for the good eduction and nurture of poore fatherlesse or helplesse children, maintenance and reliefe of poore widowes, aged, sick, and lame persons. And to that end, that all the Gleabe-Lands in the Kingdome, may be converted to the maintenance and use of those charitable houses.

Concerning Commons inclosed.

That all grounds which anciently lay in Common for the poore, and are now impropriate, inclosed, and fenced in, may forthwith (in whose hands soever they are) be cast out, and laid open againe to the free and common use and benefit of the poore.

Concerning Petitions.

That strong provision be made that neither the Parliament, nor any inferior Court, Officer, or Minister of the Law whatsoever, may in any wise let, disturb, or molest any person or persons, from contriving, promoting or presenting any Petition or Petitions concerning their grievances, liberties, to the High Court of Parliament.

FINIS.

7 The (first) Agreement of the People

The first Agreement of the People, *written before the end of October 1647 and published early in November, is a landmark in the history of the Levellers. It followed* The Case of the Armie Truly Stated *(15 October), which has been discussed in the Introduction. Its first substantive clause was to provide the basis for a large part of the Putney Debates which followed shortly after (no. 8). The* Agreement's *authorship is unknown. It seems unlikely that it was really written by the Agents (alias Agitators) of the five cavalry regiments named in the text. The Levellers' platform may well have seemed more likely to win the Army's support if it could appear as a spontaneous expression of feeling among the soldiers, rather than as a programme given to the Army by a group of civilians in London. Although Lilburne was still in the Tower, he may well have had a hand in it, with Sexby or Wildman acting as intermediary. The* Agreement *itself is short and simple. Clauses I–III set out the Leveller–Agitator position on the present Parliament and on its successors. Clause IV makes clear what was already implicit from Leveller principles: that even future reformed parliaments should be bound by certain specific fundamental laws, and should not enjoy unlimited legislative sovereignty. The matters on which no legislation was to be allowed are limited to five, and of these the last is somewhat anodyne. The rest of the pamphlet is more to do with the method of the* Agreement's *presentation to the people; the authors seem especially concerned to explain the Army's feelings and its necessities to civilian readers.*

The principle of submitting a new constitution to the people follows logically enough from the position reached in Overton's Appeale. *The authors speak of creating 'a just and equall government', and the Postscript describes the* Agreement *as an extract from the* Case of the Armie: *a distillation would have been a more apt description. The final emphasis on its compatibility with the* Declaration of the Armie, *of 14 June, was significant because at Putney the Levellers and Agitators were to try to arraign the Generals for having gone back on this* Declaration *in their* Heads of the Proposals *(composed in July, published at the beginning of August). The* Case *and the* Agreement *may indeed be seen as the radical reply to the* Heads. *Of course the* Agreement *was never submitted to the people of England; nor is it easy to imagine how in practice it could have been. But if the Agitators and through them the Levellers had gained control of the Army, an attempt might have been made to implement a new constitution along these lines.*

Comparison with the second and third Leveller Agreements *(of December 1648 and May 1649) shows a process of elaboration. The later versions contain more detailed provisions, but also more restrictions and qualifications. The third Agreement (no. 14) gains in coherence and comprehensiveness, but loses in simplicity and directness by comparison with the first. Never again were the Levellers to speak so unequivocally – or so innocently.*

AN
AGREEMENT
OF THE
PEOPLE
FOR
A firme and present Peace, Upon
grounds of common-right and freedome;

As it was proposed by the Agents of the five
Regiments of Horse; and since by the generall
approbation of the Army, offered to the joynt
concurrence of all the free COMMONS of ENGLAND.

The Names of the Regiments which have already appeared for the
Case, of The Case of the Army truly stated, and for this
present Agreement, VIZ.

OF HORSE	OF FOOT
1. Gen. Regiment.	1. Gen. Regiment.
2. Life–Guard.	2. Col. Sir Hardresse Wallers Reg.
3. Lieut. Gen. Regiment.	3. Col. Lamberts Reg.
4. Com. Gen. Regiment.	4. Col. Rainsboroughs Regiment.
5. Col. Whaleyes Reg.	5. Col. Overtons Reg.
6. Col. Riches Reg.	6. Col. Lilburns Reg.
7. Col. Fleetwoods Reg.	7. Col. Backsters Reg.
8. Col. Harrisons Reg.	
9. Col. Twisldens Reg.	

PRINTED Anno. Dom. 1647.

An Agreement of the People, for a firme
and present Peace, upon grounds of Common-Right.

Having by our late labours and hazards made it appeare to the world at how high a rate wee value our just freedome, and God having so far owned our cause, as to deliver the Enemies thereof into our hands: We do now hold our selves bound in mutual duty to each other, to take the best care we can for the future, to avoid both the danger of returning into a slavish condition, and the chargable remedy of another war: for as it cannot be imagined that so many of our Country-men would have opposed us in this quarrel, if they had understood their owne good; so may we safely promise to our selves, that when our Common Rights and

89

liberties shall be cleared, their endeavours will be disappointed, that seek to make themselves our Masters: since therefore our former oppressions, and scarce yet ended troubles have beene occasioned, either by want of frequent Nationall meetings in Councell, or by rendring those meetings ineffectuall; We are fully agreed and resolved, to provide that hereafter our Representatives be neither left to an uncertainty for the time, nor made uselesse to the ends for which they are intended: In order whereunto we declare,

I

That the People of England being at this day very unequally distributed by Counties, Cities, & Burroughts, for the election of their Deputies in Parliament, ought to be more indifferently proportioned, according to the number of the Inhabitants: the circumstances whereof, for number, place, and manner, are to be set down before the end of this present Parliament.

II

That to prevent the many inconveniences apparently arising from the long continuance of the same persons in authority, this present Parliament be dissolved upon the last day of September, which shall be in the year of our Lord, 1648.

III

That the People do of course chuse themselves a Parliament once in two years, viz. upon the first Thursday in every 2d. March, after the manner as shall be prescribed before the end of this Parliament, to begin to sit upon the first Thursday in Aprill following at Westminster, or such other place as shall bee appointed from time to time by the preceding Representatives; and to continue till the last day of September, then next ensuing, and no longer.

IV

That the power of this, and all future Representatives of this Nation, is inferiour only to theirs who chuse them, and doth extend, without the consent or concurrence of any other person or persons; to the enacting, altering, and repealing of Lawes; to the erecting and abolishing of Offices and Courts; to the appointing, removing, and calling to account Magistrates, and Officers of all degrees; to the making War and peace, to the treating with forraign States: and generally, to whatsoever is not expresly, or implyedly reserved by the represented to themselves.

Which are as followeth,

1. That matters of Religion, and the wayes of Gods Worship, are not at all intrusted by us to any humane power, because therein wee cannot remit or exceed a tittle of what our Consciences dictate to be the mind of

God, without wilfull sinne: neverthelesse the publike way of instructing the Nation (so it be not compulsive) is referred to their discretion.

2. That the matter of impressing and constraining any of us to serve in the warres, is against our freedome; and therefore we do not allow it in our Representatives; the rather, because money (the sinews of war) being alwayes at their disposall, they can never want numbers of men, apt enough to engage in any just cause.

3. That after the dissolution of this present Parliament, no person be at any time questioned for anything said or done, in reference to the late publike differences, otherwise then in execution of the Judgments of the present Representatives, or House of Commons.

4. That in all Laws made, or to be made, every person may be bound alike, and that no Tenure, Estate, Charter, Degree, Birth, or place, do confer any exemption from the ordinary Course of Legall proceedings, whereunto others are subjected.

5. That as the Laws ought to be equall, so they must be good, and not evidently destructive to the safety and well-being of the people.

These things we declare to be our native Rights, and therefore are agreed and resolved to maintain them with our utmost possibilities, against all opposition whatsoever, being compelled thereunto, not only by the examples of our Ancestors, whose bloud was often spent in vain for the recovery of their Freedomes, suffering themselves, through fraudulent accommodations, to be still deluded of the fruit of their Victories, but also by our own wofull experience, who having long expected, & dearly earned the establishment of these certain rules of Government are yet made to depend for the settlement of our Peace and Freedome, upon him that intended our bondage, and brought a cruell Warre upon us.

For the noble and highly honoured the Free-born People of England, in their respective Counties and Divisions, these.

Deare Country-men, and fellow-Commoners,

For your sakes, our friends, estates and lives, have not been deare to us; for your safety and freedom we have cheerfully indured hard labours and run most desperate hazards, and in comparison to your peace and freedome we neither doe nor ever shall value our dearest bloud and wee professe, our bowells are and have been troubled, and our hearts pained within us, in seeing & considering that you have been so long bereaved of these fruites and ends of all our labours and hazards, wee cannot but sympathize with you in your miseries and oppressions. It's greife and vexation of heart to us; to receive your meate or moneyes, whilest you have no advantage, nor yet the foundations of your peace and freedom surely layed: and therefore upon most serious considerations, that your principall right most essentiall to your well-being is the clearnes, certaintie, sufficiencie and freedom of your power in your representatives in Parliament, and considering that the original of most of your oppressions & miseries hath been either from the obscuritie and doubtfulnes of the power you have committed to your representatives in your elections, or from the want of courage in those whom you have betrusted to claime and exercise their power, which might probably proceed from their uncertaintie of your assistance and maintenance of their power, and minding that for this right of yours and ours wee engaged our lives; for the King raised the warre against you and your Parliament, upon the ground, that hee would not suffer your representatives to provide for your peace safetie and freedom that were then in danger, by disposing of the Militia and otherwise, according to their trust; and for the maintenance that was deare to us, and God hath borne witnesse to the justice of our Cause. And further minding that the only effectual meanes to settle a just and lasting peace, to obtaine remedie for all your greivances, & to prevent future oppressions, is the making clear & secure the power that you betrust to your representatives in Parliament, that they may know their trust, in the faithfull execution whereof you wil assist them. Vpon all these grounds, we propound your joyning with us in the agreement herewith sent unto you; that by vertue thereof, we may have Parliaments certainly cal'd and have the time of their sitting & ending certain & their power or trust cleare and unquestionable, that hereafter they may remove your burdens, & secure your rights, without oppositions or obstructions, & that the foundations of your peace may be so free from uncertainty, that there may be no grounds for future quarrels, or contentions to occasion warre and bloud-shed; & wee desire you would consider, that as these things wherein we offer to agree with you, are the fruites & ends of the Victories which God hath given us: so the settlement of these are the most absolute meanes to preserve you & your Posterity, from slavery, oppression, distraction, & trouble; by this, those whom your selves shall chuse, shall have power to restore you to, and secur you in, all your rights; & they shall be in a capacity to tast of subjection, as well as rule, & so shall be equally concerned with your selves, in all they do. For they must equally suffer with you under any common burdens, & partake with you in any freedoms; & by this they shal be disinabled to defraud or wrong you, when the lawes shall bind all alike, without priviledge or exemption; & by this your Consciences shall be free from tyrannie & oppression, & those occasions of endlesse strifes, & bloudy warres, shall be perfectly removed; without controversie by your joyning with us in this Agreement, all your particular & common grievances will be redressed forthwith without delay; the Parliament must then make your reliefe and common good their only study.

Now because we are earnestly desirous of the peace and good of all our Country-men, even of those that have opposed us, and would to our utmost possibility provide for perfect peace and freedome, & prevent all suites, debates, & contentions that may happen amongst you, in relation to the late war: we have therefore inserted it into this Agreement, that no person shall be questionable for any thing done, in relation to the late publike differences, after the dissolution of this present Parliament, further then in execution of their judgment; that thereby all may be secure from all sufferings for what they have done, & not liable hereafter to be troubled or punished by the judgment of another Parliament, which may be to their ruine, unlesse this Agreement be joyned in, whereby any acts of indempnity or oblivion shal be made unalterable, and you and your posterities be secure.

But if any shall enquire why we should desire to joyn in an Agreement with the people, to declare these to be our native Rights, & not rather petition to the Parliament for them; the reason is evident: No Act of Parliament is or can be unalterable, and so cannot be sufficient security to save you or us harmlesse, from what another Parliament may determine, if it should be corrupted; and besides Parliaments are to receive the extent of their power, and trust from those that betrust them; and therefore the people are to declare what their power and trust is, which is the intent of this Agreement; and its to be observed, that though there hath formerly been many Acts of Parliament, for the calling of Parliaments every yeare, yet you have been deprived of them, and inslaved through want of them; and therefore both necessity for your security in these freedomes, that are essentiall to your well-being, and wofull experience of the manifold miseries and distractions that have been lengthened out since the war ended, through want of such a settlement, requires this Agreement and when you and we shall be joyned together therein, we shall readily joyn with you, to petition the Parliament, as they are our fellow Commoners equally concerned, to joyn with us.

· And if any shall inquire, Why we undertake to offer this Agreement, we must professe, we are sensible that you have been so often deceived with Declarations and Remonstrances, and fed with vain hopes that you have sufficient reason to abandon all confidence in any persons whatsoever, from whom you have no other security of their intending your freedome, then bare Declaration: And therefore, as our consciences witnesse, that in simplicity and integrity of heart, we have proposed lately in the Case of the Army stated, your freedome and deliverance from slavery, oppression, and all burdens: so we desire to give you satisfying assurance thereof by this Agreement whereby the foundations of your freedomes provided in the Case, &c. shall be setled unalterably, & we shall as faithfully proceed to, and all other most vigorous actings for your good that God shall direct and enable us unto; And though the malice of our enemies, and such as they delude, would blast us by scandalls, aspersing us with designes of Anarchy, and community; yet we hope the righteous God will not onely by this our present desire of setling an equall just Government, but also by directing us unto all righteous undertakings, simply for publike good, make our uprightnesse and faithfulnesse to the interest of all our Countrey-men, shine forth so clearly, that malice it selfe shall be silenced, and confounded. We question not, but the longing expectation of a firme peace, will incite you to the most speedy joyning in this Agreement: in the prosecution whereof, or of any thing that you shall desire for publike 93 good; you may be confident, you shall never want the assistance of Your most faithfull fellow-Commoners, now in Armes for your service.

Edmond Bear Robert Everard LIEUT. GEN. REGIMENT.
George Garret Thomas Beverley COM. GEN. REGIMENT.
William Pryor William Bryan COL. FLEETWOODS REGIMENT.
Matthew Weale William Russell CON. WHALIES REGIMENT.
John Dover William Hudson COL. RICHES REGIMENT.

Agents coming from other Regiments unto us, have subscribed the Agreement to be proposed to their respective Regiments, and you.

For Our much honoured, and truly worthy Fellow-Commoners, and Souldiers, the Officers and Souldiers under Command of His Excellencie Sir THOMAS FAIRFAX.

Gentlemen and Fellow Souldiers;

The deepe sense of many dangers and mischiefes that may befall you in relation to the late War, whensoever this Parliament shall end, unlesse sufficient prevention be now provided, hath constrained Us to study the most absolute & certain means for your security; and upon most serious considerations, we judge that no Act of Indempnity can sufficiently provide for your quiet, ease, and safety; because, as it hath formerly been, a corrupt Party (chosen into the next Parliament by your Enemies meanes) may possibly surprize the house, and make any Act of Indemnity null, seeing they cannot faile of the Kings Assistance and concurrence, in any such actings against you, that conquered him.

And by the same meanes, your freedome from impressing also, may in a short time be taken from you, though for the present, it should be granted; wee apprehend no other security, by which you shall be saved harmlesse, for what you have done in the late warre, then a mutuall Agreement between the people & you, that no person shall be questioned by any Authority whatsoever, for any thing done in relation to the late publike differences, after the dissolution of the present house of Commons, further then in execution of their judgment; and that your native freedome from constraint to serve in warre, whether domestick or forraign, shall never be subject to the power of Parliaments, or any other; and for this end, we propound the Agreement that we herewith send to you, to be forthwith subscribed.

And because we are confident, that in judgment and Conscience, ye hazarded your lives for the settlement of such a just and equall Government, that you and your posterities, and all the free borne people of this Nation might enjoy justice & freedome, and that you are really sensible that the distractions, oppressions, and miseries of the Nation, and your want of your Arreares, do proceed from the Want of the establishment, both of such certain rules of just Government, and foundations of peace, as are the price of bloud, and the expected fruites of all the peoples cost:

94

Therefore in this Agreement wee have inserted the certaine Rules of equall Government, under which the Nation may enjoy all its Rights and Freedomes securely; And as we doubt not but your love to the freedome and lasting peace of the yet distracted Country will cause you to joyn together in this Agreement.

So we question not: but every true English man that loves the peace and freedome of England will concurre with us; and then your Arrears and constant pay (while you continue in Armes) will certainly be brought in out of the abundant love of the people to you, and then shall the mouthes of those be stopped, that scandalize you and us, as endeavouring Anarchy, or to rule by the sword; & then will so firm an union be made between the people and you, that neither any homebred or forraigne Enemies will dare to disturbe our happy peace. We shall adde no more but this; that the knowledge of your union in laying this foundation of peace, this Agreement, is much longed for, by

Yours, and the Peoples most faithfull Servants.

Postscript.

GENTLEMEN,

We desire you may understand the reason of our extracting some principles of common freedome out of those many things proposed to you in the Case truly stated, and drawing them up into the forme of an Agreement. Its chiefly because for these things wee first ingaged gainst the King, He would not permit the peoples Representatives to provide for the Nations safety, by disposing of the Militia, and otherwayes, according to their Trust, but raised a Warre against them, and we ingaged for the defence of that power, and right of the people, in their Representatives. Therefore these things in the Agreement, the people are to claime as their native right, and price of their bloud, which you are obliged absolutely to procure for them.

And these being the foundations of freedom, its necessary, that they should be setled unalterably, which can be by no meanes, but this Agreement with the people.

And we cannot but mind you, that the ease of the people in all their Grievances, depends upon the setling those principles or rules of equal Government for a free people, & were but this Agreement established, doubtlesse all the Grievances of the Army and people would be redressed immediately, and all things propounded in your Case truly stated to be insisted on, would be forthwith granted.

Then should the House of Commons have power to helpe the oppressed people, which they are now bereaved of by the chiefe Oppressors, and then they shall be equally concerned with you and all the people, in the settlement of the most perfect freedome: for they shall equally suffer with you under any Burdens, or partake in any Freedome. We shall onely adde, that the summe of all the Agreement which we herewith offer to you, is 95 but in order to the fulfilling of our Declaration of June the 14. wherein we promised to the people, that we would with our lives vindicate and cleare their right and power in their Parliaments.

Edmond Bear Robert Everard Lieut. Gen. Reg.
George Garret Thomas Beverley Com. Gen. Reg.
William Pryor William Bryan Col. Fleetwood Reg.
Matthew Wealey William Russell Col. Whaley. Reg.
John Dober William Hudson Col. Rich Reg.

Agents coming from other Regiments unto us, have subscribed the Agreement, to be proposed to their respective Regiments and you.

8 The Putney Debates

This extract is much the longest of these texts, being the greater part of the proceedings on the second day of the debates in the General Council of the Army, held in Putney church, at the end of October–beginning of November 1647. Of all the episodes in English seventeenth-century history, these meetings must surely be amongst the most extraordinary. Fundamental political principles were at issue in the debates between Oliver Cromwell and Henry Ireton on the one hand and the various radical spokesmen, including common soldiers, on the other. Besides the fact of their ever having taken place at all, it is hardly less remarkable that we have so full and apparently accurate a record of these proceedings. From his other papers we know that William Clarke, Secretary to the Army Council, used his own kind of 'short-hand' writing. The existing manuscript text of the debates is obviously a fair copy, based on Clarke's original or rough copy (which has not survived). Sir Charles Firth, whose edition appeared in 1891, believed that Clarke had transcribed the debates soon after the Restoration, in 1661–2; but unfortunately he gave no evidence in support of this view. The terminal dates are 1647 to 1666 (Clarke's own death). It seems just as plausible that he made his fair copy to while away the time in Scotland, where he was stationed as Secretary to successive Commanders-in-Chief from 1651 to 1659.

In editing the debates I have occasionally parted from the published versions, both as edited by Firth and by Professor A. S. P. Woodhouse (in 1938). Unlike them, I have abstained from altering the order of speeches, or of sentences, phrases and words within speeches; and I have indicated, by the use of square brackets or notes, wherever I have departed from the original, except in the matter of spelling, capital letters, and (the most difficult and controversial) punctuation. Remembering the provenance of the text, the reader must be prepared for obscurities.

The Levellers' and Agitators' main opponent in the debates was Henry Ireton (1611–51), a Nottinghamshire country gentleman, educated at Oxford and the Inns of Court, who had risen to be Commissary-General of Horse in the New Model Army. In 1646 he had entered parliament as a 'recruiter' (in the batches of by-elections held to make up the numerous vacancies since 1640), and he had also married Cromwell's eldest daughter Bridget. From the start we see Ireton taking the initiative. He believed, or purported to believe, that clause I of the Agreement (no. 7) implied universal manhood suffrage, that the case for this depended upon an appeal to 'natural right', which was unbounded, undefinable, and contrary to existing 'civil rights', and that this in turn would lead to an attack on property – that is, to 'levelling' in the economic sense – and, as his father-in-law was to put it, 'to anarchy'.

One of the first to argue on the other side was the other Commissary-General (for Victuals), Nicholas Cowling. He evidently subscribed to the prevalent historical myth of Anglo-Saxon freedom and democracy, lost since the imposition of the 'Norman Yoke'. But those who sustained the debate against Ireton for most of its length comprised three distinct groups, although there were marked signs of disagreement among their individual members. Of the few pro-Leveller, democratically-inclined officers, Colonel Thomas Rainsborough (? 1610–48), MP, was easily the most prominent and important. From his speeches here Rainsborough emerges as a genuine radical political idealist. But it was his high military reputation and his seat in the Commons which made him the Levellers' most influential ally, and potentially a formidable rival to Cromwell and Ireton. His brother, Major William Rainsborough, who also spoke up for the Leveller viewpoint, was to be in serious trouble a few years later as an associate of the deviant radical religious sect, the Ranters. Then there were the Agitators: in theory two men from each regiment, but we cannot be sure how many were actually present in Putney church. Edward Sexby (? 1616–58) was much the most articulate of them, and the readiest to throw down an open challenge to the Generals and their supporters. 'Buff-coat', alias Robert Everard, ostensibly co-author of the Agreement, was the only other whom Clarke himself succeeded in identifying. Lastly there were the two representatives of the civilian Levellers in London – attending evidently by courtesy of the senior officers, in recognition of the Agitators' ties with Lilburne and his party. Why John Wildman (1623–93) and Maximilian Petty (? 1618–?62) were selected, rather than Overton or Walwyn is unclear, even if Lilburne himself was disqualified by still being in the Tower. In the debate Petty appears as the most moderate of Ireton's opponents, while Wildman emerges as intellectually even more formidable than Colonel Rainsborough or Sexby, if emotionally a less powerful speaker.

To make sense of some passages, we must remember that whereas there was a uniform 40s. freehold franchise in the counties, the qualifications for the vote varied widely between different cities and boroughs. Moreover the distribution of parliamentary seats already bore little resemblance to the actual distribution either of wealth or of population. By the seventeenth century there were numerous 'rotten' and 'pocket' boroughs, just as there were sizeable manufacturing and trading towns without representation except as part of the counties in which they were situated. Ireton and the Levellers were at one in criticizing the existing system, and in wanting a redistribution of seats; their disagreement was over the way in which this was to be remedied. Various other officers spoke in favour of compromise, or else to warn against the dangers of excessive delay. Hugh Peter (1598–1660), who was presumably present in his capacity as an army chaplain, tried to act as a bridge-builder by suggesting the appointment of a small drafting sub-committee. But it is hard to see how the differences between the main protagonists could have been papered over. Later, after the debates cease to be fully recorded by Clarke, a large committee did indeed agree, by an overwhelming majority vote, to the suffrage as proposed by Petty; so, on the face of things, a compromise was reached. Credit for suggesting this must apparently go to Captain Edmund Rolfe, once a servant of Cromwell, next a cornet in his regiment, and *by 1647 a captain of foot under Cromwell's cousin Colonel 'Robin' Hammond, who was shortly to become the King's jailer in the Isle of Wight. As the debate wore on, more of the other officers present joined in. One can sense a growing impatience with both the contending parties and also a genuine desire to reach agreement. Part of the long speech by the Agitator Robert Everard is a reminder of the extraordinary ascendancy enjoyed by Cromwell, even among many who disagreed with his political and constitutional views. Finally, following Rainsborough's call for a general rendezvous of the whole army, the debate shifted back to the question of 'engagements', of who was being true or false to the Army's declarations of the previous June: the Generals or their critics. References made to the debates held at Reading in July and to* The Heads of the Proposals *show that even Petty – the least radical of the Leveller spokesmen – was committed to the abolition of monarchy and House of Lords, or at least of their powers.*

Any decisions which might be taken about troop movements were bound to raise the central issues of military discipline and control of the Army. It is hard to see that any, even temporary compromise was possible there. Finally, Wildman maintained that it was people's duty to break unjust agreements, and tried to explain what the Agitators found so obnoxious about the Heads. *In trying to rebut these charges, Ireton ascribed to Wildman authorship of the* Case of the Armie. *Whatever the truth, Wildman's disavowal is not wholly convincing.*

THE PUTNEY DEBATES

From the second day's debate in the General Council of the Army, Putney Church, 29 October 1647. The text is as follows:

The Paper called the Agreement read.
Afterwards the first Article read by itself.

Commissary [General] Ireton: The exception that lies in it is this, it is said, they are to be distributed according to the number of the inhabitants, The People of England, etc. And this doth make me think, that the meaning is that every man that is an inhabitant is to be equally considered, and to have an equal voice in the election of those representers, the persons that are for the general representative, and if that be the meaning then I have something to say against it, but if it be only, that those people, that by the civil constitution of this kingdom, which is original and fundamental, and beyond which I am sure no memory of record does go.
[Interjection] Not before the Conquest.
But before the Conquest it was so. If it be intended, that those that by that constitution that was before the Conquest that hath been beyond memory, such persons that have been before that constitution should be the electors I have no more to say against it.
Colonel Rainsborough: Moved, That others might have given their hands to it.
Captain Denne: Denied, That those that were set of their Regiment, that they were their hands.

99

Ireton: Whether those men whose hands are to it, or those that brought it do know so much of the matter as that they mean that all that had a former right of election, or those that had no right before are to come in? *Commissary [General] Cowling:* In the time before the Conquest, and since the Conquest the greatest part of the kingdom was in vassalage. *Mr Pettus [Maximilian Petty]:* We judge, that all inhabitants that have not lost their birthright should have an equal voice in elections. *Rainsborough:* I desired that those that had engaged in it, for really I think that the poorest he that is in England hath a life to live as the greatest he; and therefore truly, sir, I think it's clear, that every man that is to live under a government ought first by his own consent to put himself under that government; and I do think that the poorest man in England is not at all bound in a strict sense to that government that he hath not had a voice to put himself under; and I am confident that, when I have heard the reasons against it, that something will be said to answer those reasons, insomuch that I should doubt whether I was an Englishman or no, that should doubt of these things. *Ireton:* That's this.

Give me leave to tell you, that if you make this the rule, I think you must fly for refuge to an absolute natural right, and you must deny all civil right; and I am sure it will come to that in the consequence. This, I perceive, is pressed as that which is so essential and due, the right of the people of this kingdom, and as they are the people of this kingdom, distinct and divided from other people, as that we must for this right lay aside all other considerations. This is so just; this is so due; this is so right to them; and those that they must thus choose, and that those that they do thus choose, must have such a power of binding all, and loosing all, according to those limitations. This is pressed as so due, and so just, as is argued, that it is an engagement paramount all others, and you must for it lay aside all others; if you have engaged any others, you must break it; so look upon these as thus held out to us; so it was held out by the gentleman that brought it yesterday. For my part, I think it is no right at all. I think that no person hath a right to an interest or share in the disposing of the affairs of the kingdom, and in determining or choosing those that shall determine what laws we shall be ruled by here, no person hath a right to this that hath not a permanent fixed interest in this kingdom, and those persons together are properly the represented of this kingdom, who taken together, and consequently are to make up the represents of this kingdom, are the represents, who taken together do comprehend whatsoever is of real or permanent interest in the kingdom, and I am sure there is otherwise (I cannot tell what), otherwise any man can say why a foreigner coming in amongst us, or as many as will coming in amongst us, or by force or otherwise settling themselves here, or at least by our permission having a being here, why they should not as well lay claim to it as any other. We talk of birthright. Truly birthright there is thus much claim: men may justly have by birthright, by their very being born in England, that we should not seclude them out of England. That we should not refuse to give them air and place and ground, and the freedom of the highways and other things, to live amongst us, not any man that is born here, though he in birth, or by his birth there come nothing at all that is part of the permanent interest of this kingdom to him. That I think is due to a man by birth. But that by a man's being born here he shall have a share in that power that shall dispose of the lands here, and of all things here, I do not think it a sufficient ground, but I am sure if we look upon that which is the utmost, within man's view, of what was originally the constitution of this kingdom, upon that which is most radical and fundamental, and which if you take away, there is no man hath any land, any goods, you take away any civil interest, and that is this: that those that choose the representers for the making of laws by which this state and kingdom are to be governed, are the persons who taken together, do comprehend the local interest of this kingdom; that is, the persons in whom all land lies, and those in corporations in whom all trading lies. This is the most fundamental constitution of this kingdom, and which if you do not allow, you allow none at all. This constitution hath limited and deter-mined it, that only those shall have voices in elections. It is true, as was said by a gentleman near me, the meanest man in England ought to have. I say this: that those that have the meanest local interest, that man that hath but forty shillings a year, he hath as great voice in the election of a knight for the shire as he that hath ten thousand a year or more, if he had never so much, and therefore there is that regard had to it. But this still the constitution of this government hath had an eye to, and what other government hath not an eye to this, it doth not relate to the interest of the kingdom if it do not lay the foundation of the power that's given to the representers, in those who have a permanent and a local interest in the kingdom, and who taken altogether do comprehend the whole, and if we shall go to take away this, we shall plainly go to take away all property and interest that any man hath, either in land by inheritance, or in estate by possession, or anything else, if you take away this fundamental part of the civil constitution. There is all the reason and justice that can be: if I will come to live in a kingdom, being a foreigner to it, or live in a king-dom, having no permanent interest in it, if I will desire as a stranger, or claim as one freeborn here, the air, the free passage of highways, the protection of laws, and all such things, and if I will either desire them, or claim them, I (if I have no permanent interest in that kingdom) must submit to those laws and those rules, who taken together do comprehend the whole interest of the kingdom.

Rainsborough: Truly, sir, I am of the same opinion I was, and am resolved to keep it till I know reason why I should not. I confess my memory is bad, and therefore I am fain to make use of my pen. I remember that in a former speech this gentleman brought before this, he was saying that in some cases he should not value whether a king or no king, whether lords or no lords, whether a property or no property. For my part I differ in that. I do very much care whether a king or no king, lords or no lords, property or no property; and I think, if we do not all take care, we shall all have none of these very shortly. But as to this present business, I do hear nothing at all that can convince me, why any man that is born in England ought not to have his voice in election of burgesses. It is said that if a man have not a permanent interest, he can have no claim; and we must be no freer than the laws will let us to be, and that there is no chronicle will let us be freer than that we enjoy. Something was said to this yesterday, and I do think that the main cause why Almighty God gave men reason, it was that they should make use of that reason, and that they should improve it for that end and purpose that God gave it them, and truly I think that half a loaf is better than none if a man be an-hungry; yet I think there is nothing that God hath given a man that any else can take from him, and therefore I say, that either it must be the law of God or the law of man that must prohibit the meanest man in the kingdom to have this benefit as well as the greatest. I do not find anything in the law of God, that a lord shall choose twenty burgesses, and a gentleman but two, or a poor man shall choose none: I find no such thing in the law of nature, nor in the law of nations, but I do find that all Englishmen must be subject to English laws, and I do verily believe that there is no man but will say that the foundation of all law lies in the people, and if in the people, I am to seek for this exemption; and truly I have thought something: in what a miserable distressed condition would many a man that hath fought for the Parliament in this quarrel be? I will be bound to say that many a man whose zeal and affection to God and this kingdom hath carried him forth in this cause, hath so spent his estate that, in the way the state, the army are going this way, he shall not hold up his head, and when his estate is lost, and not worth forty shillings a year, a man shall not have any interest; and there are many other ways by which men have estates (if that be the rule which God in his providence does use) do fall to decay; a man, when he hath an estate, he hath an interest in making laws; when he hath none, he hath no power in it. So that a man cannot lose that which he hath for the maintenance of his family but he must lose that which God and nature hath given him; and therefore I do, and am still of the same opinion, that every man born in England cannot, ought not, neither by the law of God nor the law of nature, to be exempted from the choice of those who are to make laws and for him to live under, and for him (for aught I know) to lose his life under, and therefore I think there can be no great stick in this.

Truly I think that there is not this day reigning in England a greater fruit or effect of tyranny than this very thing would produce, for, sir, what is it, the King he grants a patent under the Broad-Seal of England to such a corporation to send burgesses. He grants to a city to send burgesses. Truly I know nothing free but only the knight of the shire, nor do I know anything in a parliamentary way that is clear from the height and fulness of tyranny, but as for this of corporations, it is as contrary to freedom as may be; when a poor base corporation from the King shall send two burgesses, when five hundred men of estate shall not send one, when those that are to make their laws are called by the King, or cannot act by such a call, truly I think that the people of England have little freedom.

Ireton: I think there was nothing that I said to give you occasion to think that I did contend for this, that such a corporation should have the electing of a man to the parliament. I think I agreed to this matter, that all should be equally distributed, but the question is, whether it should be distributed to all persons, or whether the same persons that are the electors should be the electors still, and it equally distributed amongst them. I do not see anybody else that makes this objection; and if nobody else be sensible of it I shall soon have done. Only I shall a little crave your leave to represent the consequences of it, and clear myself from one misrepresentation of the thing that was misrepresented by the gentleman that sat next me. I think, if the gentleman remember himself, he cannot but remember that what I said was to this effect: that if I saw the hand of God leading so far as to destroy King, and destroy lords, and destroy property, and no such thing at all amongst us, I should acquiesce in it; and so I did not care, if no king, no lords, or no property, how in comparison of the tender care that I have of the honour of God, and of the people of God, whose name is so much concerned in this Army. This I did deliver, and not absolutely.

All the main thing that I speak for, is because I would have an eye to property. I hope we do not come to contend for victory, but let every man consider with himself that he do not go that way to take away all property; for here is the case of the most fundamental part of the constitution of the kingdom, which if you take away, you take away all by that. Here are men of this and this quality are determined to be the electors of men to the parliament, and they are all those who have any permanent interest in the kingdom, and who, taken together, do comprehend the whole interest of the kingdom. I mean by permanent, local, that is not anywhere else. As for instance, he that hath a freehold, and that freehold cannot be removed out of the kingdom. And so there's a corporation, a place which hath the privilege of a market and trading, which if you should allow to all places equally, I do not see how you could preserve any peace in the kingdom, and that is the reason why in the constitution we have but some few market towns. Now those people by the former constitution were looked upon to comprehend the permanent interest of the kingdom, and those are the freemen of corporations; for he that hath his livelihood by his trade, and by his freedom of trading in such a corporation, which he cannot exercise in another, he is tied to that place, his livelihood depends upon it; and secondly, that man hath an interest, hath a permanent interest there, upon which he may live, and live a freeman without dependence. These constitutions this kingdom hath looked at. Now I wish we may all consider of what right you will challenge, that all the people should have right to elections. Is it by the right of nature? If you will hold forth that as your ground, then I think you must deny all property too, and this is my reason. For thus: by that same right of nature, whatever it be that you pretend, by which you can say, a man hath an equal right with another to the choosing of him that shall govern him, by the same right of nature, he hath the same right in any goods he sees: meat, drink, clothes, to take and use them for his sustenance; he hath a freedom to the land, the ground, to exercise it, till it. He hath the freedom to anything that any one doth account himself to have any propriety in. Why now I say, then if you will, against the most fundamental part of civil constitution (which I have now declared), will plead the law of nature, that a man should, paramount this, and contrary to this, have a power of choosing those men that shall determine what shall be law in this state, though he himself have no permanent interest in the state, whatever interest he hath he may carry about with him, if this be allowed, we are free, we are equal, one man must have as much voice as another. Then show me what step or differ-ence, why by the same right of necessity to sustain nature, it is for my better being, and possibly not for it neither; possibly I may not have so real a regard to the peace of the kingdom as that man who hath a perman-ent interest in it; but he that hath no permanent interest, that is here to-day and gone tomorrow, I do not see that he hath such a permanent interest. Since you cannot plead to it by anything but the law of nature, but for the end of better being, and that better being is not certain, and more destruc-tive to another; upon these grounds, if you do, paramount all constitu-tions, hold up this law of nature, I would fain have any man show me their bounds, where you will end, and take away all property?

Rainsborough: I shall now be a little more free and open with you than I was before. I wish we were all true hearted, and that we did all carry ourselves with integrity; if I did mistrust you, I would use such asservera-tions. I think it doth go on mistrust, and things are thought too matters of reflection that were never intended for my part; as I think you forgot something that was in my speech. You forgot something in my speech, and you do not only yourselves believe, that men are inclining to anarchy, but you would make all men believe that; and, Sir, to say because a man pleads that every man hath a voice, that therefore it destroys the same that there's a property, the law of God says it, else why God made that law, thou shalt not steal. I am a poor man, therefore I must be prest; if I have no interest in the kingdom, I must suffer by all their laws, be they right or wrong. Nay thus, a gentleman lives in a county and hath three or four lordships as some men have, God knows how they got them, and when a parliament is called, he must be a parliament-man; and it may be he sees some poor men they live near, this man he can crush them. I have known an evasion to make sure he hath turned the poor man out of doors, and I would fain know whether the potency of men do not this, and so keep them under the greatest tyranny that was thought of in the world; and therefore I think that to that it is fully answered. God hath set down that thing as to property with this law of his, thou shalt not steal. And for my part I am against any such thought, and I wish you would not make the world believe that we are for anarchy, as for yourselves.

Lieut.-General [Cromwell]: I know nothing but this, that they that are the most yielding have the greatest wisdom; but really Sir, this is not right as it should be. No man says that you have a mind to anarchy, but the consequence of this rule tends to anarchy, must end in anarchy; for where is there any bound or limit set, if you take away this, that men that have no interest but the interest of breathing [should have no voice]. Therefore I am confident on't, we should not be so hot one with another.

Rainsborough: I know that some particular men we debate with [believe – or say – we] are for anarchy.

Ireton: I have, with as much plainness and clearness of reason as I could, showed you how I did conceive the doing of this takes away that which is the most original, the most fundamental civil constitution of this King-dome, and which is above all that constitution by which I have any property and if you will take away that and set up what ever a man may claim as a thing paramount, that by the law of nature, though it be not a thing of necessity to him for the sustenance of nature, if you do make this your rule, I desire clearly to understand where then remains property. Now then, that which (I would misrepresent nothing) the great and main answer which had any thing of matter in it that seemed to be the answer upon which that which hath been said against this rests, I profess I must clear myself as to that point; I desire, I would not, I cannot allow my self to lay the least scandal upon any body, and truly for that gentleman that did take so much offence I do not know why he should take it so: we speak to the paper, not to persons, and to the matter of the paper, and I hope that no man is so much engaged to the matter of the paper. I hope our persons, and our hearts, and judgments are not pinned to papers, but that we are ready to hear what good or ill consequence will flow from it. Now then, as I say to that which is to the main answer, that it will not make the breach of property, then that there is a law, thou shalt not steal: the same law says, honour thy father, and mother: and that law doth likewise hold out that it doth extend to all that, in that place where we are in, are our governors, so that by that there is a forbidding of breaking a civil law when we may live quietly under it, and a divine law; and again it is said, indeed before, that there is no law, no divine law that tells us, that such a corporation must have the election of burgesses, of such a shire or the like. Divine law extends not to particular things; and so on the other side, if a man were to demonstrate his property by divine law, it would be very remote, but our property descends from other things, as well as our right of sending burgesses; that divine law doth not determine particulars but generals in relation to man & man, and to property, and all things else, and we should be as far to seek if we should go to prove a property in divine law as to prove that I have an interest in choosing burgesses of the parliament by divine law; and truly under favour I refer it to all whether these be any thing of solution to that objection that I made, if it be understood. I submit it to any man's judgment.

Rainsborough: To the thing itself property, I would fain know how it comes to be the property: as for estates, and those kind of things and other things that belong to men, it will be granted that it is property, but I deny that that is a property, to a lord, to a gentleman, to any man more than another in the kingdom of England, if it be a property, it is a property by a law; neither do I think, that there is very little property in this thing by the law of the land, because I think, that the law of the land in that thing is the most tyrannical law under heaven, and I would fain know what we have fought for; and this is the old law of England and that which enslaves the people of England, that they should be bound by laws in which they have no voice at all. So the great dispute is who is a right father & a right mother. I am bound to know who is my father & mother, and I take it in the same sense you do. I would have a distinction, a character whereby God commands me to honour and for my part I look upon the people of England so, that wherein they have not voices in the choosing of their fathers & mothers, they are not bound to that commandment.

Petty: I desire to add one word, concerning the word property.

It is for something that anarchy is so much talk't of. For my own part I cannot believe in the least, that it can be clearly derived from that paper. 'Tis true, that somewhat may be derived in the paper against the King, the power of the King, and somewhat against the power of the Lords; and the truth is when I shall see God going about to throw down King and Lords and property, then I shall be contented; but I hope that they may live to see the power of the King and the Lords thrown down, that yet may live to see property preserved. And for this of changing the representative of the nation, of changing those that choose the representative, making of them more full, taking more into the number than formerly, I had verily thought we had all agreed in it: that more should have chosen, all that had desired a more equal representation than now we have. For now those only choose who have forty shillings freehold. A man may have a lease for one hundred pounds a year, a man may have a lease for three lives; but for this, that it destroys all right that every Englishman that is an inhabitant of England should choose and have a voice in the representatives, I suppose it is the only means to preserve all property. For I judge every man is naturally free; and I judge the reason why the men when they are in so great numbers that every man could not give his voice, was that they who were chosen might preserve property; and therefore men agreed to come into some form of government that they might preserve property, and I would fain know, if we were to begin a government: you have not forty shillings a year, therefore you shall not have a voice. Whereas before there was a government every man had such a choice, and afterwards, and for this very cause, they did choose representatives, and put themselves into forms of government that they may preserve property, and therefore it is not to destroy it.

Ireton: I think we shall not be so apt to come to a right understanding in this business, if one man, and another man, and another man do speak their several thoughts and conceptions to the same purpose, as if we do consider what the objection is, and where the answer lies to which it is made; and therefore I desire we may do so too. That which this gentleman spake last, the main thing that he seemed to answer was this, that he would make it appear that the going about to establish this government, such a government, is not a destruction of property, nor does not tend to the destruction of property, because the people's falling into a government is for the preservation of property. What weight there [is] lies in this: since there is a falling into a government, and government is to preserve property, therefore this cannot be against property. The objection does not lie in that, the making of it more equal, but the introducing of men into an equality of interest in this government, who have no property in this kingdom, or who have no local permanent interest in it; for if I had said that I would not wish at all that we should have any enlargement of the bounds of those that are to be the electors, then you might have excepted against it, but that I would not go to enlarge it beyond all bounds, so that upon the same ground you may admit of so many men from foreign states as would outvote you. The objection lies still in this, that I do not mean that I would have it restrained to that proportion, but to restrain it still to men who have a local, a permanent interest in the kingdom, who have such an interest that they may live upon it as freemen, and who have such an interest as is fix't upon a place, and is not the same equally everywhere. If a man be an inhabitant upon a rack rent for a year, for two years, or twenty years, you cannot think that man hath any fixed permanent interest; that man, if he pay the rent that his land is worth, and he hath no advantage but what he hath by his land, that man is as good a man, may have as much interest in another kingdom, but here I do not speak of an enlarging this at all, but of keeping this to the most fundamental constitution in this kingdom. That is, that no person that hath not a local and permanent interest in the kingdom should have an equal dependence in election; but if you go beyond this law, if you admit any man that hath a breath and being, I did show you how this will destroy property. It may come to destroy property thus: you may have a major part, you may have such men chosen, or at least the major part of them, why those men may not vote against all property. You may admit strangers by this rule, if you admit them once to inhabit, and those that have interest in the land may be voted out of their land; it may destroy property that way, but here is the rule that you go by: for that by which you infer this to be the right of the people, of every inhabitant, and that because this man hath such a right in nature, though it be not of necessity for the preserving of his being; therefore you are to overthrow the most fundamental constitution for this. By the same rule, show me why you will not, by the same right of nature, make use of anything that any man hath, for the necessary sustenance of mee [men?]. Show me what you will stop at, wherein you will fence any man in a property by this rule.

Rainsborough: I desire to know how this comes to be a property in some men, and not in others.

Colonel Rich: I confess that objection that the Commissary-General last insisted upon; for you have five to one in this kingdom that have no permanent interest. Some men [have] ten, some twenty servants, some more, some less; if the master and servant shall be equal electors, then clearly those that have no interest in the kingdom will make it their interest to choose those that have no interest. It may happen, that the majority may by law, not in a confusion, you may destroy property; there may be a law enacted, that there shall be an equality of goods and estate. I think that either of the extremes may be urged to inconveniency; that is, men that have no interest as to estate should have no interest as to election. But there may be a more equal division and distribution than that he that hath nothing should have an equal voice; and certainly there may be some other way thought of, that there may be a representative of the poor as well as the rich, and not to exclude all. I remember there were many workings and revolutions, as we have heard, in the Roman Senate; and there was never a confusion that did appear, and that indeed was come to, till the state came to know this kind of distribution of election: that is how the people's voices were bought and sold, and that by the poor; and thence it came that he that was the richest man, and of some considerable power among the soldiers made himself a perpetual dictator and one they resolved on. And if we strain too far to avoid monarchy in kings that we do not call for emperors to deliver us from more than one tyrant.

Rainsborough: I should not have spoken again. I think it is a fine gilded pill, but there is much danger, and it may seem to some that there is some kind of remedy. I think that we are better as we are, that the poor shall choose many; still the people be in the same case, be over-voted still. And therefore truly, sir, I should desire to go close to the business; and the thing that I am unsatisfied in is how it comes about that there is such a propriety in some freeborn Englishmen, and not others.

Cowling: Whether the younger son have not as much right to the inheritance as the eldest?

Ireton: Will you decide it by the light of nature?

Cowling: Why election was only forty shillings a year, which was more than forty pounds a year now, the reason was: that the Commons of England were overpowered by the Lords, who had abundance of vassals, but that still they might make their laws good against encroaching prerogatives; therefore they did exclude all slaves. Now the case is not so; all slaves have bought their freedoms, they are more free that in the commonwealth are more beneficial. There are men in the country in Staines: there is a tanner in Staines worth three thousand pounds, and another in Reading worth three horseskins.

Ireton: In the beginning of your speech you seem to acknowledge by law, by civil constitution, the propriety of having voices in election was fix't in certain persons. So then your exception of your argument does not prove that by civil constitution they have no such propriety, but your argument does acknowledge by civil propriety. You argue against this law, that this law is not good.

Mr Wildman: Unless I be very much mistaken we are very much deviated from the first question. And instead of following the first proposition to inquire what is just, I conceive we look to prophecies, and look to what may be the event, and judge of the justness of a thing by the consequence. I desire we may recall whether it be right or no. I conceive all that hath been said against it will be reduced to this, that it is against a fundamental law, and another reason that every person ought to have a permanent interest, because it is not fit that those should choose parliaments that have no lands to be disposed of by parliament.

Ireton: If you will take it by the way, it is not fit that the representees should choose the representees, or the persons who shall make the law in the kingdom, who have not a permanent fix't interest in the kingdom.

Wildman: Sir, I do so take it; and I conceive that that is brought in for the same reason, that foreigners might come as well to have a notice in our elections as well as the native inhabitants.

Ireton: That is upon supposition, that these should be all inhabitants.

Wildman: I shall begin with the last first. The case is different from the native inhabitant and foreigner. If a foreigner shall be admitted to be an inhabitant in the nation, he may so he will submit to that form of government as the natives do; he hath the same right as the natives but in this particular. Our case is to be considered thus: that we have been under slavery, that's acknowledged by all. Our very laws were made by our conquerors; and whereas it's spoken much of chronicles, I conceive there is no credit to be given to any of them; and the reason is because those that were our lords, and made us their vassals, would suffer nothing else to be chronicled. We are now engaged for our freedom; that's the end of parliaments, not to constitute what is already according to the just rules of government. Every person in England hath as clear a right to elect his representative as the greatest person in England. I conceive that's the undeniable maxim of government: that all government is in the free consent of the people. If then upon that account, there is no person that is under a just government, or hath justly his own, unless he by his own free consent be put under that government. This he cannot be unless he be consenting to it, and therefore, according to this maxim, there is never a person in England; if, as that gentleman says be true, there are no laws that in this strictness and rigour of justice, that are not made by those who he doth consent to. And therefore I should humbly move, that if the question be stated, which would soonest bring things to an issue, it might rather be this: Whether any person can justly be bound by law not by his own consent, who doth not give his consent that such persons shall make laws for him.

Ireton: Let the question be so: Whether a man can be bound to any law that he doth not consent to? And I shall tell you, that he may and ought to be, that he doth not give a consent to, nor doth not choose any; and I will make it clear. If a foreigner come within this kingdom, if that stranger will have liberty who hath no local interest here, he is a man, it's true, hath air that by nature we must not expel our coasts, give him no being amongst us, nor kill him because he comes upon our land, comes up our stream, arrives at our shore. It is a piece of hospitality, of humanity, to receive that man amongst us. But if that man be received to a being amongst us, I think that man may very well be content to submit himself to the law of the land; that is, the law that is made by those people that have a property, a fix't property in the land. I think, if any man will receive protection from this people, though he nor his ancestors, not any betwixt him and Adam, did ever give concurrence to this constitution, I think this man ought to be subject to those laws, and to be bound by those laws, so long as he continues amongst them; that is my opinion. A man ought to be subject to a law, that did not give his consent, but with this reservation, that if this man do think himself unsatisfied to be subject to this law, he may go into another kingdom; and so the same reason doth extend in my under-standing, that a man that hath no permanent interest in the kingdom, if he hath money, his money is as good in another place as here; he hath nothing that doth locally fix him to this kingdom. If that man will live in this kingdom, or trade amongst us, that man ought to subject himself to the law made by the people who have the interest of this kingdom in us. And yet I do acknowledge that which you take to be so general a maxim, that in every kingdom, within every land the original of power, of making laws, of determining what shall be law in the land, does lie in the people that are possess't in the permanent interest in the land. But whoever is extraneous to this, that is, as good a man in another land, that man ought to give such a respect to the property of men that live in the land. They do not determine why should I have any interest of determining what shall be the law of this land.

Major [William] Rainsborough: I think if it can be made to appear that it is a just and reasonable thing, and that it is for the preservation of all the freeborn men, I think it ought to be made good unto them; and the reason is, that the chief end of this government is to preserve persons as well as estates, and if any law shall take hold of my person, it is more dear than my estate.

Colonel Rainsborough: I do very well remember that the gentleman in the window [said] that, if it were so, there were no propriety to be had, because a fifth [five?] part[s] of the poor people are now excluded and would then come in. So I say one on the other side said, if otherwise, then rich men shall be chosen; then, I say, the one part shall make hewers of wood and drawers of water of the other five, and so the greatest part of the nation be enslaved. And truly I think we are where we were still; and I do not hear any argument given but only that it is the present law of the kingdom. I say what shall become still of those many that have laid out themselves for the parliament of England in this present war, that have ruined themselves by fighting, by hazarding all they had. They are

Englishmen. They have now nothing to say for themselves.

Rich: I should be very sorry to speak anything here that should give offence, or that may occasion personal reflection that we spoke against just now. I did not urge anything so far as was represented, and I did not at all urge them that there should be a consideration, and that man that is, shall be without consideration, he deserves to be made poor and not to live at all. But all that I urged was this: that I think it worthy consideration, whether they should have an equality in their interest, but however, I think we have been a great while upon this point, and if we be as long upon all the rest, it were well if there were no greater difference than this.

Mr Peters [Hugh Peter]: I think that this may be easily agreed on, that is, there may be a way thought of; but I would fain know whether that will answer the work of your meeting. I think you should do well to sit up all night, but I think that three or four might be thought of in this company: you will be forced to put characters upon electors or elected. Therefore I do suppose that if there be any here that can make up a representative to your mind, the thing is gained. But the question is, whether you can state any one question for the present danger of the kingdom, if any one question or no will dispatch the work.

Sir, I desire, that some question may be stated to finish the present work, to cement us wherein lies the distance; and if the thoughts of the commonwealth, the people's freedom, I think that's soon cured; but I desire that all manner of plainness may be used, that we may not go on with the lapwing and carry one another off the nest. There is something else in that must cement us where the awkwardness of our spirits lies.

Rainsborough: For my part, I think we cannot engage one way or other in the Army if we do not think of the people's liberties; if we can agree where the liberty and freedom of the people lies, that will do all.

Ireton: I cannot consent so far before. As I said before, when I see the hand of God destroying King, and Lords, and Commons too, any foundation of human constitution, when I see God hath done it, I shall, I hope, comfortably acquiesce in it; but first, I cannot give my consent to it, because it is not good, and secondly, as I desire that this Army should have regard to engagements wherever they are lawful, so I would have them have regard to this: that they should not bring that scandal upon the name of God, that those that call themselves by that name, those whom God hath owned and appeared with, that we should not represent ourselves to the world as men so far from being of that peaceable spirit which is suitable to the Gospel, as we would have bought peace of the world upon such terms; we would not have peace in the world but upon such terms as should destroy all property. If the principle upon which you move this alteration, or the ground upon which you press that we should make this alteration, do destroy all kind of property or whatsoever a man hath by human constitution. The law of God doth not give me property, nor the law of nature, but property is of human constitution. I have a property and this I shall enjoy. Constitution founds property. If either the thing itself that you press or the consequence that you press, though I shall acquiesce in having no property, yet I cannot give my heart or hand to it; because it is a thing evil in itself, and scandalous to the world, and I desire this Army may be free from both.

Mr Sexby: I see that though it [liberty?] were our end, there is a degeneration from it. We have engaged in this kingdom and ventured our lives, and it was all for this: to recover our birthrights and privileges as Englishmen; and by the arguments urged there is none. There are many thousands of us soldiers that have ventured our lives; we have had little propriety in the kingdom as to our estates, yet we have had a birthright; but it seems now, except a man hath a fix't estate in this kingdom, he hath no right in this kingdom. I wonder we were so much deceived. If we had not a right to the kingdom, we were mere mercenary soldiers. There are many in my condition, that have as good a condition; it may be little estate they have at present, and yet they have as much a right as those too who are their lawgivers, as any in this place. I shall tell you in a word my resolution. I am resolved to give my birthright to none, whatsoever may come in the way; and be thought that I will give it to none, if this thing that with so much pressing after. There was one thing spoken to this effect: that if the poor and those in low condition.[. . .] I think this was but a distrust of providence. I do think the poor and meaner of this kingdom, I speak as in that relation in which we are, have been the means of the preservation of this kingdom. I say, in their stations, and really I think that to their utmost possibility; and their lives have not been dear for purchasing the good of the kingdom. Those that act to this end are as free from anarchy or confusion as those that oppose it, and they have the law of God and the law of their conscience. But truly I shall only sum up this in all: I desire that we may not spend so much time upon these things. We must be plain. When men come to understand these things, they will not loose that which they have contended for. That which I shall beseech you is to come to a determination of this question.

Ireton: I am very sorry we are come to this point, that from reasoning one to another we should come to express our resolutions. I profess for my part, what I see is good for the kingdom, and becoming a Christian to contend for, I hope through God I shall have strength and resolution to do my part towards it, and yet I will profess direct contrary in some kind to what that gentleman said. For my part, rather than I will make a disturbance to a good constitution of a kingdom wherein I may live in godliness and honesty, and peace and quietness, I will part with a great deal of my birthright. I will part with my own property rather than I will be the man that shall make a disturbance in the kingdom for my property; and therefore if all the people in this kingdom, or representative of them all together, should meet and should give away my property, I would submit to it, I would give it away. But that gentleman, and I think every Christian spirit, ought to bear that, to carry that in him, that he will not make a public disturbance upon a private prejudice. Now let us consider where our difference lies. We all agree that you should have a representative to govern, but this representative to be as equal as you can; but the question is, whether this distribution can be made to all persons equally, or whether amongst those equals that have the interest of England in them? That which I have declared my opinion, I think we ought to keep to; that both because it is a civil constitution, it is the most fundamental constitution that we have, and there is so much justice and reason and prudence, as I dare confidently undertake to demonstrate, as that there are many more evils that will follow in case you do alter than there can in the standing of it. But I say but this in the general, that I do wish that they that talk of birthrights, we any of us when we talk of birthrights, would consider what really our birthright is. If a man me[a]n by birthright, whatsoever he can challenge by the law of nature, suppose there were no constitution at all, supposing no civil law and civil constitution, that that I am to contend for against constitution; you leave no property, nor no foundation for any man to enjoy anything. But if you call that your birthrights which is the most fundamental part of your constitution, then let him perish that goes about to hinder you or any man of the least part of your birthright, or will do it. But if you will lay aside the most fundamental constitution, and I will give you consequence for consequence, of good upon constitution as you for your birthright, which is as good for aught you can discern as anything you can propose, at least it is a constitution; and if you were merely upon pretence of a birthright, of the right of nature, which is only true as for your better being, if you will upon that ground pretend that this constitution, the most fundamental constitution, the thing that hath reason and equity in it, shall not stand in your way, is the same principle to me (say I), but for your better satisfaction you shall take hold of anything that a man calls his own.

Rainsborough: Sir, I see that it is impossible to have liberty but all property must be taken away. If it be laid down for a rule, and if you will say it, it must be so, but I would fain know what the soldiers have fought for all this while; he hath fought to enslave himself, to give power to men of riches, men of estates, to make him a perpetual slave. We do find in all presses that go forth none must be pres't that are freehold men. When these gentlemen fall out among themselves, they shall press the poor shrubs[1] to come and kill them.

Ireton: I must confess I see so much right in the business that I am not easily satisfied with flourishes. If you will lay the stress of the business upon the consideration of reason, or right relating to anything of human constitution, or anything of that nature, but will put it upon consequences, I will show you greater ill consequences; I see enough to say that, to my apprehensions, I can show you greater ill consequences to follow upon that alteration which you would have, by extending to all that have a being in this kingdom, than that by this a great deal. This is a particular ill

[1] 'Shrub' could=a 'mean, inferior, or insignificant person' (*OED*).

consequence. This is a general ill consequence, and that is as great as this or any else, though I think you will see that the validity of that argument must lie, that for one ill lies upon that which now is, and I can show you a thousand upon this. Give me leave but this one word. I tell you what the soldier of the kingdom hath fought for. First, the danger that we stood in was that one man's will must be a law. The people of the kingdom must have this right at least, that they should not be concluded by the representative of those that had the interest of the kingdom. So men fought in this because they were immediately concerned and engaged in it; other men who had no other interest in the kingdom but this, that they should have the benefit of those laws made by the representative, yet that they should have the benefit of this representative. They thought it was better to be concluded by the common consent of those that were fix't men, and settled men, that had the interest of this kingdom, and from that way I shall know a law and have a certainty. And every man that was born in it that hath a freedom is a denizen; he was capable of trading to get money, and to get estates by; and therefore this man, I think, had a great deal of reason to build up such a foundation of interest to himself; that is, that the will of one man should not be a law, but that the law of this kingdom should be by a choice of persons to represent, and that choice to be made by the generality of the kingdom. Here was a right that induced men to fight, and those men that had not this interest, and though this be not the utmost interest that other men have, yet they had some interest. Now why we should go to plead whatsoever we can challenge by the right of nature against whatsoever any man can challenge by constitution; I do not see where that man will stop, as to point of property, that he shall not use that right he hath by the law of nature against that constitution. I desire any man to show me where there is a difference. I have been answered, now we see liberty cannot stand without property. Liberty may be had and property not be destroyed; first, the liberty of all those that have the permanent interest in the kingdom, that is provided for, and in a general sense liberty cannot be provided for[1] if property be preserved. For, if property be preserved, that I am not to meddle with such a man's estate, his meat, his drink, his apparel, or other goods, then the right of nature destroys liberty. By the right of nature I am to have sustenance rather than perish; yet property destroys it for a man to have by the light of nature, suppose there be no human constitution.

Peter: I will mind you of one thing, that upon the will of one man abusing us, and so forth. So that I profess to you for my part I hope it is not denied by any man, that any wise, discreet man that hath preserved England or the government of it; I do say still under favour there is a way to cure all this debate. I think they will desire no more liberty if there were time to dispute it. I think he will be satisfied and all will be satisfied, and if the safety of the Army be in danger, for my part I am clear it should be

[1] 'in a general sense' is repeated in the text here.

amended, the point of election should be mended.

Cromwell: I confess I was most dissatisfied with that I heard Mr Sexby speak of any man here, because it did savour so much of will. But I desire that all of us may decline that, and if we meet here really to agree to that which is for the safety of the kingdom, let us not spend so much time in such debates as these are, but let us apply ourselves to such things as are conclusive, and that shall be this: everybody here would be willing that the representative might be mended, that is, it might be better than it is. Perhaps it may be offered in that paper too lamely, if the thing be insisted upon too limited; why perhaps there are a very considerable part of copy-holders by inheritance that ought to have a voice; and there may be some-what too reflects upon the generality of the people. I know our debates are endless if we think to bring it to an issue this way, if we may but resolve upon a committee. If I cannot be satisfied to go so far as these gentlemen that bring this paper, I say it again, I profess it, I shall freely and willingly withdraw myself, and I hope to do it in such a manner that the Army shall see that I shall by my withdrawing, satisfying the interest of the Army, the public interest of the kingdom, and those ends these men aim at. And I think if you do bring this to a result it were well.

Rainsborough: If these men must be advanced, and other men set under foot, I am not satisfied; if their rules must be observed, and other men, that are in authority, do not know how this can stand together, I wonder how that should be thought wilfulness in one man that is reason in another; for I confess I have not heard anything that doth satisfy me, and though I have not so much wisdom or notions in my head, but I have so many that I could tell an hundred to the ruin of the people. I am not at all against a committee's meeting; and as you say, and I think every Christian ought to do the same, for my part I shall be ready, if I see the way that I am going, and the thing that I would insist on, will destroy the kingdom, I shall withdraw it as soon as any. And therefore, till I see that, I shall use all the means, and I think it is no fault in any man to sell that which is his birthright.

Sexby: I desire to speak a few words. I am sorry that my zeal to what I apprehend is good should be so ill resented. I am not sorry to see that which I apprehend is truth, but I am sorry the Lord hath darkened some so much as not to see it, and that is in short. Do you think it were a sad and miserable condition, that we have fought all this time for nothing? All here, both great and small, do think that we fought for something. I confess, many of us fought for those ends which, we since saw, was not that which caused us to go through difficulties and straits to venture all in the ship with you; it had been good in you to have advertised us of it, and I believe you would have fewer under your command to have commanded. But if this be the business, that an estate doth make men capable, it is no matter which way they get it, they are capable, to choose those that shall represent them; but I think there are many that have not estates that in honesty have as much right in the freedom their choice as free as any that have great estates. 115

Truly, sir, your putting off this question and coming to some other, I dare say, and I dare appeal to all of them, that they cannot settle upon any other until this be done; it was the ground that we took up arms, and it is the ground which we shall maintain. Concerning my making rents and divisions in this way, as to a particular, if I were but so, I could lie down and be trodden there. Truly I am sent by a regiment; if I should not speak, guilt shall lie upon me, and I think I were a covenant-breaker. And I do not know how we have answered in our arguments, and I conceive we shall not accomplish them to the kingdom when we deny them to ourselves. For my part I shall be loath to make a rent and division, but for my own part unless I see this put to a question, I despair of an issue.

Captain Clarke: The first thing that I shall desire was, and is, this: that there might be a temperature and moderation of spirit within us; that we should speak with moderation, not with such reflection as was boulted one from another, but so speak and so hear as that which may be the droppings of love from one another to another's hearts. Another word I have to say is the grand question of all is, whether or no it be the property of every individual person in the kingdom to have a vote in election; and the ground is the law of nature, which, for my part, I think to be that law which is the ground of all constitutions. Yet really properties are the foundation of constitutions; for if so be there were no property, that the law of nature does give a principle to have a property of what he has, or may have, which is not another man's. This property is the ground of *meum* and *tuum*. Now there may be inconveniences on both hands, but not so great freedom, the greater freedom, as I conceive, that all may have whatsoever. And if it come to pass that there be a difference, and that the one doth oppose the other, then nothing can decide it but the sword, which is the wrath of God.

Captain Audley: I see you have a long dispute that you do intend to dispute here till the tenth of March. You have brought us into a fair pass, and the kingdom into a fair pass, for if your reasons are not satisfied, and we do not fetch all our waters from your wells, you threaten to withdraw yourselves. I could wish, according to our several protestations, we might sit down quietly, and there throw down ourselves where we see reason. I could wish we might all rise, and go to our duties, and see our work in hand. I see both at a stand, and if we dispute here both are lost.

Cromwell: Really, for my own part I must needs say, whilst we say we would not make reflections, we do make reflections; and if I had not come hither with a free heart, to do that that I was persuaded in my conscience is my duty, I should a thousand times rather have kept myself away; for I do think I had brought upon myself the greatest sin that I was guilty of, if I should have come to have stood before God in that former duty which is before you, and if that my saying, which I did say, and shall persevere to say, that I should not, I cannot against my conscience do anything. They that have stood so much for liberty of conscience, if they will not grant that liberty to every man but say it is a deserting I know not what. If that be denied me, I think there is not that equality that I profes't to be amongst us. I said this, and I say no more, that make your businesses as well as you can, we might bring things to an understanding; it was to be brought to a fair composure. And when you have said: if you should put this paper to the question without any qualification, I doubt whether it would pass so freely; if we would have no difference, we ought to put it. And let me speak clearly and freely; I have heard other gentlemen do the like. I have not heard the Commissary-General answered, not in a part to my knowledge, not in a tittle; if therefore, when I see there is an extremity of difference between you, to the end it may be brought nearer to a general satisfaction; and if this be thought a deserting of that interest, if there can be anything more sharply said, I will not give it an ill word. Though we should be satisfied in our consciences in what we do, we are told we purpose to leave the Army, or to leave our commands, as if we took upon us to do it in matter of will. I did hear some gentlemen speak more of will than anything that was spoken for this way, for more was spoken by way of will than of satisfaction; and if there be not a more equality in our minds, I can but grieve for it. I must do no more.

Ireton: I should not speak, but reflections do necessitate, do call upon us to vindicate ourselves, as if we who have led men into engagements and services, that we had divided because we did not concur with them. I will ask that gentleman whom I love in my heart that spoke, whether when they drew out to serve the Parliament in the beginning, whether when they engaged with the Army at Newmarket, whether then they thought of any more interest or right in the kingdom than this, whether they did think that they should have as great interest in Parliament-Men as freeholders had, or whether from the beginning we did not engage for the liberty of parliaments, and that we should be concluded by the laws that such did make, unless somebody did make you believe before now that you should have an equal interest in the kingdom; unless somebody do make that to be believed, there is no reason to blame men for leading so far as they have done; and if any man was far enough from such an apprehension, that man hath not been deceived. And truly I shall say but this word more for myself in this business, because the whole objection seems to be prest to me and maintained by me. I will not arrogate that I was the first man that put the Army upon the thought either of successive parliaments or more equal parliaments. Yet there are some here that know who they were put us upon that foundation of liberty, of putting a period to this Parliament, that we might have successive parliaments, and that there might be a more equal distribution of elections. Here are many here that know who were the first movers of that business in the Army. I shall not arrogate that but I can argue this with a clear conscience: that no man hath prosecuted that with more earnestness, and that will stand to that interest more than I do, of having parliaments successive and not perpetual, and the distributions of it; but notwithstanding my opinion stands good, that it ought to be a distribution amongst the fix't and settled people of this nation; it's more prudent and safe, and more upon this ground of right for it. Now it is the fundamental constitution of this kingdom; and that which you take away for matter of wilfulness notwithstanding this universal conclusion, that all inhabitants as it stands, though I must declare that I cannot yet be satisfied. Yet for my part I shall acquiesce; I will not make a distraction in this Army, though I have a property in being one of those that should be an elector; though I have an interest in the birthright, yet I will rather lose that birthright, and that interest, than I will make it my business, if I see but the generality of those whom I have reason to think honest men, and conscientious men, and godly men, to carry them another way. I will not oppose, though I be not satisfied to join with them, and I desire. I am agreed with you, if you insist upon a more equal distribution of elections; I will agree with you, not only to dispute for it, but to fight for it, and contend for it. Thus far I shall agree with you; on the other hand, those who differ their terms, I will not agree with you except you go further; thus far I can go with you; I will go with you as far as I can if you will appoint a committee to consider of some of that, so as you preserve the equitable part of that constitution who are like to be freemen, and men not given up to the wills of others, keeping to the latitude which is the equity of constitutions, I will go with you as far as I can. I will sit down. I will not make any disturbance among you.

Rainsborough: If I do not speak my soul and conscience, I do think that there is not an objection made, but that it hath been answered; but the speeches are so long. I am sorry for some passion and some reflections, and I could wish where it is most taken, the cause had not been given. It is a fundamental constitution of the kingdom; there I would fain know, whether the choice of burgesses in corporations should not be altered. The end wherefore I speak is only this: you think we shall be worse than we are, if we come to a conclusion by a vote. If it be put to the question, we shall all know one another's mind; if it be determined, and the resolutions known we shall take such a course as to put it in execution. This gentleman says, if he cannot go he will sit still. He thinks he hath a full liberty; we think we have not. There is a great deal of difference between us two. If a man hath all he doth desire, but I think I have nothing at all of what I fought for, I do not think the argument holds that I must desist as well as he.

Petty: The rich would very unwillingly be concluded by the poor. And there is as much reason, and indeed no reason, that the rich should conclude the poor as the poor the rich, but there should be an equal share in both. I understood your engagement was, that you would use all your endeavours for the liberties of the people, that they should be secured. If there is a constitution, that the people are not free, that should be annulled. That constitution which is now set up in a constitution of forty shillings a year, but this constitution doth not make people free.

Cromwell: Here's the mistake: whether that's the better constitution in that paper, or that which is. But if you will go upon such a ground as that is, although a better constitution was offered for the removing of the worse, yet some gentlemen are resolved to stick to the worse. There might be a great deal of prejudice upon such an apprehension. I think you are by this time satisfied, that it is a clear mistake; for it is a dispute whether or not this be better, nay whether it be not destructive to the kingdom.

Petty: I desire to speak one word to this business, because I do not know whether my occasions will suffer me to attend it any longer. The great reason that I have heard is the constitution of the kingdom, the utmost constitution of it; and if we destroy this constitution, there is no property. I suppose that if constitutions should tie up all men in this nature, it were very dangerous.

Ireton: First, the thing itself were dangerous, if it were settled to destroy propriety. But I say the principle that leads to this is destructive to property; for by the same reason that you will alter this constitution, merely that there's a greater constitution by nature, by the same reason, by the law of nature, there is a greater liberty to the use of other men's goods, which that property bars you of. And I would fain have any man show me why I should destroy that liberty, which the freeholders and burghers in corporations have in choosing burgesses, that which if you take away, you leave no constitution; and this because there is a greater freedom due to me from some men by the law of nature, more than that I should take another man's goods because the law of nature does allow me.

Rainsborough: I would grant something that the Commissary-General says. But whether this be a just propriety, the propriety says that forty shillings a year enables a man to elect; if it were stated to that, nothing would conduce so much whether some men do agree or no.

Captain Rolfe: I conceive that, as we are met here, there are one or two things mainly to be prosecuted by us; that is especially unity, preservation of unity in the Army, and so likewise to put ourselves into a capacity thereby to do good to the kingdom. And therefore I shall desire that there may be a tender consideration had of that which is so much urged, in that of an equal, as well as of a free, Representative. I shall desire that a medium, or some thoughts of a composure in relation to servants, or to foreigners, or such others as shall be agreed upon. I say then, I conceive, excepting those, there may be a very equitable sense resented to us from that offer in our own declarations wherein we do offer the common good of all, unless they have made any shipwreck or loss of it.

Chillenden: In the beginning of this discourse there were overtures made of imminent danger. This way we have taken this afternoon is not the way to prevent it. I should humbly move that we should put a speedy end to this business, and that not only to this main question of the paper, but also according to the Lieutenant-General's motion, that a committee may be chosen seriously to consider the things in that paper, and compare them with divers things in our declarations and engagements, that so as we have all professed, to lay down ourselves before God, if we take this course of debating upon one question a whole afternoon, if the danger be so near as it is supposed, it were the ready way to bring us into it. That things may be put into a speedy dispatch.

Clarke: I presume that the great stick here is this: that if every one shall have his propriety, it does bereave the kingdom' of its principal fundamental constitution, that it hath. I presume that all people and all nations whatsoever have a liberty and power to alter and change their constitutions, if they find them to be weak and infirm. Now if the people of England shall find this weakness in their constitution, they may change it if they please. Another thing is this: if the light of nature be only in this, it may destroy the propriety which every man can call his own. The reason is this, because this principle and light of nature doth give all men their own: as for example the clothes upon my back because they are not another man's. If every man hath this propriety of election to choose those whom you fear may beget inconveniencies, I do not conceive that anything may be so nicely and precisely done, but that it may admit of inconveniency. If it be in that wherein it is now, there may those inconveniences rise from them. For my part I know nothing but the want of love in it, and the sword must decide it. I shall desire before the question be stated, it may be moderated as for foreigners.

Sir Hardress Waller: This was that I was saying: I confess I have not spoken yet, and I was willing to be silent, having heard so many speak, that I might learn to. But it is not easy for us to say when this dispute will have an end; but I think it is easy to say when the kingdom will have an end. But if we do not breathe out ourselves, we shall be kicked and spurned of all the world. I would fain know how far the question will decide it; for certainly we must not expect, while we have tabernacles here, to be all of one mind. If it be to be decided by a question, and that all parties are satisfied in that, I think the sooner you hasten to it the better. If otherwise, we shall needlessly discover our dividing opinion, which as long as it may be avoided I desire it may. Therefore I desire to have a period.

Audley: I chanced to speak a word or two. Truly there was more offence taken at it. For my part I spoke against every man living, not only against yourself and the Commissary, but every man that would dispute till we have our throats cut. I profess, if so be there were none but you and the Commissary-General alone to maintain that argument, I would die in any place in England, in asserting that it is the right of every free-born man to elect, according to the rule, *Quod omnibus spectat, ab omnibus tractari debet*, that which concerns all ought to be debated by all. He knew no reason why that law should oblige when he himself had no finger in appointing the law-giver, and therefore I desire I may not lie in any prejudice before your persons.

Captain Bishop: You have met here this day to see if God would show you any way wherein you might jointly preserve the kingdom from its destruction, which you all apprehend to be at the door. God is pleased not to come in to you. There is a gentleman, Mr Saltmarsh, did desire what he has wrote may be read to the General Council. If God do manifest anything by him, I think it ought to be heard.

Ireton: That you will alter that constitution from a better to a worse, from a just to a thing that is less just in my apprehension; and I will not repeat the reasons of that, but refer to what I have declared before. To me, if there were nothing but this, that there is a constitution, and that constitution which is the very last constitution which if you take away you leave nothing of constitution, and consequently nothing of right or property. I would not go to alter that, though a man could propound that which in some respects might be better, unless it could be demonstrated to me that this were unlawful, or that this were destructive. Truly, therefore, I say for my part, to go on a sudden to make such a limitation as that in general, if you do extend the latitude that any man shall have a voice in election who has not that interest in this kingdom that is permanent and fixed, who hath not that interest upon which he may have his freedom in this kingdom without dependence, you will put it into the hands of men to choose, of men to preserve their liberty who will give it away.

I have a thing put into my heart which I cannot but speak. I profess I am afraid, that if we from such apprehensions as these are, of an imaginable right of nature, opposite to constitution, if we will contend and hazard the breaking of peace upon this enlargement of that business, I am confident our discontent and dissatisfaction, in that if ever they do well they do in this, if there be anything at all that is a foundation of liberty, it is this: that those who shall chose the law makers shall be men freed from dependence upon others. I think if we, from imaginations and conceits, will go about to hazard the peace of the kingdom, to alter the constitution in such a point, I am afraid we shall find the hand of God will follow it; we shall see that that liberty, which we so much talk of and contended for, shall be nothing at all by this our contending for it, by putting it into the hands of those men that will give it away when they have it.

Cromwell: If we should go about to alter these things, I do not think that we are bound to fight for every particular proposition. Servants, while servants, are not included. Then you agree that he that receives alms is to be excluded.

Lieutenant-Colonel Reade: I suppose it's concluded by all, that the choosing of representatives is a privilege; now I see no reason why any man that is a native ought to be excluded that privilege, unless from voluntary servitude.

Petty: I conceive the reason why we would exclude apprentices, or servants, or those that take alms, it is because they depend upon the will of other men and should be afraid to displease. For servants and apprentices, they are included in their masters, and so for those that receive alms from door to door; but if there be any general way taken for those that are not bound, it would do well.

Everard: I being sent from the Agents of five regiments with an answer unto a writing, the committee was very desirous to inquire into the depth of our intentions. Those things that they had there manifested in the paper,

I declared it was the Lieutenant-General's desire for an understanding with us, and what I did understand as a particular person, I did declare, and were presuming those things I did declare did tend to unity. And if so, you will let it appear by coming unto us. We have gone thus far: we have had two or three meetings to declare and hold forth what it is we stand upon, the principles of unity and freedom. We have declared in what we conceive these principles do lie, I shall not name them all because they are known unto you. Now in the progress of these disputes and debates we find that the time spends, and no question but our adversaries are harder at work than we are. I heard that there were meetings (but I had no such testimony as I could take hold of), that there are meetings daily and contrivances against us. Now for our parts I hope you will not say all is yours, but we have nakedly and freely unbosomed ourselves unto you. Though these things have startled many at the first view, yet we find there is good hopes; we have fixed our resolutions, and we are determined, and we want nothing but that only God will direct us to what is just and right. But I understand that all these debates, if we shall agree upon any one thing, This is our freedom; this is our liberty; this liberty and freedom we are debarred of, and we are bereaved of all those comforts. In case we should find half a hundred of these, yet the main business is how we should find them, and how we should come by them. Is there any liberty that we find ourselves deprived of; if we have grievances let us see who are the hindrances, and when we have pitched upon that way. I conceive I speak humbly in this one thing as a particular person, that I conceive myself, that these delays, these disputes, will prove little encouragement. As it was told me by these gentlemen, that he had great jealousies that we would not come to the trial of our spirits and that perhaps there might happen another design in hand. I said to his Honour again, if they would not come to the light, I would judge they had the works of darkness in hand. Now as they told me again on the other hand, when it was questioned by Colonel Hewson,[1] they told me: These gentlemen, not naming any particular persons, they will hold you in hand, and keep you in debate and dispute till you and we come all to ruin. Now I stood as a moderator between these things. When I heard the Lieutenant-General speak I was marvellously taken up with the plainness of the carriage. I said, I will bring them to you. You shall see if their hearts be so; for my part I see nothing but plainness and uprightness of heart made manifest unto you. I will not judge, nor draw any long discourses upon our disputes this day. We may differ in one thing, that you conceive this debating and disputation will do the work; we must put ourselves into the former privileges which we want.

Waller: I think this gentleman hath dealt very ingenuously and plainly with us. I pray God we may do so too, and for one I will do it. I think our disputings will not do the thing. I think if we do make it our resolution

[1] 'on the other hand' is repeated in the text here.

that we do hold it forth to all powers, Parliament or King, or whoever they are, to let them know that these are our rights, and if we have them not we must get them the best way we can.

Cromwell: I think you say very well; and my friend at my back, he tells me that [there] are great fears abroad; and they talk of some things such as are not only specious to take a great many people with, but real and substantial, and such as are comprehensive of that that hath the good of the kingdom in it. And truly if there be never so much desire of carrying on these things, never so much desire of conjunction, yet if there be not liberty of speech to come to a right understanding of things, I think it shall be all one as if there were no desire at all to meet. And I may say it with truth, that I verily believe there is as much reality and heartiness amongst us, to come to a right understanding, and to accord with that, that hath the settlement of the kingdom in it, though when it comes to particulars we may differ in the way. Yet I know nothing but that every honest man will go as far as his conscience will let him; and he that will go farther, I think he will fall back. And I think, when that principle is written in the hearts of us, and when there is not hypocrisy in our dealings, we must all of us resolve upon this, that 'tis God that persuades the heart. If there be a doubt of sincerity, it's the devil that created that effect; and 'tis God that gives uprightness. And I hope with such an heart that we have all met withal; if we have not, God find him out that came without it; for my part I do it.

Ireton: When you have done this according to the number of inhabitants, do you think it is not very variable, I would have us fall to something that is practicable, with as little pains and dissatisfaction as may be. I remember that in the proposals that went out in the name of the Army, it is propounded as a rule to be distributed according to the rates that the counties bear in the kingdom. And remember then you have a rule, and though this be not a rule of exactness for the number will change every day; yet there was something of equality in it, and it was a certain rule, where all are agreed; and therefore we should come to some settling. Now I do not understand wherein the advantage does lie from a sudden danger upon a thing that will continue so long, and will continue so uncertain as this is.

Waller: 'Tis thought there's imminent danger; I hope to God we shall be so ready to agree for the future that we shall all agree for the present to rise as one man if the danger be such, for it is an impossibility to have a remedy in this. The paper says that this Parliament is to continue a year, but will the great burden of the people be ever satisfied with papers? You eat and feed upon them. I shall be glad that there be not any present danger; if not that you will think of some way to ease the burden, that we may take a course, and when we have satisfied the people that we do really intend the good of the kingdom. Otherwise, if the four Evangelists were here, and lay free quarter upon them, they will not believe you.

Colonel Rainsborough: Moved, that the Army might be called to a rendezvous, and things settled.

Ireton: We are called back to engagements. I think the engagements we have made and published, and all the engagements of all sorts, have been better kept by those that did not so much cry out for it than by those that do, and if you will in plain terms better kept than by those that have brought this paper. Give me leave to tell you, in that one point, in the engagement of the Army not to divide, I am sure that he that understands the engagement of the Army not to divide or disband for satisfaction, that we are not to divide for quarters, for the ease of the country, or the satisfaction of service; he that does understand it in that sense, I am not capable of his understanding. But there was another sense in it, and that is, that we should not suffer ourselves to be torn into pieces, such a dividing as is really a disbanding; and for my part I do not know what disbanding is if not that dividing. That I do not see the authors of this paper, the subscribers of that book that is called The Case of the Army, I say that they have gone the way of disbanding. For my part I do not know what disbanding is, if that disbanding of an army is not parting in a place, for if that be so, did not we at that night disband to several quarters? Did we not then send several regiments, and yet the authors of that paper and the subscribers of them, for I cannot think the authors and subscribers all one, we all know, and they may know it, that there is not one part of the Army is divided farther than the outcries of the authors of it. Colonel Scroope's regiment into the West, we know where it was first; Colonel Horton's regiment into Wales for preventing of insurrection there; Colonel Lambert's, Colonel Lilburne's regiment then sent down for strengthening such a place as York? They go to scandalize an engagement or divide. There's no part of the Army is dispersed to quarters farther than that, whereupon that outcry is. But he that will go to understand this to be a dividing that we engaged against, he looks at the name, and not at the time. That dividing which is a disbanding, that dividing which makes no army, and if that dissolving of that order and government which is as essential to an army as life is to a man, which if it be taken away I think that such a company are no more an army than a rotten carcass is a man; and those that have gone to divide the Army. And what else is there in this paper that we have acted so vigorously for? They do not propose that this Parliament should end till the beginning of September. I say plainly, the way hath been the way of disunion and division, and that of that order and government by which we shall be enabled to act, and I shall appeal to all men: the dividing from that General Council wherein we have all engaged we would be concluded by that, and the endeavouring to draw the soldiers to run this way. When all comes upon the matter, it is but a critical difference and the very substance of that we have declared before. For my part I profess it seriously, that we shall find it in the issue, that the principle of that division, of disbanding is no more than this: whether such or such shall have the managing of the business. And let it be judged whether by this or that way we have taken, or that they have taken be not the same as to the matter. I shall

appeal: whether there can be any breach of the Army higher than that breach we have now spoke of, that word dividing the Army; whether we will not divide with such satisfaction, whether that dividing were not more truly and properly in every man's heart, this dividing wherein we do go apart one from another, and consequently those that have gone this way have not broke the Engagement, the other dividing whether that were a dividing a keeping of the Engagement. And those that do judge the one, I do not think that we have been fairly dealt with.

Rainsborough: I do not make any great wonder that this gentleman hath sense above all men in the world. But for these things, he is the man that hath undertaken them all. I say this gentleman hath the advantage of us; he hath drawn up the most part of them; and why he may not keep a sense that we do not know of. It is a huge reflection, a taxing of persons, if this gentleman had declared to us at first that this was the sense of the Army in dividing, and it was meant that men should not divide in opinions. To me that is a mystery, and because I will avoid further reflections, I shall say no more.

Agitator: Whereas you say the Agents did it, the soldiers did put the Agents upon these meetings. It was the dissatisfactions that were in the Army which provoked, which occasioned, those meetings, which you suppose tends so much to dividing; and the reason of such dissatisfactions are because those whom they had to trust to act for them were not true to them.

Ireton:[1] If this be all the effect of your meetings to agree upon this paper, here is but one thing in this that hath not been insisted upon and propounded by the Army heretofore, all along. Here it is put according to the number of inhabitants; here it is put according to the inhabitants, there according to the taxes. This says a period at such a day, the 8th of September; the other says a period within a year at most. That these have the power of making law, and determining what is law, without the consent of another. 'Tis true that Proposals said not that. And for my part, if any man will put that to the question whether we shall concur with it, I am in the same mind if you put it in any other hands than those that are free men. But if you shall put the question and with that limitation that hath been all along acknowledged by the Parliament, till we can acquit ourselves justly from any engagement, old or new, that we stand in, to preserve the person of the King, the persons of Lords, and their rights, so far as they are consistent with the common right – till that be done, I think there is reason that exception should continue, which hath been all along, that is, where the safety of the kingdom is concerned. This they seem to hold out. I would hold to positive constitution where I would not do real mischief. And therefore where I find that the safety of the kingdom is not concerned, I would not for every trifling make that this shall be a law, though neither the Lords, who have a claim to it, nor the King, who hath a claim to it,

---

[1] The speaker's name is omitted, but this is obviously Ireton and not still the Agitator speaking.

will consent. But where this is concerned upon the whole matter, let men but consider those that have thus gone away to divide from the Army. Admit that this Agreement of the People be the advantage; it may be we shall agree to that without any limitation. I do agree that the King is bound by his oath at his coronation, is bound at his coronation to agree to the law that the Commons shall choose without Lords or anybody else. But where I see things I would neither be thought to be a wrong-doer or disturber; so long as I can with safety continue a constitution, I will do it. If I can agree any further, that if the King do not confirm with his authority the laws that the people shall choose, we know what will follow.

Petty: I had the happiness sometimes to be at the debate of the Proposals, and my opinion was then as it is now, against the King's vote and the Lords'. But not so as I do desire since it hath pleased God to raise a company of men that do stand up for the power of the House of Commons, which is the representative of the people, and deny the negative voice of King and Lords. For my part I was much unknown to any of them, but only as I heard their principles; and hearing of their principles I cannot but join with them in my judgment, for I think it is reasonable that all laws are made by their consent. Whereas you seem to make the King and Lords so light a thing as that it may be to the destruction of the kingdom to throw them out, and without prejudice; for my part I cannot but think that both the power of King and Lords was ever a branch of tyranny. And if ever a people shall free themselves from tyranny, certainly it is after seven years' war and fighting for their liberty. For my part if the constitution of this kingdom shall be established as formerly, it might rivet tyranny into this kingdom more strongly than before. For when the people shall hear that for seven years together the people were plundered, and after they had overcome the King and kept the King under restraint, and at last the King comes in, then it will rivet the King's interest; and so when any men shall endeavour to free themselves from tyranny, we may do them mischief and no good. I think it's most just and equal, since a number of men have declared against it, they should be encouraged in it, and not discouraged. And I find by the Council that their thoughts are the same against the King and Lords, and if so be that a power may be raised to do that, it would do well.

Wildman: Truly, sir, I being desired by the Agents yesterday to appear at council or committees, either at that time, I suppose I may be bold to make known what I know of their sense, and a little to vindicate them in their way of proceeding, and to show the necessity of this way of proceeding that they have entered upon. Truly, sir, as to breaking of engagements, the Agents do declare their principle, that whensoever any engagement cannot be kept justly, but when they cannot act justly they must break that engagement. Now though its urged they ought to condescend to what the General Council do, I conceive it's true so long as it is for their safety. I conceive just and righteous for them to stand up for some more speedy vigorous actings. I conceive it's no more than what the Army did when the Parliament did not only delay deliverance, but opposed it. And I conceive this way of their appearing hath not appeared to be in the least way anything tending to division, since they proceed to clear the rights of the people; and so long as they proceed upon those righteous principles, I suppose it cannot be laid to their charge that they are dividers. And though it be declared, that the malice of the enemies would have bereaved you of your liberties as Englishmen, therefore as Englishmen they are deeply concerned to regard the due observation of their rights, as I, or any commoner, have right to propound to the kingdom my conceptions what is fit for the good of the kingdom. Whereas it is objected: How will it appear that their proceedings shall tend for the good of the kingdom? The matter is different. Whereas it was said before, it was propounded there must be an end to the Parliament, an equality as to elections, I find it to be their minds when they came there, they found many aversions from matters that they ought to stand to as soldiers and not as Englishmen; and therefore I find it concerning the matter of the thing, I conceive it to be a very vast difference in the whole matter of Proposals. The foundation of slavery was riveted more strongly than before: as where the militia is instated in the King and Lords, and not in the Commons, there is a foundation of a future quarrel constantly laid.

However, the main thing was that the right of the militia was acknowledged by the King. They found in the Proposals propounded, to be before any redress of any one of the people's grievances, any one of their burdens; and so to be brought in as with a negative voice, whereby the people and Army that have fought against him when he had propounded such things. And finding they perceived they were, as they thought, in a sad case; for they thought, he coming in thus with a negative, the Parliament are but as so many ciphers, so many round O's, for if the King would not do it, he might choose, *Sic volo, sic jubeo, Etc.*, and so the corrupt party of the kingdom must be so settled in the King. The godly people are turned over and trampled upon already in the most places of the kingdom. And I find this to be their thoughts. But whereas it is said, How will this paper provide for anything for that purpose? I shall say that this paper doth lay down the foundations of freedom for all manner of people. It doth lay the foundations of soldiers', whereas they found a great uncertainty in the Proposals, that they should go to the King for an Act of Indemnity, and thus the King might command his judges to hang them up for what they did in the wars, because, the present constitution being left as it was, nothing was law but what the King signed, and not any ordinance of Parliament. I speak but the words of the Agents. And considering of this, that they thought it should be by an Agreement with the people, whereby a rule between the Parliament and the people might be set, that so they might be destroyed neither by the King's prerogative nor Parliament's privileges. They are not bound to be subject to the laws as other men; why men cannot recover their estates. They thought there must be a necessity of a rule between the Parliament and the people, so that the Parliament should know what they were entrusted to, and what they were not; and that there might be no doubt for the Parliament's power, to lay foundations of future quarrels. The Parliament shall not meddle with a soldier after indemnity, it is agreed amongst the people. Whereas between a parliament and king, if the King were not under restraint should make an Act of Indemnity, whereas another Parliament cannot alter this. That these foundations might be established, that there might be no dispute between Lords and Commons, but, these things being settled, there should be no more disputes, but that the Parliament should redress the people's grievances. Whereas now all are troubled with King's interests, almost if this were settled, and besides the Parliament should be free from these temptations, which for my own part I do suppose to be a truth. That this very Parliament, by the King's voice in this very Parliament, may destroy, whereas now they shall be free from temptations and the King cannot have an influence upon them as he hath.

Ireton: Gentlemen, I think there is no man is able to give a better account of the sense of the Agents, and so readily; he hath spoke so much as they have in their book, and therefore I say he is very well able to give their sense. And I wish their senses had not been prejudicial to other men's senses, but, as I fear it will prove, really prejudicial to the kingdom, how plausible soever it seems to be carried. That paper of The Case of the Army that doth so abuse the General and General Council of the Army, that such and such things have been done that made them do thus and thus. And first as to the material points of the paper, you know as to the business of the Lords, the way we were then in admitted no other. This gentleman that speaks here, and the other gentleman that spake before, when we were at Reading framing the Proposals, did not think of this way. I am sure they did not think of this way; and according to the best judgments of those that were entrusted by the General Council to draw up the Proposals, it was carried by a question clearly, that we should not. In these Proposals our business was to set forth particulars; we had set forth general declarations, which did come to as much in effect as this: the thing then proposed was, that we should not take away the power of the Lords in this kingdom, and it was concluded in the Proposals. But as to the King we were clear: there is not one thing in the Proposals, nor in what was declared, that doth give the King any negative. And therefore that's part of the scandal amongst others: we do not give the King any negative voice; we do but take the King as a man with whom we have been at a difference; we propound terms of peace. We do not demand that he shall have no negative, but we do not say that he shall have any. There's another thing, that we have, as they say, gone from our engagements in our declarations, in that we go in the Proposals to establish the King's rights before the people's grievances. In our general declarations we first desire a purging of this Parliament, a period of this Parliament, and provision for the certainty of future parliaments; and if the King shall agree in these things

and what else the Parliament shall propound, that are necessary for the safety of the kingdom, then we desire his rights may be considered so far as may consist with the rights of the people. We did so in the declarations, and you shall see what we did in the Proposals. In the Proposals, things that are essential to peace, and it distinguishes those from the things that conduce to our better being, and things that lay foundations of an hopeful constitution in the future; when those are passed, then they say that, these things having the King's concurrence, we desire that his right may be considered. There were many other grievances and particular matters which we did not think so necessary that they should precede the settling of a peace, which is the greatest grievance of the kingdom. Our way was to take away that. Then we say, these propounding what things we thought in our judgments are to be essential and necessary as to peace. And then it says, there yet we desire that the Parliament would lose no time from the consideration of them. These gentlemen would say now we have gone from our declarations, that we propose the settling of the King: it stands before those grievances. We say, those grievances are not so necessary as that the remedying of them should be before the settling of the peace of the kingdom. What we thought in our consciences to be essential to the peace of the kingdom we did put preceding to the consideration of the King's personal right; and the concurrence of those is a condition without which we cannot have any right at all, and without there can be no peace, and have before named the consideration of the King's rights in the settling of a peace, as a thing necessary to the constitution of a peace. That, therefore, we should prefer the King's rights before a general good, was as unworthy and as unchristian an injury as ever was done to men that were in society with them, and as merely equivocation. But it was told you, that the General Council hath seemed to do so and so, to put the soldiers out of the way; and it is suggested that the Engagement is broken by our dividing to quarters; and whether that be broken or not, and it is suggested in other things, but it is said that the General Council hath broken the Engagement in this: that whereas before we were not a mercenary army, now we are. Let any man but speak what hath given the occasion of that. It hath been pressed by some men that we should have subjected to the Parliament, and we should stand to the propositions whatever they were; but the sense of the General Council was this: that, as they had sent their propositions to the Parliament, that they would see what the Parliament would do before they would conclude what themselves would do; and that there was respect to that which we have hitherto accounted the fundamental council of the kingdom. If all the people to a man had subscribed to this, then there would be some security to it, because no man would oppose; but otherwise our concurrence amongst ourselves is no more than our saying ourselves we will be indemnified. But our indemnity must be to something that at least we will uphold, and we see we cannot hold to be a conclusive authority of the kingdom; and for that of going to the King for indemnity, we propose an Act of Oblivion only for the King's party; we propose for ourselves an Act of

Indemnity and Justification. Is this the asking of a pardon? Then let us resort to the first petition of the Army, wherein we all were engaged once, which we made the basis of all our proceedings. In that we say, that an ordinance might be passed, to which the royal assent might be desired; but we have declared that, if the royal assent could not be had, we should account the authority of the Parliament valid without it. We have desired, in the General Council, that for security for arrears we might have the royal assent. And let me tell you, though I shall be content to lose my arrears to see the kingdom have its liberty, and if any man can do it, unless it be by putting our liberty into the hands of those that will give it away when they have done; but I say that I do not think that true in this: Whoever talk't either of the endeavours of the soldiers or of any other indemnity by the sword in their hands, is the perpetuating of combustions; so that word cannot take place, and does not suppose the settling of a peace, and by that authority which hath been here, by the legislative power of the kingdom; and he that expects to have the arrears of the soldiers, so I think he does but deceive himself. For my own part I would give up my arrears, and for my part lose my arrears, if we have not settlement; no arrears or want of indemnity, nor anything in the world, shall satisfy me to have a peace upon any terms, wherein that which is really the right of this nation is not as far provided for as can be provided for by men. I could tell you many other particulars wherein there are divers gross injuries done to the General and General Council, and such a wrong as is not fit to be done among Christians, and so wrong and so false that I cannot think that they have gone so far in it.

Wildman: I do not know what reason you have to suppose I should be so well acquainted with The Case of the Army, and the things proposed. I conceive them to be very good and just; but for that which I give as their sense, which you are pleased to say are scandals cast upon the Army. The legislative power had been acknowledged to be in the King with Lords and Commons; and then considering that, and what you said before was a scandal, that you propounded to bring in the King with his negative voice. I do humbly propound to your consideration, when you restrain the King's negative in one particular, which is in restraining unequal distributions, but whereas you do say the legislative power to be now partly in him, and say directly, in these very words, shall be restored to his personal rights.

And therefore I conceive, if I have any reason, the King is proposed to be brought in with his negative voice. And whereas you say it is a scandal for the King to come in with his personal rights, that the King consenting to those things, the King to be restored to all his personal rights.

There's his restoration. Not a bare consideration what his rights are before the people's grievances, but a restoration to his personal rights. These things being done, is the Parliament not to lose their rights; and for that of Indemnity, I do not say it was an asking of the King pardon, it is rendering us up, and therefore it is null in law.

9 The Humble Petition

After their defeat at Ware, in November 1647, the Levellers turned their main energies back to pamphleteering, party organization, and mass petitioning, especially in London. This Petition, *of September 1648, is their fullest policy statement since the 'large'* Petition *of eighteen months earlier (no. 5). Its relatively restrained tone contrasts with the bitter attacks that had been made on the Army leaders and on the Long Parliament in publications during 1647 and early 1648, and with those that were to follow in 1649. The Second Civil War had by this time been fought and won, but the parliamentary majority were still bent on an accommodation with the King; Lilburne had already abstained from attacking Cromwell after his own and Wildman's release from prison by Parliament in August (he had been re-arrested, and Wildman also committed, for contempt earlier in the year). Any treaty between King and Parliament was almost bound to be made at the expense of the Army, the radical Puritan sects, and the popular movement. Yet the tone of this* Petition *suggests that the Levellers still wanted to keep their options open, and perhaps to increase their support by statesmanlike moderation, or to put out feelers for reconciliation with the Army leaders. On the face of it, they do not yet seem to be finally convinced that the Long Parliament was beyond hope of redemption. If the use of argument from 'right reason' suggests Overton's influence, the general tenor and implied irony, when the authors emphasize Parliament's failings and inconsistencies, point to Walwyn. Its comprehensive treatment of immediate political issues, constitutional demands for the future – with reserved powers as in the* Agreement – *legal reforms, and measures to remedy economic grievances makes this obviously composite work the logical successor to Overton's* Appeals *and to the first* Agreement, *as well as to the 'large'* Petition. *Whatever its merits, or its potential popular appeal, the* Petition *was accorded a temporising, even polite reception by the House of Commons. But events in the months that followed were to move rapidly away from constitutional compromise or political reasonableness.*

TO THE
RIGHT HONORABLE,
THE
COMMONS OF ENGLAND
In Parliament Assembled.

The humble Petition of divers wel affected Persons
inhabiting the City of London, Westminster, the
Borough of Southwark, Hamblets, and places adjacent.
With the Parliaments Answer thereunto.

Sheweth,

That although we are as earnestly desirous of a safe and wel-grounded
Peace, and that a finall end were put to all the troubles and miseries of the
Common-wealth, as any sort of men whatsoever: Yet considering upon
what grounds we engaged on your part in the late and present Wars, and
how far (by our so doing) we apprehend ourselves concerned, Give us
leave (before you conclude as by the Treaty in hand) to acquaint you first
with the ground and reason which induced us to aid you against the King
and his Adherents. Secondly, What our Apprehensions are of this Treaty.
Thirdly, What we expected from you, and do still most earnestly desire.

Be pleased therefore to understand, that we had not engaged on your
part, but that we judged this honourable House to be the supream
Authority of England, as chosen by, and representing the People; and
entrusted with absolute power for redresse of Grievances, and provision
for Safety: and that the King was but at the most the chief publike Officer
of this Kingdom, and accomptable to this House (the Representative of
the People, from whom all just Authority is, or ought to be derived) for
discharge of his Office, And if we had not bin confident hereof, we had
bin desperately mad to have taken up Armes or to have bin aiding and
assisting in maintaining a War against Him: the Lawes of the Land making
it expresly a crime no lesse than Treason for any to raise War against the
King.

But when we considered the manifold oppressions brought upon the
Nation, by the King, His Lords, and Bishops; and that this Honourable
House declared their deep sence thereof; and that (for continuance of that
power which had so opprest us) it was evident the King intended to raise
Forces, and to make War; and that if he did set up his Standard, it tended
to the dissolution of the Government: upon this, knowing the safety of
the People to be above Law, and that to judge thereof appertained to the
Supream Authority, and not to the Supream Magistrate, and being
satisfyed in our Consciences, that the publike safety and freedom was in
imminent danger, we concluded we had not only a just cause to maintain;
but the supream Authority of the Nation, to justifie, defend, and indemp-
nifie us in time to come, in what we should perform by direction thereof;

132

though against the known Law of the Land, or any inferiour Authority, though the highest.

And as this our understanding was begotten in us by principles of right reason, so were we confirmed therein by your own proceedings, as by your condemning those Judges who in the case of Ship-money had declared the King to be Judge of safety; and by your denying Him to have a Negative voice in the making of Laws; where you wholly exclude the King from having any share in the supream Authority: Then by your casting the Bishops out of the House of Lords, who by tradition also, had bin accounted an essential part of the supream Authority; And by your declaring to the Lords, That if they would not joyn with you in se[t]lling the Militia, (which they long refused) you would settle it without them, which you could not justly have done, and they had any real share in the supream Authority.

These things we took for real Demonstrations, that you undoubtedly knew your selves to be the supream Authority; ever weighing down in us all other your indulgent expressions concerning the King or Lords. It being indeed impossible for us to believe that it can consist either with the safety or freedom of the Nation, to be governed either by 3. or 2. Supreams, especially where experience hath proved them so apt to differ in their Judgements concerning Freedom or Safety, that the one hath been known to punish what the other hath judged worthy of reward; when not only the freedom of the people is directly opposite to the Prerogatives of the King and Lords, but the open enemies of the one, have been declared friends by the other, as the Scots were by the House of Lords.

And when as most of the oppressions of the Common-wealth have in all times bin brought upon the people by the King and Lords, who nevertheless would be so equal in the supream Authority, as that there should be no redress of Grievances, no provision for safety, but at their pleasure. For our parts, we profess our selves so far from judging this to be consistent with Freedom or Safety, that we know no great cause Wherefore we assisted you in the late Wars, but in hope to be delivered by you from so intollerable, so destructive a bondage, so soon as you should (through Gods blessing upon the Armies raised by you) be enabled.

But to our exceeding grief, we have observed that no sooner God vouchsafeth you victory, and blesseth you with success, and thereby enablet you to put us and the whole Nation, into an absolute condition of freedom and safety: but according as ye have bin accustomed, passing by the ruine of a Nation, and all the bloud that hath bin spilt by the King and his Party, ye betake your selvs to a Treaty with him, thereby puting him that is but one single person, and a publike Officer of the Commonwealth, in competition with the whole body of the people, whom ye represent; not considering that it is impossible for you to erect any authority equall to your selves; and declared to all the world that you will not alter the ancient Government, from that of King, Lords, and Commons: not once mentioning (in case of difference) which of them is supream, but leaving that point (which was the chiefest cause of all our publike differences, disturbances Wars and miseries) as uncertain as ever.

In so much as we who upon these grounds have laid out our selves every way to the uttermost of our abilities: and all others throughout the land, Souldiers and others who have done the like in defence of our supream authority, and in opposition to the King, cannot but deem our selves in the most dangerous condition of all others, left without all plea of indemnity, for what we have done; as already many have found by losse of their lives & liberties, either for things done or said against the King; the law of the land frequently taking place, and precedency against and before your authority, which we esteemed supreame, and against which no law ought to be pleaded. Nor can we possibly conceive how any that have any waies assisted you, can be exempt from the guilt of murders and robbers, by the present laws in force, if you persist to disclaime the Supreame Authority, though their owne conscience do acquit them, as having opposed none but manifest Tyrants, Oppressors and their adherents.

And whereas a Personall Treaty, or any Treaty with the King, hath been long time held forth as the only means of a safe & wel-grounded peace; it is well known to have been cryed up principally by such as have been dis-affected unto you; and though you have contradicted it: yet it is believed that you much fear the issue; as you have cause sufficient, except you see greater alteration in the King and his party then is generally observed, there having never yet been any Treaty with him, but was accompanied with some underhand dealing; and whilst the present force upon him (though seeming liberty) will in time to come be certainly pleaded, against all that shall or can be agreed upon: nay, what can you confide in if you consider how he hath been provoaked; and what former Kings upon lesse provocations have done, after Oaths, Laws, Charters, Bonds, Excommunications, and all ties of Reconsilliations, to the destruction of all those that had provoked and opposed them: yea, when your selves so soone as he had signed those bils in the beginning of this Parliament, saw cause to tell him, That even about the time of passing those bils, some design or other was one fact which if it had taken effect would not only have rendred those bills fruitlesse, but have reduced you [to] a worse condition of confusion than that wherein the Parliament found you.

And if you consider what new wars, risings, revolting invasions, and plottings have been since this last cry for a Personall Treaty, you will not blame us if we wonder at your hasty proceedings thereunto: especially considering the wonderfull victories which God hath blessed the Army withall.

We professe we cannot chuse but stand amazed to consider the inevitable danger we shall be in, though all things in the Propositions were agreed unto, the Resolutions of the King and his party have been perpetually violently and implacably prosecuted & manifested against us; and that with such scorn and indignation, that it must be more than such ordinary bonds that must hold them.

And it is no lesse a wonder to us, that you can place your own security therein, or that you can ever imagine to see a free Parliament any more in England.

The truth is (and we see we must either now speak it [or] for ever be silent.) We have long expected things of an other nature from you, and such as we are confident would have given satisfaction to all serious people of all Parties.

1. That you would have made good the supreme of the people, in this Honourable House, from all pretences of Negative Voices, either in King or Lords.

2. That you would have made laws for election of representatives yearly and of course without writ or summons.

3. That you would have set expresse times for their meeting Continuance and Dissolution: as not to exceed 40 or 50 daies at the most, and to have fixed an expressed time for the ending of this present Parl.

4. That you would have exempted matters of Religion and God, worship, from the compulsive or restrictive power of any Authoritie upon earth, and reserved to the supreme authorities an un compulsive power only of appointing a way for the publick, whereby abundance of misery, prosecution and hart-burning would for ever be avoyded.

5. That you would have disclaimed in your selvs and all future Representatives, a power of Pressing and forcing any sort of men to serve in warrs, there being nothing more opposite to freedom, nor more unreasonable in an authoritie impowered for raising monies in all occasions, for which, and a just cause, assistants need not be doubted: the other way serving rather to maintain in justice and corrupt parties.

6. That you would have made both Kings, Queens, Princes, Dukes, Earls, Lords, and all Persons, alike liable to every Law of the Land, made or to be made; that so all persons even the Highest might fear & stand in aw and neither violate the publick peace, nor private right of person or estate, (as hath been frequent) without being lyable to accompt as other men.

7. That you would have freed all Commoners from the jurisdiction of the Lords in all cases: and to have taken care that all tryalls should be only of twelve sworn men, and no conviction but upon two or more sufficient known witnesses.

8. That you would have freed all men from being examined against themselves, and from being questioned or punished for doing of that against which no Law hath bid provided.

9. That you would have abbreviated the proceedings in Law, mitigated and made certain the charge thereof in all particulars.

10. That you would have freed all Trade and Marchandising from all Monopolizing and Engrossing, by Companies or otherwise.

11. That you would have abolished Excise, and all kind of taxes, except subsidies, the old and onely just way of England.

12. That you would have laid open all late Inclosures of Fens, and 135

other Commons, or have enclosed them onely or chiefly to the benefit of the poor.

13. That you would have considered the many thousands that are ruined by perpetual imprisonment for debt, and provided to their enlargement.

14. That you would have ordered some effectual course to keep people from begging and beggery, in so fruitful a Nation as through Gods blessing this is.

15. That you would have proportioned Punishments more equal to offences; that so mens Lives and Estates might not be forfeited upon trivial and slight occasions.

16. That you would have removed the tedious burthen of Tythes, satisfaying all Impropriators, and providing a more equal way of maintenance for the publike Ministers.

17. That you would have raised a stock of Money or[1] of those many confiscated Estates you have had, for payment of those who contributed voluntoarily above their abilities, before you had provided for those that disbursed out of their superfluities.

18. That you would have bound your selves and all future Parliaments from abolishing propriety, levelling mens Estats, or making all things common.

19. That you would have declared what the duty or busines of the Kingly office is, and what not, and ascertained the Revenue, past increase or diminution, that so there might never be more quarrels about the same.

20. That you would have rectified the election of publike Officers for the Citie of London, of every particular Company therin, restoring the Comunalty thereof to their just Rights, most unjustly withheld from them, to the producing and maintaining of corrupt interest, opposite to common Freedom, and exceedingly prejudecal to the trade and manufactures of this Nation.

21. That you would have made full and ample reparations to all persons that had bin oppressed by sentences in high Commission, Star-Chamber, and Council Board, or by any kind of Monopolizers, or projectors, and that out of the estates of those that were authors, actors or promoters of so intollerable mischiefs, and that without much attendance.

22. That you would have abolished all Committees, and have conveyed all businesses into the true method of the usuall Tryalls of the Commonwealth.

23. That you would not have followed the example of former tyrannous and superstitious Parliaments, in making Orders, Ordinances or lawes, or in appointing punishments concerning opinions or things super-naturall stiling some blasphemies others heresies; when as you know your selves easily mistaken and that divine truths need no human helps to support them: such proceedings having bin generally invented to divide

[1] For 'or' read 'out'.

the people against themselves, and to affright men from that liberty of discourse by which Corruption & tyranny would be soon discovered.

24. That you would have declared what the businesse of the Lords [w]as, and ascertain their condition, not derogating them the Liberties of oither men, that so there might be an end of striving about the same.

25. That you would have done Justice upon the Capitall Authors and Promoters of the former or late Wars, many of them being under your power; Considering that mercy to the wicked, is cruelty to the innocent: and that all your lenity doth but make them the more insolent and presumptuous.

26. That you would have provided constant pay for the Army, now under the Command of the Lord Gen. Fairfax, and given rules to all Judges, and all other publike Officers throughout the Land for their indempnity, and for the saving harmlesse all that have any wayes assisted you, or that have said or done any thing against the King, Queen, or any of his party since the beginning of this Parl. without which any of his party are in a better condition then those who have served you; nothing being more frequent with them, then their reviling of you and your friends.

The things and worthy Acts which have bin done and atchived by this Army and their Adherents (how ever ingratefully suffered to be scandalized as Sectaries and men of corrupt Judgements) in defence of the just authority of this honourable House, and of the common liberties of the Nation, and in opposition to all kind of Tyranny and oppression, being so far from meriting an odious Act of Oblivion, that they rather deserve a most honourable Act of perpetual remembrance, to be as a patern of publike vertue, fidelity, and resolution to all posterity.

27. That you would have laid to heart all the abundance of innocent bloud that hath bin spilt, and the infinite spoil and havock that hath been made of peaceable harmlesse people, by express Commissions from the King; and seriously to have considered whether the justice of God be likely to be satisfyed, or his yet continuing wrath appeased, by an Act of Oblivion.

These and the like we have long time hoped you would have minded, and have made such an establishment for the Generall peace and contentfull satisfaction of all sorts of people, as should have bin to the happines of all future generations, and which we most earnestly desire you would set your selves speedily to effect; whereby the almost dying honour of this most honourable House, would be again revived, and the hearts of our Petitioners and all other well affected people, be a fresh renewed unto you, the Freedom of the Nation (now in perpetuall hazard) would be firmly established, for which you would once more be so strengthened with the love of the people, that you should not need to cast your eyes any other wayes (under God) for your security: but if all this availeth noteing,[1] God

[1] nothing

be our Guide, for men sheweth us not a way for our preservation.

The house received this Petition, and returned answer thereunto which was to this effect viz. That the house gave them thanks for their great paines, and care to the publike good of the Kingdom, and would speedily take their humble desires into their serious consideration

FINIS.

10 The Whitehall Debates

*Like number 8, these brief extracts are again based on William Clarke's fair copy
of his original notes. They belong to the resumed discussions between the Army
leaders and the Levellers which took place in November–December 1648. Apart
from Lilburne's full but retrospective and obviously partisan account in his* Legall
Fundamentall Liberties *(published in the summer of 1649), Clarke's records of
the discussions on particular days are all that we have; and these are clearly
incomplete. The surviving texts mainly relate to debates on the relations of church
and state, notably to the powers – if any – which the civil magistrate should have
in matters of religion under the proposed compromise* Agreement of the People,
*which was then in the process of being drafted. The officers present at these
meetings of the Council of the Army (the General Council, including Agitators,
having ceased to exist a year or so earlier) were now joined by several Independents or Congregationalists, both army chaplains and London clergymen, as
well as by Leveller spokesmen, who at one stage included Lilburne, Overton and
Wildman.*

*The conservative viewpoint, that the magistrate should have some limited
powers to repress blasphemous, atheistical and perhaps Papist or Episcopalian
expressions, which were offensive to all true religion, was sustained by Ireton
almost entirely. One or two of the less radical divines present gave him some,
qualified support. Wildman's contributions have been chosen for reproduction
here, partly because he proved himself the most articulate of the Leveller spokesmen. They are also the most comprehensible taken out of context; and suggest his
sceptical, if not materialist viewpoint.*

The second Leveller Agreement *(published the day after this debate, and
therefore written in anticipation of the failure to agree on a compromise) and the
officers'* Agreement, *presented to Parliament on 20 January, differed fundamentally on the right to religious freedom as an absolute, unqualified reserved
power. The Levellers appear to adopt the principle of an officially supported form
of worship and of religious education, but leave the magistrate no other scope to
repress unwelcome or heterodox views; the officers' proposals are more or less in
line with Ireton's position in the debates. But even the officers' policy, in so far as
it was implemented under the Commonwealth and – perhaps more fully – under
Cromwell's Protectorate, was less repressive, and more tolerant over a wider
range, than anything which was yet in prospect from either Anglicans or Presbyterians.*

THE WHITEHALL DEBATES

Wildman's speeches in the General Council of Officers,
Whitehall, 14 December 1648.

The text is as follows:

Wildman: I suppose the difference is concerning the stating of the question. For what that learned gentleman was pleased to say, whether it were proper for this Council to conceive, whether it were matter of conscience. Through the judgment of God upon the nation all authority hath been broken to pieces, or at least it hath been our misery that it hath been uncertain where the supreme authority hath been, that none have known where the authority of the magistrate is, or his office. For the remedy of this your Excellency hath thought fit to propound a new way of settling this nation, which is a new constitution. Your Excellency thinks it that it can be no other way for to govern the people than this way.

And though this Agreement were resolved here, and therefore the question is now what power the people will agree to give to the magistrates that they will set over them to be their governors. Now the great misery of our nation hath been the magistrates' trust not being known. Now we being about settling the supreme power, I think it is clearly to declare what this power is; therefore I think the question will be: whether we shall entrust the magistrate in matters of religion or not; whether it be necessary to exercise it or not. That then the question must be thus: whether it be necessary that, after we have had a war for the power, to show what power we do give them, and what not. And I desire that the question may be stated: Whether it is necessary clearly to express in this constitution whether to entrust the magistrate in matters of religion or not; whether it be necessary to express it or not?

Mr Wildman's Question: Whether the magistrate have any restrictive or compulsive power in the time or manner of God's worship, or faith or opinion concerning him?

Wildman: I suppose the gentleman that spoke last[1] mistakes the question. He seems to speak as in relation to the people's giving that power the gentleman spoke before.[2] But to that which he spoke this may be answered, *de futuro.* That it is not lawful to entrust the magistrate with such a power. That it was not merely typical. The question was whether it were moral. If it were not moral, it were perpetual. If it were moral, it must go to all magistrates in the world. That the magistrate should act to his conscience, destroy and kill all men that would not come to such a worship as he had. God hath not given a command to all magistrates to destroy idolatry, for in consequence it would destroy the world. To that which the gentleman said, that the people might confer such a power upon the magistrate in

---

[1] Philip Nye, one of the leading Independent divines.
140 [2] John Goodwin, the most radical of the leading Independent ministers.

relation to a common good, I answer: that matters of religion or the worship of God are not a thing trustable, so that either a restrictive or a compulsive power should make a man to sin. To the second thing, that not only in relation to a common good, but to the prevention of evil, because by the magistrate's preventing such things as are contrary to the light of nature [to that end there might be such a power] to that I answer, it is not easily determinable what is sin by the light of nature. And if the gentleman speak of things between man and man, of things that tend to human society, he is besides the question; if concerning matters of the worship of God, it is an hard thing to determine. It is not easy by the light of nature to determine there is a God. The sun may be that God. The moon may be that God. To frame a right conception or notion of the First Being, wherein all other things had their being, is not by the light of nature. Indeed, if a man consider there is a will of the Supreme Cause, it is an hard thing for the light of nature to conceive how there can be any sin committed. And therefore the magistrate cannot easily determine what sins are against the light of nature, and what not. And to both of those considerations together it may be said this: however, supposing both things were [these] thus, yet [it] is but to put the magistrate in a probable condition to do good, or in a capacity probably to prevent the sin; because the magistrate must be conceived to be as erroneous as the people by whom he is restrain'd, and more probable to err than the people that have no power in their hands, the probability is greater that he will destroy what is good than prevent what is evil. So that to both of them, they do not put the commonwealth into so much as a probability of any good by such a trust committed to them. I humbly conceive that, while there is a new-seeming question, whether such things be nulled by the Gospel, the ground which the Commissary-General says: that which was sin then is sin now. This is your argument: that what was sin then, and is sin now, and ought to be punished then, it ought to be punished now. I suppose there is no consequence at all because, if it were punished then, it ought to be punished now; because it was upon a judicial law which was not[1] moral, but not naturally moral, and yourself said that the punishment was not naturally. And if so, I would desire to know how we should distinguish which part of it was naturally moral and what was not. The Decalogue contains the whole Law. If you will extend it beyond its[elf], I would know whether you will terminate it. Besides, if it were naturally moral, you should find it natural. If it had been given as a thing naturally moral, and as a magistrate, then it must belong to every magistrate that was in the world but not *quatenus* magistrates; and then you must hold that God had ordained such a power to them in every magistrate. I must confess that what was given to them was as Jewish magistrates. Not determining what a magistrate shall be, you leave us to an uncertainty. We find no such power at all in any magistrate.

---

[1] ?delete this 'not'.

11 Englands New Chains Discovered
JOHN LILBURNE

Lilburne is generally thought to have been the principal, if not the sole author of
Englands New Chains Discovered. Its appearance reflected the renewed
breach between the Levellers and the Army leaders together with the now purged
'Rump' House of Commons, which followed hard upon the dramatic events of
December 1648–January 1649. Lilburne, and those who supported him in
presenting this in the form of a 'petition' to Parliament, saw the country's new
rulers rapidly consolidating a formidable combination of political and military
power, of legislative, executive and judicial authority. The MP whose censure
is mentioned was a religious deviant, John Fry, who sat for Shaftesbury. He was
forgiven his apparent unitarianism and unconcealed anti-clericalism in 1649, but
was expelled from the House for repeating his offences two years later. The
'grand contrivers' who are portrayed as manipulating both Army and Parliament
for their own sinister ends are, of course, Cromwell and Ireton. In reality things
were not quite so clear-cut. For instance Ireton was not elected to the first Council
of State chosen by the Rump earlier in February. The military-civilian jealousies
and resentments, which were ultimately to destroy the Commonwealth, were
already at work. Once more we meet the theme of consistency to the Army's
engagements, that is the declarations of summer 1647. As in the autumn of that
year, it became increasingly clear in the early spring of 1649 that the real issue
was going to be over control of the Army. At the same time Lilburne seems, if only
for propaganda purposes, to have been appealing to the Rump to take steps, before
it was too late, against the incipient military dictatorship. Apart from the by now
familiar issues of tithes and law reform, many positive aspects of the Levellers'
programme had been temporarily squeezed out by the crisis of the moment.
   The second part of Englands New Chains, presented a month later, precipitated their enemies' counter-blow against the Levellers. It provided the
Council of State with the occasion – one might say the pretext – for having the
leaders arrested, before wider opposition could be aroused or army discipline
further undermined.

ENGLANDS NEW CHAINS DISCOVERED[1]

For where is that good, or where is that liberty so much pretended, so
deerly purchased? If we look upon what this House hath done since it hath
voted it self the Supreme Authority, and disburthened themselves of the

[1] Sigs. A3v–B3.

power of the Lords. First, we find a high Court of Justice erected, for Tryal of Criminal causes; whereby that great and strong hold of our preservation, the way of tryal by 12. sworn men of the Neighbourhood is infringed, all liberty of exception against the tryers, is over-ruled by a Court consisting of persons pickt and chosen in an un-usual way; the practise whereof we cannot allow of, though against open and notorious enemies; as well because we know it to be an usual policy to introduce by such means all usurpations, first against Adversaries, in hope of easier admission; as also, for that the same being so admited, may at pleasure be exercised against any person or persons whatsoever. This is the first part of our new liberty. The next is the censuring of a Member of this House, for declaring his judgement in a point of Religion, which is directly opposite to the Reserve in the Agreement concerning Religion. Besides the Act for pressing of Sea-men, directly contrary to the Agreement of the Officers. Then the stoping of our mouths from Printing, is carefully provided for, and the most severe and unreasonable Ordinances of Parliament that were made in the time of Hollis and Stapletons reign, to gag us from speaking truth, and discovering the tyrannies of bad men, are refered to the care of the General, and by him to his Marshal, to be put in execution; in searching, fining, imprisoning, and other waies corporally punishing all that any waies be guilty of unlicensed Printing; They dealing with us as the Bishops of old did with the honest Puritan, who were exact in geting Laws made against the Papist, but really intended them against the Puritan, and made them feel the smart of them: Which also hath bin, and is dayly exercised most violently, whereby our Liberties have him more deeply wounded, than since the begining of this Parliament; and that to the dislike of the Souldiery, as by their late Petition in that behalf plainly appeareth. Then whereas it was expected that the Chancery, and Courts of Justice in Westminster, and the Judges and Officers thereof should have bin surveyed, and for the present regulated, till a better and more equal way of deciding controversies could have bin constituted, that the trouble and charge of the people in their suits should have bin abated: Insteed hereof, the old and advanced fees are continued, and new thousand pounds Annual stipends alotted; when in the corruptest times the ordinary fees were thought a great and a sore burden; in the mean time, and in lieu thereof, there is not one perplexity or absurdity in proceedings taken away. Those Petitioners that have moved in behalf of the people, how have they bin entertained? Sometimes with the complement of empty thanks, their desires in the mean time not at all considered; at other times meeting with Reproches and Threats for their constancy and publike affections, and with violent motions, that their Petitions be burnt by the common Hangman, whilst others are not taken in at all; to so small an account are the people brought, even while they are flattered with notions of being the Original of all just power. And lastly, for compleating this new kind of liberty, a Councel of State is hastily erected for Guardians thereof, who to that end are possessed with power to order and dispose all the forces appertaining to England by Sea or Land, to dispose of the publike Treasure, to command any person whatsoever before them, to give oath for the discovering of Truth, to imprison any that shall dis-obey their commands, and such as they shall judge contumatious. What now is become of that liberty that no mans person shall be attached or imprisoned, or otherwise dis-eased of his Free-hold, or free Customs, but by lawful judgement of his equals? We entreat you give us leave to lay these things open to your view, and judge impartially of our present condition, and of your own also, that by strong and powerfull influences of some persons, are put upon these and the like proceedings, which both you and we ere long (if we look not to it) shall be inforced to subject our selves unto; then we have further cause to complain, when we consider the persons: as first, the chief of the Army directly contrary to what themselves thought meet in their Agreement for the People. 2. Judges of the Law, and Treasurers for monies. Then 5. that were Members of the Lords House, and most of them such as have refused to approve of your Votes and proceedings, concerning the King and Lords. 2. of them Judges in the Star-chamber, and approvers of the bloudy and tyrannical sentences issuing from thence.

Some of your own House, forward men in the Treaty, and decliners of your last proceedings; all which do cleerly manifest to our understandings that the secret contrivers of those things doe think themselves now so surely guarded by the strength of an Army, by their dayly Acts and Stratagems, to their ends inclined, and the captivation of this House, that they may now take off the Vail and Cloak of their designes as dreadlesse of what ever can be done against them. By this Councel of State, all power is got into their own hands, a project which hath been long and industriously laboured for; and which being once firmly and to their liking established their next motions may be upon pretense of ease to the People, for the dissolution of this Parliament, half of whose time is already swallowed up by the said Councel now, because no obstacle lies in their way, to the full establishment of these their ends, but the uncorrupted part of the Souldiery, that have their eyes fixed upon their ingagements and promises of good to the People, and resolve by no threats or allurements to decline the same; together with that part of the people in Citie and Countries, that remain constant in their motions for Common good, and still persist to run their utmost hazards for procurement of the same, by whom all evil mens designes both have, and are still likely to find a check and discovery. Hereupon the grand contrivers fore-mentioned, whom we can particular by name, do begin to raise their spleen, and manifest a more violent enmitie against Souldiers and People, disposed as afore-said, than ever heretofore, as appeareth by what lately past, at a meeting of Officers, on Feb. 22. last, at White-Hall, where after expressions of much bitternesse against the most Conscientious part of the Souldiery, and others, it was insisted upon, (as we are from very creditable hands certainly informed) that a motion should be made to this House for the procurement

144

of a Law enabling them to put to death all such as they should judge by Petitions or otherwise to disturbe the present proceedings; and upon urging that the Civil Magistrate should do it, It was answered, that they could hang twenty ere the Magistrate one. It was likewise urged that Orders might be given to seize upon the Petitioners, Souldiers, or others, at their meetings, with much exclamation against some of greatest integritie to your just Authority, whereof they have given continual and undenyable assurances. A Proclamation was likewise appointed, forbidding the Souldiers to Petition you, or any but their Officers, prohibiting their correspondencies; And private Orders to be given out for seizing upon Citizens and Souldiers at their meetings. And thus after these fair blossoms of hopefull liberty, breaks forth this bitter fruit, of the vilest and basest bondage that ever English men groan'd under: whereby this notwith-standing is gained (viz.) an evident and (we hope) a timely discovery of the instruments, from whence all the evils, contrivances, and designes (which for above these eighteen moneths have been strongly suspected) took their rise and original, even ever since the first breach of their Promises and engagements made at New Market, Triploe Heath, with the Agitators and People. It being for these ends that they have so violently opposed all such as manifested any zeal for Common right, or any regard to the Faith of the Army, sentencing some to death, others to reproachfull punish-ments, placing and dis-placing Officers according as they shewed them-selves serviceable or opposite to their designes, listing as many as they thought good, even of such as have served in Arms against you: And then again upon pretence of easing the charge of the People, disbanding Super-numeraries, by advantage thereof picking out, such as were most cordial and active for Common good; thereby moulding the Army (as far as they could) to their own bent and ends premised; exercising Martial Law with much cruelty, thereby to debase their spirits, and make them subservient to their wils and pleasures; extending likewise their power (in many cases) over persons not Members of the Army.

And when in case of opposition and difficult services, they have by their creatures desired a Reconciliation with such as at other times they re-proached, vilified, and otherwise abased; and through fair promises of good, and dissembled repentance gained their association and assistance, to the great advantage of their proceedings: yet their necessities being over, and the Common enemy subdued, they have sleighted their former promises, and renewed their hate and bitternesse against such their assist-ances, reproaching them with such appellations as they knew did most distaste the People, such as Levellers, Jesuites, Anarchists, Royalists, names both contradictory in themselves, and altogether groundlesse in relation to the men so reputed; merely relying for releese thereof upon the easinesse and credulity of the People.

And though the better to insinuate themselves, and get repute with the People, as also to conquer their necessities, they have bin fane to make use of those very principles and productions, the men they have so much 145 traduced, have brought to light: yet the producers themselves they have and doe still more eagerly maligne than ever, as such whom they know to bee acquainted to their deceipts, and deviations and best able to discover the same.

So that now at length, guessing all to be sure, and their own (the King being removed, the House of Lords nulled, their long plotted Councel of State erected, and this House awed to their ends,) the edge of their mallice is turning against such as have yet so much courage left them as to appear for the well establishment of Englands Liberties: and because God hath preserved a great part of the Army untainted with the guilt of the designes afore-mentioned, who cannot without much danger to the designers themselves be suppressed, they have resolved to put this House upon raising more new forces, (notwithstanding the present necessities of the People, in maintaining those that are already) in doing whereof, though the pretence be danger, and opposition, yet the concealed end is like to be the over-ballancing those in the Army, who are resolved to stand for true Freedome, as the end of all their labours, the which (if they should be permitted to do) they would not then doubt of making themselves absolute seizures, Lords and Masters, both of Parliament and People; which when they have done we expect the utmost of misery, nor shall it grieve us to expire with the liberties of our native Country: for what good man can with any comfort to himself survive then? But God hath hitherto preserved us, and the Justice of our desires, as integrity of our intentions are dayly more and more manifest to the impartial and unprejudiced part of men; insomuch that it is no smal comfort to us, that notwithstanding we are upon all these disadvantages that may be, having neither power nor preheminence, the Common Idols of the world; our Cause and principles, do through their own natural truth and lustre get ground in mens understandings, so that where there was one, twelve moneths since, that owned our principles, we beleeve there are now hundreds, so that though we fail, our Truths prosper.

And posterity we doubt not shall reap the benefit of our endeavours, what ever shall become of us. However though we have neither strength nor safety before us, we have discharged our Consciences, and emptied our breasts unto you, knowing well that if you will make use of your power, and take unto you that courage which becomes men of your Trust and condition, you may yet through the goodnesse of God prevent the danger and mischief intended, and be instrumental in restoring this long enthralled and betrayed Nation into a good and happy condition.

[1.] For which end we most earnestly desire and propose, as the main prop and support of the work, that you will not dissolve this House, nor suffer your selves to be dissolved, until as aforesaid, you see a new Representative the next day ready to take your room; which you may confidently and safely insist upon, there being no considerable number in the Army or else-where, that will be so unworthy as to dare to disturb you

therein.

2. That you will put in practise the self-denying Ordinance, the most just and useful that ever was made, and continually cryed out for by the people; whereby a great infamy that lies upon your cause will be removed, and men of powerful influences, and dangerous designes, deprived of those means and opportunities which now they have, to prejudice the publike.

3. That you will consider how dangerous it is for one and the same persons to be continued long in the highest commands of a Military power, especially acting so long distinct, and of themselves, as those now in being have done, and in such extraordinary waies whereunto they have accustomed themselves, which was the original of most Regalities and Tyrannies in the world.

4. That you appoint a Committee of such of your own members, as have bin longest establisht upon those rules of Freedom upon which you now proceed; to hear, examine, and conclude all controversies between Officers and Officers, and between Officers and Souldiers; to consider and mitigate the Law-Martial; and to provide that it be not exercised at all upon persons not of the Army: Also to release and repair such as have thereby unduly suffered, as they shall see cause: To consider the condition of the private Souldiers, both Horse and Foot in these deer times, and to allow them such increase of pay, as wherewithal they may live comfortably, and honestly discharge their Quarters: That all disbanding be refered to the said Committee, and that such of the Army as have served the King, may be first disbanded.

5. That you will open the Press, whereby all trecherous and tyranical designes may be the easier discovered, and so prevented, which is a liberty of greatest concernment to the Commonwealth, and which such only as intend a tyrannie are engaged to prohibit: The mouths of Adversaires being best stopped, by the sensible good which the people receive from the actions of such as are in Authority.

6. That you wil (whilst you have opportunity) abate the charge of the Law, and reduce the stipends of Judges, and all other Magistrates and Officers in the Common-wealth, to a less, but competent allowance, converting the over-plus to the publike Treasury, whereby the taxes of the people may be much eased.

7. But above all, that you will dissolve this present Councel of State, which upon the grounds fore-mentioned so much threatneth Tyrannie; and mannage your affairs by Committees of short continuance, and such as may be frequently and exactly accountable for the discharge of their Trusts.

8. That you will publish a strict prohibition, and severe penalty against all such, whether Committees, Magistrates, or Officers of what kind soever, as shall exceed the limits of their Commission, Rules, or Directions, and incourage all men in their informations and complaints against them.

9. That you will speedily satisfie the expectations of the Souldiers in

point of Arrears, and of the people in point of Accounts, in such a manner, as that it may not as formerly, prove a snare to such as have bin most faithful, and a protection to the most corrupt, in the discharge of their trust and duties.

10. That the so many times complained of Ordinance for Tyths upon treble damages, may be forthwith taken away; all which, together with due regard shewed to Petitioners, without respect to their number and strength, would so fasten you in the affections of the people, and of the honest Officers and Souldiers, as that you should not need to fear any opposite power whatsoever: and for the time to come, of your selves enjoy the exercise of your Supreme Authority, whereof you have yet but the name onely; and be inabled to vindicate your just undertakings; wherein we should not onely rejoyce to have occasion to manifest how ready we should be to hazard our lives in your behalf, but should also bend all our studies and endeavours to render you Honourable to all future generations.

12 The Hunting of the Foxes

RICHARD OVERTON and/or JOHN LILBURNE

The Hunting of the Foxes from New-Market and Triploe Heaths to
Whitehall, By five small Beagles (late of the Armie). Or, the Grandie-
Deceivers Unmasked. *(21 March 1649) belongs to the same phase of
Leveller activity as the previous document. It purported to be written by five
ex-cavalry troopers, recently cashiered for mutinous behaviour, but Richard
Overton was probably the true author. (Some authorities ascribe it to Lilburne,
but stylistically this seems less likely.) Like Wildman's* Putney Projects *of
December 1647 (see Introduction), it concentrates almost wholly on the alleged
dishonesty of Cromwell and Ireton, tracing their hypocritical behaviour and their
tyrannous designs step by step from their betrayal of the engagements entered into
in 1647. As with* Englands New Chains *(especially part two) it was clearly
aimed at public opinion in the Army and among the people at large. There is no
longer any pretence at a dialogue with their opponents: a coming struggle for
power is envisaged, even if a call to arms is not yet sounded.*

*This short passage is one of the classic accounts of Oliver Cromwell the great
hypocrite, as seen by his erstwhile radical allies. The same treatment of him can
be found, but at far greater length, in Edmund Ludlow's* Memoirs. *Joyce is of
course the man who as a mere cornet had seized the King on behalf of the Army
in the summer of 1647, Cromwell's attitude towards this action having been
outwardly equivocal but probably extending to secret approval. Vernon, by now
no longer a member of the Army, was a regimental officer who had attacked the
leaders and their policies in a pamphlet of the previous December. No doubt these
instances were cited because of their significance for ex-Agitators and other rank
and file.*

THE HUNTING OF THE FOXES *(extract)*

Was there ever a generation of men so Apostate so false and so perjur'd as
these? did ever men pretend an higher degree of Holinesse, Religion, and
Zeal to God and their Country than these? these preach, these fast, these
pray, these have nothing more frequent then the sentences of sacred
Scripture, the Name of God and of Christ in their mouthes: You shall
scarce speak to *Crumwell* about any thing, but he will lay his hand on his
breast, elevate his eyes, and call God to record, he will weep, howl and
repent, even while he doth smite you under the first rib. Captain *Ioyce*
and Captain *Vernam* can tell you sufficient stories to that purpose.

13 A Manifestation

WILLIAM WALWYN

A Manifestation *(14 April 1649) is one of several pamphlets written by Lilburne and the other Leveller leaders in the Tower of London and smuggled out for publication. While it purports to be the joint work of the four leaders, Walwyn has generally been credited with the main, indeed perhaps the sole authorship. This is convincing on grounds both of style and content. The worthy Thomas Prince, while by no means totally inarticulate, may none the less be excluded as lacking the necessary intellectual and political range. The tone and manner are insufficiently truculent for Overton, and there is not enough self-dramatization for Lilburne; moreover the text is blessedly free from references and citations. But even if substantially the work of Walwyn, it may be taken as the Levellers' fullest and – surprisingly in the circumstances – their calmest collective self-justification. It is one of their very few pamphlets – one is tempted to say, one of the few pieces of political writing of any age – which is both compelling and a pleasure to read, maintaining as it does a remarkable consistency and evenness of tone. The author or authors succeed in the difficult task of vindicating themselves without appearing excessively self-righteous. In rebutting the various charges brought against them by their enemies, they elaborate their own position. Economic levelling is again condemned, as something which in no circumstances must be forced on people. Equality of wealth and even common ownership are not in fact condemned in themselves, but are only regarded as acceptable if brought about spontaneously, by the free choice of the whole people. Yet to go as far even as this was to give a handle to their opponents, and led to attempts by hostile pamphleteers to drive a wedge between Walwyn and the other Leveller leaders, in particular Lilburne and Prince.*

The charges of anarchism, crypto-royalism and crypto-Popery were more easily and confidently dismissed; those of atheism and anti-scripture-ism (questioning the literal truth of the Bible) were successfully rebutted, while admitting their greater religious flexibility and informality compared to those who attacked them. The charge brought against them of disappointed ambition is nicely turned to their advantage and their enemies' discomfort. This leads on to a particularly interesting discussion about the vital necessity for strict limits on the powers of rulers, even if they themselves were to form a future government. The author(s) would assuredly have agreed with Lord Acton, that 'all power tends to corrupt, and absolute power corrupts absolutely.'

How one treats false friends is perhaps the severest test of true charity. And a somewhat pained reference is reserved for the various ministers and other members of those Congregationalist and Baptist churches in London who had recently turned against them. This related especially, but not exclusively to the attack made by John Price and others on Walwyn (see Introduction).

The author(s) also refer back to the officers' Agreement of the previous January, and anticipate their own final version which was already in preparation (no. 14); they make it clear that, both here and in the Agreement which is in prospect, their appeal will be over the heads of the existing parliament to the nation at large. In fact, the Levellers' only successful appeal was to posterity.

A MANIFESTATION
from
Lieutenant Col. John Lilburn, Mr William Walwyn,
Mr Thomas Prince, and Mr Richard
Overton,
(Now Prisoners in the Tower of London) And others,
commonly (though unjustly)
Styled
LEVELLERS.

Intended for their
FULL VINDICATION

From
The many aspersions cast upon them, to render them odious
to the World, and unserviceable to the Common-wealth
And to satisfie and ascertain all Men
whereunto all their Motions and Endeavours tend, and what
is the ultimate Scope of their Engagement in the
PUBLICK AFFAIRES.
They also that render evill for good, are Our adversaries:
because We follow the thing that good is.

Printed in the year of our Lord, 1649.

A
MANIFESTATION
FROM
Lieutenant Colonel John Lilburn, Master William Walwyne,
Master Thomas Prince, and Master Richard Overton (now
prisoners in the Tower of London) and others, commonly
(though unjustly) stiled Levellers.

Since no man is born for himself only, but obliged by the Laws of Nature (which reaches all) of Christianity (which ingages us as Christians) and of Publick Societie and Government, to employ our endeavours for the advancement of a communitive Happinesse, of equall concernment to others as our selves: here have we (according to that measure of under-standing God hath dispensed unto us) laboured with much weaknesse   151 indeed, but with integrity of heart, to produce out of the Common Calamities, such a proportion of Freedom and good to the Nation, as might somewhat compensate its many grievances and lasting sufferings: And although in doing thereof we have hitherto reaped only Reproach, and hatred for our good Will, and been faine to wrestle with the violent passions of Powers and Principalities; yet since it is nothing so much as our Blessed Master and his Followers suffered before us, and but what at first we reckoned upon, we cannot be thereby any whit dismayed in the performance of our duties, supported inwardly by the Innocency and evennesse of our Consciences.

'Tis a very great unhappinesse we well know, to be alwayes struling and striving in the world, and does wholly keep us from the enjoyment of those contentments our several Conditions reach unto: So that if we should consult only with our selves, and regard only our own ease, Wee should never enterpose as we have done, in behalfe of the Common-wealth: But when so much has been done for recovery of our Liberties, and seeing God hath so blest that which has been done, as thereby to cleer the way, and to afford an opportunity which these 600 years has been desired, but could never be atained, of making this a truly happy and wholly Free Nation; We think our selves bound by the greatest obliga-tions that may be, to prevent the neglect of this opportunity, and to hinder as much as lyes in us, that the bloud which has been shed be not spilt like water upon the ground, nor that after the abundant Calamities, which have overspread all quarters of the Land, the change be onely Notionall, Nominall, Circumstantiall, whilst the reall Burdens, Grievances, and Bondages, be continued, even when the Monarchy is changed into a Republike.

We are no more concern'd indeed then other men, and could bear the Yoke we believe as easily as others; but since a Common Duty lyes upon every man to be cautious and circumspect in behalfe of his Country, especially while the Government thereof is setling, other mens neglect is so far we thinke from being a just motive to us of the like sloath and inanimiadvertency[1], as that it rather requires of us an increase of care and circumspection which if it produces not so good a settlement as ought to be, yet certainly it will prevent its being so bad as otherwise it would be, if we should all only mind our particular callings and imployments.

So that although personally we may suffer, yet our solace is that the Common-wealth is therby some gainer, and we doubt not but that God in his due time wil so cleerly dispel the Clouds of Ignominy and Obloquy which now surround us by keeping our hearts upright and our spirits sincerely publike, that every good man will give us the right hand of fellowship, and be even sorry that they have been estranged, and so hardly opinionated against us: We question not but that in time the reason of such misprisions will appear to be in their eyes and not in our Actions,

152   [1] 'Inanimiadvertency' = 'inadvertency' or 'inattentiveness' (*OED*).

in the false Representation of things to them and improper glosses that are put upon every thing we do or say: In our own behalfs we have as yet said nothing, trusting that either shame and Christian duty would restraine men from making so bold with others good Name and Reputation, or that the sincerity of our actions would evince the falsehood of these scandals, and prevent the Peoples Beliefe of them; But we have found that with too much greedinesse they suck in Reports that tend to the discredit of others, and that our silence gives encouragement to bad Rumors of us; so that in all places they are spread, and industriously propagated as well amongst them that know us, as them that know us not, the first being fed with Jealousies that there is more in our designs then appeares, that there is something of danger in the bottom of our hearts, not yet discovered: that we are driven on by others, that we are even discontented and irresolved, that no body yet knowes what we would have, or where our desires will end; whilst they that know us not are made believe any strange conceit of us, that we would Levell all mens estates, that we would have no distinction of Orders and Dignities amongst men, that we are indeed for no government, but a Popular confusion; and then againe that we have bin Agents for the King, and now for the Queen; That we are Atheists, Antiscripturists, Jesuites and indeed any thing, that is hatefull and of evill repute amongst men.

All which we could without observance pass over, remembering what is promised to be the Portion of good men, were the damage only personall, but since the ends of such Rumors are purposely to make us uselesse and unserviceable to the Common-wealth, we are necessitated to open our breasts and shew the world our insides, for removing of those scandalls that lye upon us, and likewise for manifesting plainly and particularly what our desires are, and in what we will center and acquiess: all which we shall present to publike view and consideration, not pertinatiously or Magisterially, as concluding other mens judgements, but manifesting our own, for our further vindication, and for the procuring of a Bond and lasting establishment for the Common-wealth.

First, Then it will be requisite that we express our selves concerning Levelling, for which we suppose is commonly meant an equalling of mens estates, and taking away the proper right and Title that every man has to what is his own. This as we have formerly declared against, particularly in our petition of the 11 of Sept. so do we again professe that to attempt an inducing the same is most injurious, unlesse there did precede an universall assent thereunto from all and every one of the People. Nor doe we, under favour, judge it within the Power of a Representative it selfe, because although their power is supreame, yet it is but deputative and of trust; and consequently must be restrained expresly or tacitely, to some particular essential as well to the Peoples safety and freedom as to the present Government.

The Community amongst the primitive Christians, was Voluntary, not Coactive; they brought their goods and laid them at the Apostles feet, 153 they were not enjoyned to bring them, it was the effect of their Charity and heavenly mindednesse, which the blessed Apostles begot in them, and not the Injunction of any Constitution, which as it was but for a short time done, and in but two or three places, that the Scripture makes mention of, so does the very doing of it there and the Apostles answer to him that detained a part, imply that it was not esteemed a duty, but reckoned a voluntary act occasioned by the abundant measure of faith that was in those Christians and Apostles.

We profess therefore that we never had it in our thoughts to Level mens estates, it being the utmost of our aime that the Commonwealth be reduced to such a passe that every man may with as much security as may be enjoy his propriety.

We know very well that in all Ages those men that engage themselves against Tyranny, unjust and Arbitrary proceedings in Magistrats, have suffered under such appellations, the People being purposely frighted from that which is good by insinuations of imaginary evill.

But be it so, we must notwithstanding discharge our Duties, which being performed, the successe is in Gods hand to whose good pleasure we must leave the cleering of mens spirits, our only certainty being Tranquillity of mind, and peace of Conscience.

For distinction of Orders and Dignities, We think them so far needful, as they are animosities[1] of vertue, or requisite for the maintenance of the Magistracy and Government, we thinke they were never intended for the nourishment of Ambition, or subjugation of the People but only to preserve the due respect and obedience in the People which is necessary for the better execution of the Laws.

That we are for Government and against Popular Confusion, we conceive all our actions declare, when rightly considered, our aim having bin all along to reduce it as near as might be to perfection, and certainly we know very well the pravity and corruption of mans heart is such that there could be no living without it; and that though Tyranny is so excessively bad, yet of the two extreames, Confusion is the worst: Tis somewhat a strange consequence to infer that because we have laboured so earnestly for a good Government, therefore we would have none at all; Because we would have the dead and exorbitant Branches pruned, and better sciens[2] grafted, therefore we would pluck the Tree up by the roots.

Yet thus have we been misconceived, and misrepresented to the world, under which we must suffer, till God sees it fitting in his good time to cleer such harsh mistakes, by which many, even good men keep a distance from us.

For those weake suppositions of some of us being Agents for the King or Queen, we think it needful to say no more but this, That though we

---

[1] 'Animosity' could = 'high spirit, spiritedness, courage, bravery, or excitement of strong feeling' (OED).

[2] ?stems, or scions

have not bin any way violent against the persons of them, or their Partie, as having aimed at the conversion of all, and the destruction of none, yet doe we verily beleeve that those Principles and Maxims of Government which are most fundamentally opposite to the Prerogative and the Kings interest, take their first rise and originall from us, many whereof though at first star[t]led at, and disown'd by those that professed the greatest opposition to him, have yet since been taken up by them and put in practise: and this we think is sufficient, though much more might be said to cleer us from any Agency for that Party.

It is likewise suggested that we are acted by others, who have other ends then appear to us; we answer. That that cannot be, since every thing has its rise amongst our selves, and since those things we bring to light cannot conduce to the ends of any but the publike weale of the Nation.

All our Desires, Petitions and Papers are directly opposite to all corrupt Interests; nor have any, credit with us, but persons well known, and of certain aboads, and such as have given sound and undeniable testimonies of the truth of their affection to their Country: Besides, the things we promote, are not good onely in appearance, but sensibly so: not moulded nor contrived by the subtill or politick Principles of the World, but plainly produced and nakedly sent, without any insinuating arts, relying wholly upon the apparent and universall beleefe they carry in themselves; and that is it which convinces and engages us in the promotion thereof. So that that suggestion has not indeed any foundation in itself, but is purposely framed, as we conceive, to make us afraid one of another, and to disable us in the promotion of those good things that tend to the freedom and happiness of the Common-wealth.

For our being Jesuits, either in Order or Principles, as 'tis severally reported of us; Though the easiest Negative is hardly proved; yet we can say, That those on whom the first is principally fix'd, are married, and were never over Sea: and we think Marriage is never dispenc'd withall in that Order, and that none can be admitted into the Order but such as are personally present. 'Tis hard that we are put to expresse thus much; and haply we might better passe such reports over in silence; but that we beleeve the very mentioning of them publickly, will be an answer to them, and make such as forment them asham'd of such generally condemned wayes of discrediting and blasting the Reputation of other men. For the principles of Jesuits, we professe we know not what they are; but they are generally said to be full of craft and worldly policy; and therefore exceedingly different from that plainness and simplicity that is apparently visible in all our proceedings.

Whereas its said, we are Atheists and Antiscripturists, we professe that we beleeve there is one eternall and omnipotent God, the Author and Preserver of all things in the world. To whose will and directions, written first in our hearts, and afterwards in his blessed Word, we ought to square our actions and conversations. And though we are not so strict upon the formall and Ceremonial part of his Service, the method, manner, and personall injunction being not so clearly made out unto us, nor the necessary requisites which his Officers and Ministers ought to be furnished withall as yet appearing to some of us in any that pretend thereunto: yet for the manifestations of Gods love in Christ, it is cleerly assented unto by us; and the practicall and most reall part of Religion is as readily submitted unto by us, as being, in our apprehensions, the most eminent and the most excellent in the world, and as proceeding from no other but that God who is Goodnesse it self: and we humbly desire his Goodnesse daily more and more to conform our hearts to a willing and sincere obedience thereunto.

For our not being preferred to Offices and Places of profit and credit, which is urged to be the ground of our dissatisfaction, we say, That although we know no reason why we should not be equally capable of them with other men, nor why our publick Affection should be any barr or hinderance thereunto: Yet on the other side, we suppose we can truly say of our selves, that we have not been so earnest and solicitous after them as others: and that in the Catalogue of Sutors, very few that are reckoned of us, are to be found. We are very sorry that so general a change of Officers is proposed, which we judge of no small disparagement to our Cause; and do think it best, that in removals of that kinde, the ground should not be difference in opinion, either in Religious or Civil Matters, but corruption or breach of Trust; Considering the misery which befalls whole Families upon such Changes; and that discontents are thereby increased: Whereas we hold it necessary that all wayes of composure and acquieting those storms which the preceding differences and distractions have begotten, be with utmost care and prudence endeavoured.

And whereas 'tis urged, That if we were in power, we would bear our selves as Tyrannically as others have done: We confess indeed, that the experimentall defections of so many men as have succeeded in Authority, and the exceeding differences we have hitherto found in the same men in a low, and in an exalted condition, makes us even mistrust our own hearts, and hardly beleeve our own Resolutions of the contrary. And therefore we have proposed such an Establishment, as supposing men to be too flexible and yeelding to worldly Temptations, they should not yet have a means or opportunity either to injure particulars, or prejudice the Publick, without extreme hazard and apparent danger to themselves. Besides, to the objection we have further to say, That we aim not at power in our selves, our Principles and Desires being in no measure of self-concernment: nor do we relie for obtaining the same upon strength, or a forcible obstruction; for solely upon that inbred and perswasive power that is all good and just things, to make their own way in the hearts of men, and so to procure their own Establishments.

And that makes us at this time naked and defencelesse as we are, and amidst so many discouragements on all hands to persevere in our motions and desires of good to the Nation; although disowned therein at such a time when the doing thereof can be interpreted no other but a politick delivering us up to slaughter, by such as we took for Friends our bretheren of several Churches; and for whom with truth of affection we have even in the most difficult times done many Services: all which, and whatsoever else can be done against us, we shall reckon but as badges of our sincerity, and be no whit discouraged thereby from the discharge of our duties.

For the dis-satisfaction that be upon many good mens spirits, for that they are not ascertained whereunto all our motions tend, and in what they will center.

Though, we conceive, they may have received some general satisfaction from what we have formerly at severall times propounded: yet since they were not disposed into such a form and condition as to become practicable; we have, with the best care and abilities God hath afforded us, cast the same into a Modell and Platform, which we shall speedily present unto the view and consideration of all, as the Standard and ultimate scope of our Designes, that so (in case of approvall) it may be subscribed and returned as agreed upon by the People. And thus far, we conceive, we may without offence or prejudice to Authority, proceed: and which we the rather do, because we know no better, and indeed no other way or means (but by such an Agreement) to remove (as much as may be) all disgusts and heart-burnings, and to settle the Common-Wealth upon the fairest probabilities of a lasting Peace, and contentfull Establishment.

The Agreement of the People which was presented by his Excellency and the Officers of the Army to the Right Honourable the Commons in Parliament, although in many things short (according to our apprehensions) of what is necessary for the good of the Common-wealth, and satisfaction of the People; particularly, in that it containeth no provision for the certain removall of notorious and generally complained of grievances: And although it hath some things of much hazard to the Publick, – yet, had it been put in execution, we should scarcely have interrupted the proceedings thereof, since therein is contained many things of great and important concernment to the Common-wealth. But seeing the time proposed therein for reducing the same into practice, is now past, and that likewise the generality of the people have not, or do not approve of the same, for the reasons (as we suppose) fore-mentioned: We have thought fit to revise it, making onely such alterations therein as we conceive really necessary for the welfare, security and safety of the People, together with additional Provisions for the taking away of those Burdens and Grievances which may without reall prejudice to the Management of publick Affairs be removed.

And because it is essentiall to the nature of such an Agreement to take its rise from the People, we have therefore purposely declined the presentment thereof to the Parliament: and conceive it may speedily proceed to Subscription, and so to further practice, without any interruption to this Representative, untill the season prefix'd in the Agreement, for the assembling another: By whose immediate succession, without any intervall, the Affairs of the Common-wealth may suffer no stop or intermission.

Lastly, We conceive we are much mistaken in being judged impatient, and over-violent in our motions for the publick Good. To which we answer, That could we have had any assurance that what is desired should have otherwise, or by any have been done; and had not had some taste of the relinquishment of many good things that were promised, we should not have been so earnest and urgent for the doing thereof.

Though we know likewise it hath been very customary in such heretofore as never intended any freedom to the Nation, to except only against the season, and to protract the time so long, till they became sufficiently impowred to justifie the totall denyall and refusall thereof. However, the main reason of our proceeding as we do, is because we prefer the way of a settlement by an Agreement of the People before any other whatsoever.

And thus the world may clearly see what we are, and what we aym at: We are altogether ignorant, and do from our hearts abominate all designes and contrivances of dangerous consequence which we are said (but God knows, untruly) to be labouring withall. Peace and Freedom is our Designe: by War we were never gainers, nor ever wish to be; and under bondage we have been hitherto sufferers. We desire however, that what is past may be forgotten, provided the Common wealth may have amends made it for the time to come. And this from our soul we desire.

Having no mens persons in hatred and judging it needfull that all other respects whatsoever are to give way to the good of the Common-wealth, and this is the very truth and inside of our hearts.

John Lilburne
William Walwyn
Thomas Prince
Richard Overton.

From the Tower,
April 14. 1649.

14 The (third and final) Agreement of the [Free] People

The third and final Leveller Agreement of the [Free] People of England *(1 May 1649) may be taken as the formal summing-up of their constitutional programme. The prologue seems once more to smack of Walwyn, but the text itself must surely have been a composite work in which Lilburne's experience and his prestige as leader, together with Overton's resilience as a pamphleteer, would have counted for more than Walwyn's urbanity and intellectualism. The* Agreement *specifies the future parliamentary franchise and the broad lines of electoral reform in the annual parliaments which are to be operative in the future, but leaves open the detail of constituency boundaries. Strict separation between the different branches of government – executive, legislature and judiciary – is now established as a fundamental reserved power. In general, the second and third* Agreements *multiply the number of these fundamentals, in comparison with the original* Agreement *(no. 7). The principles of rotation in office and in membership of parliament are to be seen as serving a common purpose: deliberately to limit the powers of the governors and to make them more genuinely answerable to the wishes of the governed. The fundamentals, or matters reserved as being above and beyond the scope of legislation, now include monopolies, excise, legal reforms, tithes, and other immediate grievances. In these respects the second and third* Agreements *can be seen as logical sequels to the 'large'* Petition *of March 1647 and to that of September 1648 (nos. 5 and 9) as well as to the first* Agreement. *Future reformed parliaments were to be more severely restricted in their exercise of legislative sovereignty than had been envisaged in 1647.*

Religious toleration remained a fundamental. But an important distinction was now drawn between freedom of belief and worship, which was still unqualified, and civic equality for adherents of all religions. Those who owned 'the Pope's (or other forraign) Supremacy' were to be barred from holding office in the Commonwealth. Although some English Catholics might well have found a Leveller regime more congenial than the rule of either the Rump Parliament or the Stuart kings, such a distinction – between freedom of worship and complete religious equality, implying neutrality of the state in matters of belief – can hardly be condemned in a seventeenth-century context.

Very severe measures were proposed against anyone – soldier, civilian, or MP – who tried to overthrow the Agreement *once it was in operation. This is a reminder that, while they may have been inconsistent towards direct action and the use of force, the Levellers were not pacifists, or believers in total non-violence. Like Gerrard Winstanley the Digger, they were prepared to countenance, indeed to advocate the death penalty for what would in modern times be called counter-*

revolutionary activity. This, together with the restriction placed on Catholics holding office, and the unqualified disavowal of economic levelling, perhaps make the third Agreement less humane and more conservative than A Manifestation. But the more comprehensive a political programme becomes, assuming its authors' basic sincerity, the more compromises inevitably have to be made. None the less, this is by any standards a remarkable political and constitutional blueprint for a popular movement which had started virtually from nothing only about three years earlier – amazingly enlightened, yet far from abstract or unpractical.

AN
AGREEMENT
of the
Free People of England.
Tendered as a Peace-Offering to this distressed Nation.
BY
Lieutenant Colonel John Lilburne, Master William Walwyn, Master Thomas Prince, and Master Richard Overton, Prisoners in the Tower of London, May the 1. 1649.
Matth. 5. verse 9. Blessed are the Peace-makers for they shall be called the children of God.

A Preparative to all sorts of people.

If afflictions make men wise, and wisdom direct to happinesse, then certainly this Nation is not far from such a degree thereof, as may compare if not far exceed, any part of the world: having for some yeares by-past, drunk deep of the Cup of misery and sorrow. We blesse God our consciences are cleer from adding affliction to affliction, having ever laboured from the beginning, of our publick distractions, to compose and reconcile them: & should esteem it the Crown of all our temporal felicity that yet we might be instrumentall in procuring the peace and prosperity of this Common-wealth the land of our Nativity.

And therefore according to our promise in our late Manifestation of the 14 of Aprill 1649, (being perswaded of the necessitie and justnesse thereof) as a Peace-Offering to the Free people of this Nation, we tender this ensuing Agreement, not knowing any more effectual means to put a finall period to all our feares and troubles.

It is a way of settlement, though at first much startled at by some in high authority; yet according to the nature of truth, it hath made its own way into the understanding, and taken root in most mens hearts and affections, so that we have reall ground to hope (what ever shall become of us) that our earnest desires and indeavours for good to the people will not altogether be null and frustrate.

The life of all things is in the right use and application, which is not our worke only, but every mans conscience must look to it selfe, and not dreame out more seasons and opportunities. And this we trust will satisfie all ingenuous people that we are not such wilde, irrationall, dangerous Creatures as we have been aspersed to be; This agreement being the ultimate end and full scope of all our desires and intentions concerning the Government of this Nation, and wherein we shall absolutely rest satisfied and acquiesce; nor did we ever give just cause for any to beleeve worse of us by any thing either said or done by us, and which would not in the least be doubted, but that men consider not the interest of those that have so unchristian-like made bold with our good names; but we must bear with men of such interests as are opposite to any part of this Agreement, when neither our Saviour nor his Apostles innocency could stop such mens mouthes whose interests their doctrines and practises did extirpate: And therefore if friends at least would but consider what interest men relate to, whilst they are telling or whispering their aspersions against us, they would find the reason and save us a great deale of labour in clearing our selves, it being a remarkable signe of an ill cause when aspersions supply the place of Arguments.

We blesse God that he hath given us time and hearts to bring it to this issue, what further he hath for us to do is yet only knowne to his wisedom, to whose will and pleasure we shall willingly submit; we have if we look with the eyes of frailty, enemies like the sons of Anak, but if with the eyes of faith and confidence in a righteous God and a just cause, we see more with us then against us,

John Lilburn
William Walwyn
Thomas Prince
Richard Overton.

From our causelesse captivity in the
Tower of London, May 1. 1649.

The Agreement it selfe thus followeth.

After the long and tedious prosecution of a most unnaturall cruell, homebred war, occasioned by divisions and distempers amongst our selves, and those distempers arising from the uncertaintie of our Government, and the exercise of an unlimited or Arbitrary power, by such as have been trusted with Supreme and subordinate Authority, whereby multitudes of grevances and intolerable oppressions have been brought upon us. And finding after eight yeares experience and expectation all indeavours hitherto used, or remedies hitherto applyed, to have encreased rather then diminished our distractions, and that if not speedily prevented our falling againe into factions and divisions, will not only deprive us of the benefit of all those wonderful Victories God hath vouchsafed against such as sought our bondage, but expose us first to poverty and misery, and then to be destroyed by forraigne enemies.

And being earnestly desirous to make a right use of that opportunity God hath given us to make this Nation Free and Happy, to reconcile our differences, and beget a perfect amitie and friendship once more amongst 161 us, that we may stand clear in our consciences before Almighty God, as unbyassed by any corrupt Interest or particular advantages, and manifest to all the world that our indeavours have not proceeded from malice to the persons of any, or enmity against opinions; but in reference to the peace and prosperity of the Common-wealth, and for prevention of like distractions, and removall of all grievances; We the free People of England, to whom God hath given hearts, means and opportunity to effect the same, do with submission to his wisdom, in his name, and desiring the equity thereof may be to his praise and glory: Agree to ascertain our Government, to abolish all arbitrary Power, and to set bounds and limits both to our Supreme, and all Subordinate Authority, and remove all known Grievances.

And accordingly do declare and publish to all the world,
that we are agreed as followeth,

I. That the Supreme Authority of England and the Territories therewith incorporate, shall be and reside henceforward in a Representative of the people consisting of four hundred persons, but no more; in the choice of whom (according to naturall right) all men of the age of one and twenty yeers and upwards (not being servants, or receiving alms, or having served the late King in Arms or voluntary Contributions), shall have their voices; and be capable of being elected to that Supreme Trust those who served the King being disabled for ten years onely. All things concerning the distribution of the said four hundred Members proportionable to the respective parts of the Nation, the severall places for Election, the manner of giving and taking of Voyces, with all Circumstances of like nature, tending to the compleating and equall proceedings in Elections, as also their Salary, is referred to be setled by this present Parliament, in such sort as the next Representative may be in a certain capacity to meet with safety at the time herein expressed: and such circumstances to be made more perfect by future Representatives.

II. That two hundred of the four hundred Members, and not lesse, shall be taken and esteemed for a competent Representative; and the major Voyces present shall be concluding to this Nation. The place of Session, and choice of a Speaker, with other circumstances of that nature, are referred to the care of this and future Representatives.

III. And to the end all publick Officers may be certainly accountable, and no Factions made to maintain corrupt Interests, no Officer of any salary Forces in Army or Garison, nor any Treasurer or Receiver of publick monies, shall (while such) be elected a Member for any Representative; and if any Lawyer shall at any time be chosen, he shall be uncapable of practice as a Lawyer, during the whole time of that Trust. And for the same reason, and that all persons may be capable of subjection as well as rule.

IIII. That no Member of the present Parliament shall be capable of being
elected of the next Representative, nor any Member of any future

Representative shall be capable of being chosen for the Representative immediately succeeding: but are free to be chosen, one Representative having intervened: Nor shall any Member of any Representative be made either Receiver, Treasurer, or other Officer during that imployment.

v. That for avoyding the many dangers and inconveniences apparantly arising from the long continuance of the same persons in Authority; We Agree, that this present Parliament shall end the first Wednesday in August next 1649, and thenceforth be of no power or Authority: and in the mean time shall order and direct the Election of a new and equall Representative, according to the true intent of this our Agreement: and so as the next Representative may meet and sit in power and Authority as an effectuall Representative upon the day following; namely the first Thursday of the same August, 1649.

vi. We agree, if the present Parliament shall omit to order such Election or Meetting of a new Representative; or shall by any means be hindered from performance of that Trust:

That in such case, we shall for the next Representative proceed in electing thereof in those places, & according to that manner & number formerly accustomed in the choice of Knights and Burgesses; observing onely the exceptions of such persons from being Electors or Elected, as are mentioned before in the first, third, and fourth Heads of this Agreement: It being most unreasonable that we should either be kept from new, frequent and successive Representatives, or that the Supreme Authority should fall into the hands of such as have manifested disaffection to our common Freedom, and endeavoured the bondage of the Nation.

vii. And for preserving the supreme authority from falling into the hands of any whom the people have not, or shall not chuse,

We are resolved and agreed (God willing) that a new Representative shall be upon the first Thursday in August next aforesaid: the ordering and disposing of themselves, as to the choice of a speaker: and the like circumstances, is hereby left to their discretion: but are in the extent and exercise of Power, to follow the direction and rules of this agreement; and are hereby authorised and required according to their best judgements, to set rules for future equall distribution, and election of Members as is herein intended and enjoyned to be done, by the present Parliament.

viii. And for the preservation of the supreme Authority (in all times) entirely in the hands of such persons only as shal be chosen thereunto – we agree and declare: That the next & al future Representatives, shall continue in full power for the space of one whole year: and that the people shall of course, chuse a Parliament once every year, so as all the members thereof may be in a capacity to meet and take place of the foregoing Representative: the first Thursday in every August for ever if God so please; Also (for the same reason) that the next or any future Representative being met, shall continue their Session day by day without intermission for four monthes at the least; and after that shall be at Liberty to adjourn from two months as they shall see cause untill their yeer be 163 expired, but shall sit no longer then a yeer upon pain of treason to every member that shall exceed that time: and in times of adjurnment shall not erect a Councel of State but refer the managing of affairs in the intervals to a Committee of their own members giving such instructions, and publish them, as shall in no measure contradict this agreement.

IX. And that none henceforth may be ignorant or doubtfull concerning the power of the Supreme authority, and of the affairs, about which the same is to be conversant and exercised: we agree and declare, that the power of Representatives shall extend without the consent or concurrence of any other person or persons,

1. To the conservation of Peace and commerce with forrain Nations.
2. To the preservation of those safe guards, and securities of our lives, limbes, liberties, properties, and estates, contained in the Petition of Right, made and enacted in the third year of the late King.
3. To the raising of moneys, and generally to all things as shall be evidently conducing to those ends, or to the enlargement of our freedom, redress of grievances, and prosperity of the Common-wealth.

For security whereof, having by wofull experience found the prevalence of corrupt interests powerfully inclining most men once entrusted with authority, to pervert the same to their own domination, and to the prejudice of our Peace and Liberties, we therefore further agree and declare.

X. That we do not inpower or entrust our said representative to continue in force, or to make any Lawes, Oaths, or Covenants, whereby to compell by penalties or otherwise any person to any thing in or about matters of faith, Religion or Gods worship or to restrain any person from the profession of his faith, or exercise of Religion according to his Conscience, nothing having caused more distractions, and heart burnings in all ages, then persecution and molestation for matters of Conscience in and about Religion:

XI. We doe not impower them to impresse or constraint any person to serve in war by Sea or Land every mans Conscience being to be satisfied in the justness of that cause wherein he hazards his own life, or may destroy an others.

And for the quieting of all differences, and abolishing of all enmity and rancour, as much as is now possible for us to effect.

XII. We agree, That after the end of this present Parliament, no person that be questioned for any thing said or done in reference to the late Warres, or publique differences; otherwise then in pursuance of the determinations of the present Parliament, against such as have adhered to the King against the Liberties of the people: And saving that Accomptants for publick moneys received, shall remain accomptable for the same.

XIII. That all priviledges or exemptions of any persons from the Lawes, or from the ordinary course of Legall proceedings, by vertue of any Tenure, Grant, Charter, Patent, Degree, or Birth, or of any place of residence, or refuge, or priviledge of Parliament, shall be henceforth void and null; and the like not to be made nor revived again.

XIIII. We doe not impower them to give judgment upon any ones person or estate, where no Law hath been before provided, nor to give power to any other Court or Jurisdiction so to do, Because where there is no Law there is no transgression, for men or Magistrates to take Cognisance of; neither doe we impower them to intermeddle with the execution of any Law whatsoever.

XV. And that we may remove all long setled Grievances, and thereby as farre as we are able, take away all cause of complaints, and no longer depend upon the uncertain inclination of Parliaments to remove them, nor trouble our selves or them with Petitions after Petitions, as hath been accustomed, without fruit or benefit; and knowing no cause why any should repine at our removall of them, except such as make advantage by their continuance, or are related to some corrupt Interests, which we are not to regard.

We agree and Declare,

XVI. That it shall not be in the power of any Representative to punish, or cause to be punished, any person or persons for refusing to answer to questions against themselves in Criminall causes.

XVII. That it shall not be in their power, after the end of the next Representative, to continue or constitute any proceedings in Law that shall be longer then Six months in the final determination of any cause past all Appeal, nor to continue the Laws or proceedings therein in any other Language then English, nor to hinder any person or persons from pleading their own Causes, or of making use of whom they please to plead for them.

The reducing of these and other the like provisions of this nature in this Agreement provided, and which could not now in all particulars be perfected by us, is intended by us to be the proper works of faithful Representatives.

XVIII. That it shall not be in their power to continue or make any Laws to abridge or hinder any person or persons, from trading or merchandizing into any place beyond the Seas, where any of this Nation are free to Trade.

XIX. That it shall not be in their power to continue Excise or Customs upon any sort of Food, or any other Goods, Wares, or Commodities, longer then four months after the beginning of the next Representative, being both of them extreme burthensome and oppressive to Trade, and so expensive in the Receipt, as the moneys expended therein (if collected as Subsidies have been) would extend very far towards defraying the publick charges; and forasmuch as all Moneys to be raised are drawn from the People; such burthensome and chargeable wayes, shall never more be revived, nor shall they raise Moneys by any other ways (after the aforesaid time) but only by an equal rate in the pound upon every reall and personall estate in the Nation.

xx. That it shall not be in their power to make or continue any Law, whereby mens reall or personall estates, or any part thereof shall be exempted from payment of their debts; or to imprison any person for debt of any nature, it being both unchristian in it self, and no advantage to the Creditors, and both a reproach and prejudice to the Common-wealth.

xxi. That it shall not be in their power to make or continue any Law, for taking away any mans life, except for murther, or other the like hainous offences destructive to humane Society, or for endevouring by force to destroy this our Agreement, but shall use their uttermost endeavour to appoint punishments equall to offences: that so mens Lives, Limbs, Liberties, and estates, may not be liable to be taken away upon trivial or slight occasions as they have been; and shall have speciall care to preserve, all sorts of people from wickedness misery and beggery; nor shall the estate of any capitall offender be confiscate but in cases of treason only; and in all other capitall offences recompence shall be made to the parties damnified, as well out of the estate of the Malifactor, as by loss of life, according to the conscience of his jury.

xxii. That it shall not be in their power to continue or make any Law, to deprive any person, in case of Tryals for Life, Limb, Liberty, or Estate, from the benefit of witnesses, on his, or their behalf; nor deprive any person of those priviledges and liberties, contained in the Petition of Right, made in the third yeer of the late King Charls.

xxiii. That it shall not be in their power to continue the Grievance of Tithes, longer than to the end of the next Representative; in which time, they shall provide to give reasonable satisfaction to all Impropriators: neither shall they force by penalties or otherwise any person to pay towards the maintenance of any Ministers, who out of conscience cannot submit thereunto.

xxiv. That it shall not be in their power to impose Ministers upon any the respective Parishes, but shall give free liberty to the parishioners of every particular parish, to chuse such as themselves shall approve; and upon such terms, and for such reward, as themselves shall be willing to contribute, or shall contract for, Provided, none be chusers but such as are capable of electing Representatives.

xxv. That it shal not be in their power, to continue or make a law, for any other way of Judgments, or Conviction of life, limb, liberty, or estate, but onely by twelve sworn men of the Neighborhood; to be chosen in some free way by the people; to be directed before the end of the next Representative, and not picked and imposed, as hitherto in many places they have been.

xxvi. They shall not disable any person from bearing any office in the Common-wealth, for any opinion or practice in Religion, excepting such as maintain the Popes (or other forraign) Supremacy.

xxvii. That it shal not be in their power to impose any publike officer upon any Counties, Hundreds, Cities, Towns, or Borroughs; but the people capable by this Agreement to chuse Representatives, shall chuse all their publike Officers that are in any kinde to administer the Law for their respective places, for one whole yeer, and no longer, and so from yeer to yeer: and this as an especial means to avoyd Factions, and Parties.

And that no person may have just cause to complain, by reason of taking away the Excise and Customs, we agree,

XXVIII. That the next, and all future Representatives shall exactly keep the publike Faith, and give ful satisfaction, for all securities, debts, arrears or damages, (justly chargeable) out of the publike Treasury; and shall confirm and make good all just publike Purchases and Contracts that have been, or shall be made; save that the next Representative may confirm or make null in part or in whole, all gifts of Lands, Moneys, Offices, or otherwise made by the present Parliament, to any Member of the House of Commons, or to any of the Lords, or to any of the attendants of either of them.

And for as much as nothing threateneth greater danger to the Commonwealth, then that the Military power should by any means come to be superior to the Civil Authority.

XXIX. We declare and agree, That no Forces shal be raised, but by the Representatives, for the time being; and in raising thereof, that they exactly observe these Rules, namely, That they allot to each particular County, City, Town, and Borrugh, the raising, furnishing, agreeing, and paying of a due proportion, according to the whole number to be levyed; and shall to the Electors of Representatives in each respective place, give Free liberty, to nominate and appoint all Officers appertaining to Regiments, Troops, and Companies, and to remove them as they shall see cause. Reserving to the Representative, the nominating, and appointing onely of the General, and all General-Officers; and the ordering, regulating, and commanding of them all, upon what service shall seem to them necessary for the Safety, Peace, and Freedom of the Common-wealth.

And in as much as we have found by sad experience, That generally men make little or nothing, to innovate in Government, to exceed their time and power in places of trust, to introduce an Arbitrary, and Tyrannical power, and to overturn all things into Anarchy and Confusion, where there are no penalties imposed for such destructive crimes and offences.

XXX. We therefore agree and declare, That it shall not be in the power of any Representative, in any wise, to render up, or give, or take away any part of this Agreement, nor level mens Estates, destroy Propriety, or make all things Common: And if any Representative shall endevor, as a Representative, to destroy this Agreement, every Member present in the House, not entering or immediately publishing his dissent, shall incur the pain due for High Treason, and be proceeded against accordingly; and if any person or persons, shall by force endevor or contrive, the destruction thereof, each person so doing shall likewise be dealt withal as in cases of Treason.

And if any person shal by force of Arms disturb Elections of Representatives, he shall incurr the penalty of a Riot; and if any person not
capable of being an Elector, or Elected, shal intrude themselves amongst
those that are, or any persons shall behave themselves rudely and dis-
orderly, such persons shal be liable to a presentment by a grand Inquest
and to an indictment upon misdemeanor; and be fined and otherwise
punish'd according to the discretion and verdict of a Jury. And all Laws
made, or that shall be made contrary to any part of this Agreement, are
hereby made null and void.

Thus, as becometh a free People, thankfull unto God for this blessed
opportunity, and desirous to make use thereof to his glory, in taking off
every yoak, and removing every burthen, in delivering the captive, and
setting the oppressed free; we have in all the particular Heads foremen-
tioned, done as we would be done unto, and as we trust in God will abolish
all occasion of offence and discord, and produce the lasting Peace and
Prosperity of this Common wealth: and accordingly do in the sincerity
of our hearts and consciences, as in the presence of Almighty God, give
cleer testimony of our absolute agreement to all and every part hereof by
subscribing our hands thereunto. Dated the first day of May, in the Yeer
of our Lord, 1649.

John Lilburn
William Walwyn
Thomas Prince
Richard Overton.

April 30. 1649.
Imprimatur. Gilbert Mabbot.

FINIS.

London, Printed for Gyles Calvert at the black
spread-Eagle at the West end
of Pauls

1 For instance Joseph Frank, *The Levellers: A History of the Writings of Three Seventeenth-Century Social Democrats: John Lilburne, Richard Overton, William Walwyn* (Cambridge, Mass., 1955; repr. N.Y. 1969), esp. ch. 1.

2 See Keith Thomas, 'The Levellers and the Franchise', ch. 2 in G. E. Aylmer (ed.), *The Interregnum: The Quest for Settlement 1646–1660* (1972).

3 Keith Thomas, *Religion and the Decline of Magic* (1971), p. 313 and n. 7; paperb. edn. (Harmondsworth, 1973), p. 372 and n. 154.

4 *An Apollogie of the Souldiers to all their Commission Officers in Sir Thomas Fairfax his Armie*, B.M., E.381 (18). 2 pp., signed 'Your servants so far as we may'.

5 *A New Found Stratagem Framed in the Old Forge of Machivilisme and put upon the Inhabitants of the County of Essex. To destroy the Army under his Excellency Sir Thomas Fairfax, and to inslave all the Free-borne of England on a sudden . . .* B.M., E.384 (11). Dated 18 Apr. by George Thomason. Text pp. 3–15. I cannot see conclusive evidence that this was by Overton, as is assumed by Wolfe and Frank, though it may be.

6 *Killing Noe Murder* (1657), extract repr. in G. Orwell & R. Reynolds (eds.), *British Pamphleteers*, vol. 1, *From the Sixteenth Century to the French Revolution* (1948), pp. 128–9.

7 Lilburne, *The Just Mans Justification* . . ., matter added to the 2nd edn., written 27 Aug., published 18 Sept. 1647, B.M., E.407 (26), esp. pp. 24, 28; Overton, *Eighteen Reasons Propounded to the Souldiers . . . why they ought to continue the Agitators . . .* 11 Aug. 1647, apparently not collected by Thomason. B.M., 534 d. 10; *The Humble Address of the Agitators . . . to . . . Fairfax*, 14 Aug. 1647, B.M., E.402 (8).

8 See *D.N.B.;* C. H. Firth & G. Davies, *Regimental History of Cromwell's Army* (2 vols. Oxford, 1940), p. 422. He did not in fact take up his naval command until the following January. The House of Lords approved his appointment on 1 October (*Lords Journals*, IX, 459).

9 Lilburne apparently recommended a change of Agitators as early as 21 August 1647 (see *The Juglers Discovered*, itself dated 28 Sept., B.M., 1104. a.16 (1), p. 10, for his letter of 21 Aug.).

10 Don M. Wolfe (ed.), *Leveller Manifestoes of the Puritan Revolution* (New York, 1944; repr. London, 1967), Document 5, p. 196. *The Case of the Armie* is also available in W. Haller & G. Davies (eds.), *The Leveller Tracts 1647–1653* (New York, 1944; repr. Gloucester, Mass., 1964), pp. 65–87.

11 Maurice Ashley, *John Wildman, Plotter and Postmaster* (1947), esp. ch. 1.

12 G. K. Fortescue (ed.), *Catalogue of Thomason Tracts* (1908), vol. 1, p. 566.

13 C. H. Firth (ed.), *The Clarke Papers* (Camden Society and Royal Historical Society, Camden Series. 4 vols. 1891–1901), vol. 1, pp. 176–214; also available in A. S. P. Woodhouse (ed.), *Puritanism and Liberty: Being the Army Debates (1647–9) from the Clarke Manuscripts with Supplementary Documents* (1938; repr. 1950; 2nd edn. repr. 1965), pp. 409–22.

14 Lieutenant-Colonel William Ayres or Eyres, Major Thomas Scott, MP (no connection of the better-known republican and regicide Thomas Scot MP), and Captain William Bray. Scott died in prison soon after; the other two we shall meet again.

15 PAULINE GREGG, *Free-born John: A Biography of John Lilburne* (1961), ch. 17.

16 *A Declaration of some Proceedings of Lieut. Col. John Lilburn And his Associates . . .*, 14 Feb. 1648. B.M., E.427 (6), reprinted in HALLER AND DAVIES, *Leveller Tracts*, pp. 88–134.

17 FRANK, *The Levellers*, pp. 173–4.

18 See C. H. FIRTH (ed.), *The Clarke Papers*, vol. II (Camden Soc. 1894), pp. 71–136, 139–40, 147–57, 163–86, for the most complete text; also available in WOODHOUSE (ed.), *Puritanism and Liberty*, pp. 125–78. Overton is named as a speaker on 14 Dec.

19 *Foundations of Freedom; Or, An Agreement of the People . . .*, 15 Dec. 1648. B.M., E.476 (26), repr. in WOLFE, *Leveller Manifestoes*, pp. 293–303.

20 *Several Proposals for Peace and Freedom, By an Agreement of the People*, 22 Dec. 1648. B.M., E.477 (18), repr. in WOLFE, *Leveller Manifestoes*, pp. 312–21.

21 *A Petition From His Excellency Thomas Lord Fairfax And the General Council of Officers of the Army, To the Honourable the Commons of England in Parliament assembled Concerning the Draught of an Agreement of the People . . . Together with the said Agreement*, 20 Jan. 1649. B.M., E.539 (2); repr. in WOLFE, *Leveller Manifestoes*, pp. 333–54; also a later edn. of July 1649 (B.M., 669, f.14 (59)). (By then Fairfax had succeeded to his father's title, as a Scottish peer.)

22 [?WALWYN], *The Vanitie of the present Churches, And Uncertaintie of their Preaching, discovered, . . .*, Feb.–Mar. 1649; *Walwins Wiles*, April 1649; [Humphrey Brooke MD], *The Charity of Churchmen: Or, A Vindication of Mr William Walwyn Merchant . . .* May 1649; *Walwyns Just Defence Against the Aspersions Cast upon him*, dated by Thomason 30 May 1649. All repr. in HALLER & DAVIES, *Leveller Tracts*, pp. 252–75, 286–317, 329–98.

23 LILBURNE, PRINCE AND OVERTON, *The Picture of the Councel of State, Held forth to the Free people of England . . .*, published between 4 and 11 April 1649; and (later in date) WALWYN, *The Fountain of Slaunder Discovered*, 30 May 1649. Both repr. in HALLER & DAVIES, *Leveller Tracts*, pp. 191–251 (but extracts only from the latter, the rest of it belonging to Walwyn's conflict with the Puritan churches, for which see above).

24 FIRTH AND DAVIES, *Regimental History*, vol. I, p. 223.

25 LILBURNE, *Truths Victory over Tyrants and Tyranny*, 26 Oct. 1649, B.M., E.579 (12); 'Theodorus Verax' [CLEMENT WALKER], *The Triall of Lieut.-Colonell John Lilburne at the Guild-Hall of London, 24, 25, 26 October. 1649*. B.M., E.584 (9).

26 *The New Law of Righteousness*, Jan. 1649, repr. in G. H. SABINE (ed.), *The Works of Gerrard Winstanley* (Ithaca, N.Y., 1941; repr. New York, 1965), pp. 149–244.

27 On 5 December 1648, see SABINE, *Works of Winstanley*, Appendix, pp. 611–23, 627–40, for this and its sequel, *More Light Shining in Buckinghamshire*, of 30 March 1649.

28 The imprint is 'Rotterdam. 1649'. It was dated by Thomason 14 August. B.M., E.569 (5). Part of it is repr. in G. ORWELL & R. REYNOLDS (eds.), *British Pamphleteers*, vol. I (1948), pp. 82–112. For reasons given above, and on stylistic grounds, I cannot accept H. N. Brailsford's suggestion that it was by Walwyn (see his *Levellers and the English Revolution*, ed. C. HILL (1961), p. 71, n. 1).

29 Published 25 April 1649. B.M., E.552 (1); extracts repr. in J. H. AVELING, *The Chamberlens and the Midwifery Forceps* (1882), pp. 78–80; and in ORWELL AND REYNOLDS, *British Pamphleteers*, vol. I, pp. 114–19.

30 The writer on trade, Benjamin Worsley, at this time also a strong millenarian, was there in 1648–9.

31 As was true of Pieter-Cornelis Plockhoy of Zurick-Zee, who published radical, socially oriented pamphlets as Peter Cornelius in 1659: *The Way to Peace and Settlement*, and *A Way Propounded to make the poor in these and other Nations happy*.

32 CHRISTOPHER HILL, *The World Turned Upside Down: Radical Ideas during the English Revolution* (1972), ch. 7, 'Levellers and True Levellers', esp. pp. 91–9.

33 *A Declaration of the Wel-Affected In the County of Buckinghamshire. Being A Representation of the middle sort of Men* . . . THOMASON: 10 May 1649. B.M.,

E.555 (1); repr. in SABINE, *Works of Winstanley*, APPDX., pp. 643–7. It calls for the release of the four imprisoned Leveller leaders, but is 'true Leveller' in attacking lords of manors and their oppressions.

34 WILLIAM WALWYN, Physician, *Physick for Families: Or, The new, Safe and Powerful way of Physick, upon constant proof Established;* . . ., (London, 1681) B.M., C.54.a.26. The credit for identifying the medical William Walwyn with the ex-Leveller belongs to W. SCHENK (see 'A Seventeenth-Century Radical', *Econ. Hist. Rev.*, vol. XIV (1944), pp. 74–83, and *The Concern for Social Justice in the Puritan Revolution* (1948), ch. 3, esp. pp. 58–9, 63, n. 104).

Sources of the Illustrations

Bodleian Library *Frontispiece*, 20; British Library 17, 21, 26, 27, 30, 35, 47, 54; British Museum 8, 14, 15, 29, 36, 53; National Army Museum, London 11; Reference Library, Holton Park, Oxford 44; Victoria and Albert Museum 51; Wandsworth Central Library 32.

Select Bibliography

(in order of publication within each section; place of publication is London unless otherwise stated)

SOURCES

S. R. GARDINER (ed.), *Constitutional Documents of the Puritan Revolution 1628–60* (1st edn. Oxford, 1889); *1625–1660* (2nd & 3rd edns., 1899, 1906). Includes the first modern re-publications of the Heads of Proposals, the (first) Agreement of the People, and the Officers' Agreement.

C. H. FIRTH (ed.), *The Clarke Papers* (Camden Soc., and Royal Hist. Soc., Camden series. 4 vols. 1891–1901, repr. 1965). Indispensable for the Agitators and the Army, 1647–49; the first printed text of the debates.

W. HALLER (ed.), *Tracts on Liberty in the Puritan Revolution 1638–1647* (3 vols. New York, 1934; repr. N.Y. 1965). Vol. I contains a useful introductory survey, index, etc.; vols. II and III facsimile reproductions of pamphlets. Not limited to Leveller works.

A. S. P. WOODHOUSE (ed.), *Puritanism and Liberty. Being the Army Debates (1647–9) from the Clarke Manuscripts with Supplementary Documents* (1938; London and Chicago, 1951; 1965 and 1966). A more accessible and some-times more intelligible text of the debates than Firth's; many valuable extracts, from the Agreements and other pamphlets, in the remaining sections and in the Appendix.

G. H. SABINE (ed.), *The Works of Gerrard Winstanley* (Ithaca, N.Y., 1941; repr. New York, 1965). Vital for any serious study of the Diggers, alias True Levellers.

DON M. WOLFE (ed.), *Leveller Mani-festoes of the Puritan Revolution* (New York, 1944; repr. London and New York, 1967). Covers 1646–9; prints all the Agreements, and several pamphlets not re-published elsewhere.

W. HALLER & G. DAVIES (eds.), *The Leveller Tracts 1647–1653* (New York, 1944; repr. Gloucester, Mass., 1964). Very strong on 1649 and for Walwyn; little Lilburne except the mainly auto-biographical *Legall Fundamentall Liber-ties*, and the two parts of *Englands New Chains*; some overlap with Wolfe.

GEORGE ORWELL AND REGINALD REY-NOLDS (eds.), *British Pamphleteers*, I, *From the Sixteenth Century to the French Revolution* (1948). Longish extracts from *Tyranipocrit*, Chamberlen, and some Digger or True Leveller works.

C. HILL AND E. DELL (eds.), *The Good Old Cause: The English Revolution of 1640–1660: Its Causes, Course, and Consequences* (1949; repr. London and New York, 1969). Many short extracts, some from the less well known radical pamphlets.

C. HILL (ed.), Gerrard Winstanley, *Law of Freedom and Other Writings* (Pelican, 1973). Excellent value.

REFERENCE WORKS

The Dictionary of National Biography (63 vols. 1885–1900; repr. Oxford. 22 vols. 1908–9). Still contains the best short factual biographies of several of the characters involved; most relevant articles by Firth.

172

I.H.R. LONDON, *Corrections and Additions to the D.N.B.*, . . . *1923–1963* (Boston, 1966).

G. K. FORTESCUE (and others) (ed.), *Catalogue of the pamphlets . . . collected by George Thomason 1640–1661* (2 vols. 1908). Indispensable for the British Museum collection, originally made by Thomason and donated to the nation by George III; to be supplemented by use of the two following items.

BRITISH MUSEUM, *General Catalogue of Printed Books* (revised repr. edn. 1931–66).

DONALD G. WING, *Short-Title Catalogue of Books printed* (in England, etc.) *1641–1700* (3 vols. New York, 1945–51. Rev. edn. in progress, vol. I, 1972). The best starting point for locating works not in the B.M., short of using numerous other library catalogues (which often means going to the libraries concerned).

SECONDARY WORKS

G. P. GOOCH, *The history of English democratic ideas in the 17th century* (Cambridge, 1898; rev. edn. ed. H. J. Laski, 1927). A pioneering work; still of some interest.

T. C. PEASE, *The Leveller Movement . . .* (Washington, D.C., and Oxford, 1916; repr. Gloucester, Mass., 1965). Valuable; the best account written until the 1950s–60s.

E. BERNSTEIN, *Cromwell and communism, socialism, and democracy in the great English civil war* (original German edn. 1895; Engl. transl. 1930). More of a period piece for late 19th- early 20th-century socialist attitudes than of value as a history itself.

MARGARET JAMES, *Social Problems and Policies during the Puritan revolution 1640–1660* (1930; repr. 1966). Dated in its treatment of economic developments and on some aspects of social history, but still valuable for its use of pamphlets, especially on divisions in London.

W. K. JORDAN, *The Development of Religious Toleration in England* (4 vols. 1932–40; repr. Gloucester, Mass., 1965). Vols. III and IV cover 1640–60; wider than the title suggests; deals with ideas of several Levellers and other radicals.

M. A. GIBB, *John Lilburne the Leveller, a Christian Democrat* (1947).

MAURICE ASHLEY, *John Wildman, Plotter and Postmaster* (1947).

W. SCHENK, *The Concern for Social Justice in the Puritan Revolution* (London and New York, 1948). Much concerned with continuity between earlier (medieval and reformation) religious radicals and those of the Interregnum, including the Levellers; good on the biographical side.

JOSEPH FRANK, *The Levellers: A History of The Writings of Three Seventeenth-Century Social Democrats: John Lilburne, Richard Overton, William Walwyn* (Cambridge, Mass., 1955; repr. New York, 1969). In many ways the best book on the subject; wider, with more on the movement and its other members, than the sub-title would suggest.

W. HALLER, *Liberty and Reformation in the Puritan Revolution* (New York, 1955). Largely a survey of Puritan and other radical thought from 1641 to 1649, dealing fully with the leading Leveller authors. Less satisfactory as an interpretative study than Frank or Zagorin.

PEREZ ZAGORIN, *A History of Political Thought in the English Revolution* (1954; repr. New York, 1966). Opening chapters deal with Levellers and other radicals; short, densely packed; the best analysis except for those who find his tone too secular.

PAULINE GREGG, *Free-born John: A Biography of John Lilburne* (1961). Fuller than Gibb; a more secular tone, but sympathetic to Lilburne's religious aspirations and beliefs.

H. N. BRAILSFORD, *The Levellers and the English Revolution*, ed. C. Hill (London and Stanford, California, 1961). Uneven; the fullest study of the rise and organization of the movement; some fine narrative sequences, but too inclined to take the Levellers out of their 17th-century context; perhaps more exciting reading than Frank, but where they differ Frank is usually more reliable.

C. B. MACPHERSON, *The Political Theory of Possessive Individualism: Hobbes to Locke* (Oxford, 1962 and paperback edn., 1964). Chapter III and the Appendix are concerned with the Levellers, particularly in connection with the Franchise (see below, Thomas).

HOWARD SHAW, *The Levellers* (Seminar Studies in History, 1968). A useful short introduction, with a few extracts from sources.

CHRISTOPHER HILL, *The World Turned Upside Down: Radical Ideas during the English Revolution* (1972), esp. chs. 4 and 7. The Levellers have a place in several of Hill's other books, but this is the one by which his treatment of them and his analysis of their role should be judged. An immensely stimulating, and at times truly moving book; indispensable, whether or not all his interpretations are accepted. Paperback edn. to be published shortly.

ARTICLES AND ESSAYS

J. W. GOUGH, 'The Agreements of the People', *History*, vol. 15 (1931).

MARGARET JAMES, 'The Importance of the Tithes Controversy in the English Revolution', *History*, vol. 26 (1941).

W. SCHENK, 'A Seventeenth-Century Radical', *Econ. Hist. Rev.*, 1st ser., vol. XIV (1944) on Walwyn.

H. ROSS WILLIAMSON, *Four Stuart Portraits* (1949) – the last chapter of which is on Rainsborough.

C. HILL, 'The Norman Yoke', in his *Puritanism and Revolution* (1958; New York, 1964; repr. 1965; in paperback 1968) – a substantial section of this essay (originally published in 1952) is concerned with the Levellers; one of Hill's finest pieces.

O. LUTAUD, 'Le parti politique "NIVELEUR" et la première Révolution anglaise, (Essai d'Historiographie)', *Revue Historique*, 86th Year, vol. CCXXVII (1962) – the fullest survey of the Levellers' historical reputation; includes continental European as well as British and American publications on the subject.

J. C. DAVIS, 'The Levellers and Democracy', *Past & Present*, no. 40 (1968); one of the earliest criticisms of Macpherson's interpretation.

A. L. MORTON, *The World of the Ranters* (1970) contains essays on Leveller Democracy and on Walwyn.

ROGER HOWELL, JR., and DAVID E. BREWSTER, 'Reconsidering the Levellers: the evidence of *The Moderate*', *Past & Present*, no. 46 (1970). Although *The Moderate* is discussed by Frank and Gregg, this makes more systematic use of it.

G. E. AYLMER, 'Gentlemen Levellers?', *Past & Present*, no. 49 (1970) – a short note on biographical origins and social connections.

KEITH THOMAS, 'The Levellers and the Franchise', ch. 2 in Aylmer (ed.), *The Interregnum: The Quest for Settlement 1646–1660* (London and Hamden, Conn., 1972) – the most thoroughgoing criticism of Macpherson.

C. B. MACPHERSON, *Democratic Theory* (Oxford, 1973), ch. XII, 'Servants and labourers in 17th-century England', although intended as a reply to another review of his previous book by P. Laslett (in the *Histl. Jnl.*, VII (1964), shows that the controversy is still open.

B. S. MANNING (ed.), *Religion, Politics, and the English Civil War* (1973), chs. by Patricia Higgins on women, and by J. C. Davis on the Levellers (the latter a strongly religious interpretation).

Index